Understanding Digital Imposition

by
Hal Hinderliter

GATF*Press*
PITTSBURGH

Library of Congress Catalog Card Number: 97-74139
International Standard Book Number: 0-88362-186-X

Printed in the United States of America

GATF Catalog No. 1508
First Edition
Second Printing, February 2002

INTERNATIONAL (A) **PAPER**

Printed on Williamsburg Offset, 60-lb., smooth finish by International Paper

GATF*Press*
Graphic Arts Technical Foundation
200 Deer Run Road
Sewickley, PA 15143-2600
Phone: 412/741-6860
Fax: 412/741-2311
Email: info@gatf.org
Internet: www.gain.net

Orders to:
GATF Orders
P.O. Box 1020
Sewickley, PA 15143-1020
Phone (U.S. only): 800/662-3916
Phone (Canada only): 613/236-7208
Phone (all other countries): 412/741-5733
Fax: 412/741-0609 • Internet: www.gain.net

GATF*Press* books are widely used by companies, associations, and schools
for training, marketing, and resale. Quantity discounts are available
by contacting Peter Oresick at 800/910-GATF.

Contents

This book is dedicated in loving memory of my father,
John Melvin Hinderliter. As I finish this book, I can hear him saying,
All I ask is that you do the best that you can.
Knowledge is something no one can take from you.
There's nothing wrong with making a living by working with your hands.
May these truths be things I never forget.

Preface

This book is intended as a bridge between the digital techniques used for imposition today and the traditional photomechanical approach used for most of the 20th century. The early chapters of *Understanding Digital Imposition* are designed to lead the reader through the vocabulary, tools, and processes of image assembly, presenting the details of this vanishing profession while illuminating the ways in which these historic techniques connect to the computer-based workflow of today. The menus and functions of our current digital imposition programs correspond to identical manual image assembly processes; therefore, a complete understanding of digital imposition must rest upon a thorough familiarization with impositions created "the old-fashioned way."

It would be an oversight to not mention the previous texts that have made this book possible; numerous GATF resources (such as *The Lithographers Manual* and *What the Printer Should Know about Paper)* were consulted during the creation of this manuscript. The greatest debt, however, is owed to Harold L. Peck and his classic reference, *Stripping: The Assembly of Film Images*; many illustrations originally created for Peck's book can be found scattered throughout the pages of this book. I'd also like to express my appreciation to Tom Destree, GATF's editor in chief, as well as Peter Oresick, director of technical information and education programs, for their patience through this interminable process. Special thanks go to GATF staff members Rich Adams, Greg Bassinger, Joe Marin, and Dave Watterson for working to create many of the photographs and illustrations found within. Most of all, I must acknowledge the contributions of Jack Smolevitz and Tom Lapsley, two masters of the stripper's craft.

Writing my first book has been a fascinating experience—a dance with the terrifying as well as a walk amongst the clouds. Through all the composing and editing and rewrites, I take some comfort that the process of authoring a book remains largely unchanged from the early days of the Gutenberg press. Authors struggling with manuscripts, proofs to be read, and the demands of the publisher to "hurry up and finish your book!"—these must have been commonplace occurrences, even centuries ago.

Yet other things have changed so much, Gutenberg would undoubtedly feel a stranger in today's publishing environment. Authors and editors collaborate via email, documents arrive as electronic bits and bytes, and illustrations are created by artists hunched over computer screens or by photographers with their digital cameras. Words and images can flow straight to the printing plate without the help of a graphic arts camera, or even so much as a piece of film.

It seems certain that within a few short years, the printing industry will have once again transformed itself beyond recognition. Within this atmosphere of change and upheaval, it has been a considerable challenge to create the text that follows; after all, any book that deals in electronic imaging should be as topical as the magazines and websites we all depend on to stay current.

As a final note, I have a request to make of you who have chosen to take part in this journey from the light table to digital imposition: I would be honored to hear from each and every one of you about the content and structure of *Understanding Digital Imposition*. Simply journey to the GATF website (http://www.gatf.org) and follow the links to the page devoted to this book; from there, you may easily send an email message regarding your comments. With your help, future revisions will contain the necessary information to keep this book relevant and useful; and in closing, I hope that this first edition will be of value to you.

Hal Hinderliter
Center for Imaging Excellence
Pittsburgh
June 1998

1 Introduction

In 1989 the large commercial printer I was working for had just upgraded its imagesetter to an internal drum device. This startling technological leap may now seem like only a small improvement, but the day I grasped what this new device could do, it chilled me to the bone.

It was just another shift of stripping film on the light table. I was an image assembler, and proud of it. We were the *prima donnas* of the printing industry—part artist and part laborer, our hands moving with the subtle grace of a Times Square pickpocket. Yes, 1989 was several years into the age of desktop publishing, but for many printers the result of the Macintosh explosion had so far resulted only in some jobs that had previously been furnished as artboards now being output directly to film. That film was the digital equivalent of a line shot from an artboard. These "computer films" had no usable photos, no tint screens, no tight registration of multiple colors—everything was either solid black or clear film, and it was up to the crew of strippers to breathe life and color into these stark, text-only negatives. A major part of my job at that time was spent creating screen builds—using film and Rubylith masks to expose manufactured tint screens (non-digital films) featuring tiny halftone dots. When these dots were exposed to printing plates in different combinations at precise angles, they would allow the press to create a variety of different colors from the four process color inks (cyan, magenta, yellow, and black).

Of course, I had heard some excited murmurings from my friend Buzz, our resident Macintosh guru. He had been conducting experiments for more than a year, trying to produce film with a consistent and accurate patch of dots; but due to the technical limitations of our equipment, his efforts were producing only streaked, fuzzy blotches. Then it happened:

I grabbed a new job off the stack, and took it back to my light table. Inside the jacket were sets of film, four for each page, and attached to the films was a note, proclaiming in large letters: "Use these films—the screens are good!"

I spread the films out and stared at them. It was only text, big letters in various headlines, but the screen builds had already been done. Since the page did not feature any photographs or other artwork, all that was left for me to do was to draw a layout and tape down the films—no masks, no knockouts, no compositing. The computer and this newfangled imagesetter had done it all! I called out to the other strippers in the room, telling them they had to see what was on my table.

As they gathered around to look, I told them that these tint screens were made by a computer and output onto separate films at the proper angles. As they gazed down at these films, I said something like "Do you know what this means to us? If a computer can put useable tint screens into a negative, how long can it be before they are outputting complete pages, with pictures and everything else? What will they need us for, if a computer can do all that?" Tom, the department skeptic, scoffed and said, "For every computer they buy, they'll have to hire *two* strippers to fix all the mistakes." Today that former stripper uses a computer to output fully imposed sheets of film.

You could certainly make the argument that the above scenario was possible as far back as 1980, when the first color electronic prepress systems (CEPS) became available from vendors such as Scitex or Hell. However, these machines did not achieve widespread use throughout the printing industry because of their high price tags. In fact, even if a printer could afford to buy a large CEPS it was seldom used for more than a small portion of the most difficult jobs. The vast majority of printed materials continued to be generated through typesetting and pasteup until the late 1980s. This is when the ease-of-use and affordable computing power of the Apple Macintosh inspired designers everywhere to begin doing their own typesetting, instead of buying this service from traditional typographic houses. This trend quickly became a tidal wave. We came to call this combination of affordable hardware and mass-produced software "desktop publishing."

It is immediately evident that the personal computer and desktop publishing have wrought enormous changes in the printing industry. More than any other factor, the widespread acceptance and use of desktop publishing software for document creation is responsible for converting the industry from a laborious, craft-oriented art form into a high-speed, computer-aided custom manufacturing process. Given that, why has it taken so long to complete the transition? The Apple Macintosh debuted in 1984, and Aldus PageMaker was introduced soon after—yet more than a decade after the introduction of Post-Script, many printers still output single pages of film and arrange them into position manually on a light table.

After considering a variety of implicating factors, I point to the printshop culture and its resistance to change. That might sound like an unfair statement to some—after all, we have gone from hot metal type to laser-imaged printing plates in just over a generation—but most of the meaningful advances in our industry have occurred because our customers forced us to change. To give customers the greater freedom and control they desire, we became adept at accepting and outputting *their* digital files. From digital scanning to digital proofing, decade after decade of new technology has sought to give the customers what they want—printing that can be delivered *faster* and *cheaper.* If these methods also do the job *better,* that is just icing on the proverbial cake. It also helps explain why digital imposition software has not inspired the same level of interest that QuarkXPress and Adobe Photoshop have—it just is not something that our *customers* really care about.

A stripper and a Macintosh operator examine an envelope layout.

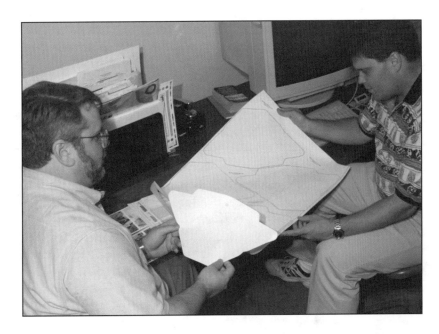

Or at least they didn't care in the past. Today the hot buzz-word is computer-to-plate (CTP). In magazine articles, Internet discussion groups, trade-show seminars, and GATF's Satellite Symposium television special, printers are telling the tale of how bypassing film to directly image printing plates with a laser beam is allowing them to print faster, cheaper, and better—and of course, customers are taking notice. Many of the printers I speak to who are involved in CTP have told me that their biggest customers pushed them into it. What has CTP got to do with digital imposition? Like Frank Sinatra sang in "Love and Marriage," you can't have one without the other. Once again the customer's desire to implement new technology is forcing the printer to abandon the comfortable present (in this case, assembling pages on a light table) for the bright promise of a better future *without film*. Even those printers who currently think they cannot afford CTP are frantically trying to get up-to-speed on digital imposition, both to achieve better utilization of their existing medium- and large-format imagesetters, and to prepare for the eventual conversion of the entire printing industry to a filmless workflow.

So what is the holdup? Why are so many printers still paying good wages to people who lean over light tables all day long, drawing layouts and staring through little magnifying glasses for the purpose of putting one register mark on top of another? I attribute this to two factors:

- Strippers with traditional backgrounds know how conventional image assembly works and can, therefore, *recognize potential problems with computer-generated film* that does not meet traditional quality standards. In most printing plants today, the stripper stands tall as the final point of quality control. Of course, it is very expensive to catch mistakes and re-output film at this late stage in the process. Companies that have gotten away from film were able to do so because they improved their digital infrastructure, training workers with conventional knowledge to become computer operators, and instituting robust error-checking procedures for incoming customer files—a process known as *preflighting.*

- The strippers themselves are afraid to change. Under-estimating the importance of their traditional knowledge, many strippers feel that they will never be a part of printing's new computer age. Too often, management feels the same way, which creates an environment where microchips and laser beams turn the customer's wishes into film, but ball-point pens and T-squares prepare these films for the press. With so few people left who understand how to plan and assemble work using the traditional methods described in the next few chapters, prepress department managers sometimes feel they must choose between the security of maintaining the status quo with strippers, and the certain upheaval of replacing conventional image assembly with digital technology.

Fortunately, this situation is changing for the better. Word is getting out that retraining strippers, platemakers, and other workers who understand the intricacies of putting ink on paper is a great investment. As I have often stated, it is easier to train a stripper how to use a computer than to teach a computer user about printing methods and the impact of bindery and finishing techniques. In fact, readers of this book are likely to be conventional workers who are about to put down their X-Acto knives and pick up a computer mouse—the same transition I made, not too many years ago.

For those of you who do not possess conventional prepress experience, you will probably be surprised by my next statement. *Truly understanding digital imposition is impossible without a clear grasp of the many processes involved in manual image assembly.* Yes, you may have the fastest mouse in town, but ability without knowledge only builds a house that cannot stand. Whether your interest lies in the current Post-Script imposition software offerings or the high-end workflows of RIP-based imposition, you will be at a loss to fully understand the capabilities of these programs without a basic knowledge of image assembly and imposition planning. That is why this book, *Understanding Digital Imposition,* will first take you through an explanation of how and why manual imposition is accomplished—fundamental issues that are as true for the users of today's imposition software as they were for the strippers of yesterday.

We will begin this explanation with the next chapter, which defines the components of a page and provides a context for further discussion of the imposition process.

2 Placing Graphics on the Sheet

Trying to explain the process of imposition to the uninitiated is akin to providing an explanation of how cement blocks are used to make up a solid foundation—for most people, it is something that "just happens." Few give much thought to the minute details surrounding the wide range of possible choices for locating each block—except the mason who has to build the wall! Imposition can be thought of as a similar process; the choices made at this stage of print preparation guarantee the creation of a solid foundation for printing, binding, and finishing the printed project. Just as with the construction of a building, we typically do not think about the imposition process unless something goes wrong.

Defining Imposition

What is **imposition?** This term refers to the process of placing graphics into predetermined positions on a sheet of paper. From this definition, however, it is difficult to distinguish between imposition and other parts of the graphic communications craft, such as pasteup and page layout. A key difference is that page layout is the process of defining where repeating elements such as headlines, text, and folios (page numbers) will appear on multiple pages throughout a document, while imposition can be thought of as defining where these completed pages will appear on much larger sheets of paper.

If that is the case, why didn't I refer to imposition as "the process of placing pages on a large sheet of paper"? The answer lies in the nature of the printing industry. While this simple definition would be applicable to most print companies most of the time, it fails to fully explain the process as employed by important segments of our trade, such as packaging, label printing, and financial printing. These types of printers deal with graphics that are not pages at all; more importantly, these types of projects present their own challenges—each graphic being imposed might be a different size and shape than the others on the sheet, or combinations of different sizes might lead to the rotation of graphics at unusual angles.

Even publications printers, who think of most projects in terms of the number of pages to be printed, will find the occasional project that breaks the rules; for example, imposing multiple business cards or printing flat envelopes before converting (see chapter 7 for more on envelope conversion). While it is important that we not underestimate the importance of these nonpublication markets, trying to speak of the imposition process in an all-inclusive manner throughout the rest of this book would result in an unreadable nightmare of political correctness. Therefore, in the interest of both clarity and brevity, I beg the indulgence of readers from the packaging, label printing, and other industry segments who are imposing graphics other than pages. I will focus on some of the special considerations for these markets later in this book, but in most places I will refer to the process of imposing *pages,* hoping that readers from these specialty printers will make the necessary substitution of appropriate terms (box, label, envelope, check, etc.) in their minds!

Throughout this book, the term *imposition* will necessarily be used many times. In a few instances, however, the term *pagination* is used instead. For the purpose of this book, assume that *imposition* and *pagination* have the same definition—even though there are a few segments of the printing industry where this is not the case. (Directory publishers, for example, refer to pagination as the process of positioning numerous small ads on the proper pages of a phone directory or other book.)

Basic Page Terminology

During my discussion of imposition, I will use several terms to refer to the components that make up a page. I will also explore some of the important stylistic rules that govern page layout, along with their connection to the imposition process.

Page Numbers

The *page number* is a simple concept to understand. Each page in a publication can be assigned a number, the value of which defines its place in the overall sequence of pages. The first page in a book or magazine, however, often is not Page One. Printers uses a variety of different numbers to designate each page's location in relation to the other pages in a specific section, and each section may or may not use a different numbering strategy. As an example, the front cover of a magazine might be designated as OFC, with the inside front cover page designated as IFC. This would allow the first page of the text to be referred to as page number one, which in this case is the first page of the text. This distinction is especially important when the cover is printed on a different type of stock than the interior pages, requiring a separate press sheet for the cover pages (as opposed to a self-cover booklet, in which the cover and text are printed on the exact same type of stock). Another commonly used style for page numbering refers to the pages in a book's introduction segment by Roman numerals (i, ii, iii, iv, and so on).

Folio

The *folio* is a similar concept, with an important distinction: Every page in a document has a page number, and knowing this number is an essential part of arranging the pages in the proper imposition order. Page numbers, however, do not have to be printed on the pages. It is quite common in shorter publications to go without visible page numbers, although these numbers still exist, whether they are visible or not. Page numbers that *are* visible (printed within the page area) are called folios. Folios include any text that is linked to the visible page number; for instance, if the page numbers within a document are shown as "Page One," "Page Two," and so on, even the word "page" is a part of the folio. This would also be

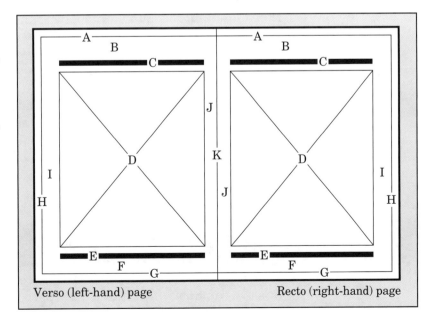

Basic page terminology: (A) head trim, (B) top, or head, margin, (C) header, (D) body of the page, (E) footer, (F) bottom, or foot, margin, (G) foot trim, (H) face, or front, trim, (I) margin at the face, or front margin, (J) margin at the gutter, or back margin, and (K) fold.

Verso (left-hand) page

Recto (right-hand) page

true in the case of a graphic symbol or art element that might appear as a part of the page number (common examples of this include small ellipses or rectangles in which the page number appears).

Footers and Headers

Words, rules, or other artwork that appear at the bottom of pages are collectively referred to as the *footer.* The footer may be exactly the same on every page, or it may change from chapter to chapter. If the page includes a folio at the bottom of the page as well as other text or graphics, this folio is part of the group that makes up the footer. A similar concept is the *header,* which refers to text and artwork (yes, even folios) that appear at the top of multiple pages. A common use of a header in book publishing is to display the title of the book at the top of the left-hand page, and the title of the chapter at the top of the right-hand page. Many times, the header is followed by a very thin horizontal rule that visually separates the repeating header information from the continuing text.

Body of the Page

The area of text between the header and the footer is the *body* of the page. Many times, this text is arranged in long lines that cover nearly the full width of the page; this is called a single *column* of text. Quite often, however, the graphic artist enhances the readability and stylistic flexibility of the design by dividing the text into two or three columns. The shorter lines of type that result from multicolumn layout are easier to read and more visually interesting than the longer lines resulting from the single-column approach.

The space between two columns of type is called the *gutter.* The term gutter also refers to the side of the page that is involved in the binding process (see discussion of margins below). For example, on a magazine that is stapled together, the edge of the page where the fold occurs can also be called the gutter. When using this term, indicate clearly whether you are referring to the space between columns of text or to the bound edge of a page. The other edges of the page are known as the *head* (top), *foot* (bottom), and *face.*

Margins

Although it is possible to have *white space* (an area that is devoid of text or graphics) anywhere on a page, the unprinted area between the body of the page and the edge of the page is known as the margin. If the white space is above the header, it is the *top margin;* if the white space is below the footer, it is the ***bottom margin.*** The white space between the body of the page and the outside edge of the page is called the ***margin at the face,*** or ***front margin.*** The white space between the body of the page and the page's inside edge (where the fold typically occurs) is called the ***margin at the gutter,*** or ***back margin.***

Trim Size

The size of the page is determined when the paper is cut down and made into a book. The intended place for the paper cutter to chop through the sheet is known as the ***trim.*** When referring to the size of each page in a book or magazine, we might use the term ***page size.*** A more versatile term, the ***trim size,*** can be used to refer to the intended size of any item that is cut out of a larger sheet of paper. After a large sheet is folded into a booklet, three separate cuts will be made to turn the booklet into a clean, sharp, finished piece. We refer to these three finishing cuts by naming the page area being cut: the ***foot trim,*** the ***head trim,*** and the ***face trim*** (or ***front trim).***

Bleeds

If the designer wants a picture or other graphic on a page to extend all the way to the trim, the image must actually extend a short distance beyond the trim to achieve the desired effect. This is due to the inexact nature of the folding and cutting that will occur after the printing is complete.

An image that bleeds off two sides of the sheet. The bleed is typically ⅛ in. (3 mm).

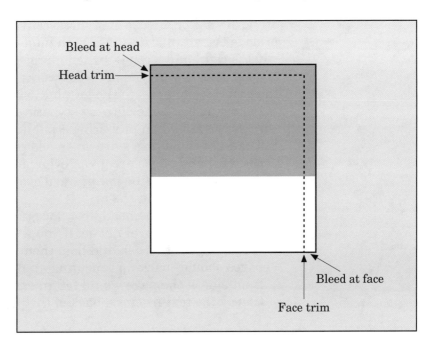

Since the location where the guillotine cutter's blade will chop through the sheet will not be absolutely consistent, this extra image allowance is required in case the trim is made farther away from the content of the page than had been intended. This extra image area which extends beyond the trim is called ***bleed***, and the standard width of this bleed in the printing industry is 0.125 in. (3 mm) beyond the trim.

Stylistic Conventions

The use of page numbers, folios, and other common page elements is governed by a concept called ***stylistic convention.*** This concept is basic to the principles of graphic design and page layout, and it means that designers will consciously limit their range of choices when deciding how to put together the artwork for a printed piece. As you might guess, the idea of following an accepted norm during the creative process goes against the very nature of some designers. Occasionally, designers break the rules of stylistic convention just for the fun or shock value of it. Often, however, these rules are broken because the designer is not trained in the principles of graphic design.

Some of the stylistic conventions in use today have evolved from centuries of design experience and have become widely accepted because they enhance the designer's ability to communicate. Other conventions are useful because they provide a standardized way of handling the print project, making processes such as imposition easier and faster. Unfortunately, the use or misuse of stylistic conventions does not provide the graphic designer with immediate feedback on what is right and wrong—when a project breaks the norms of good design, ***you*** (the prepress worker) will have to deliver the unfortunate news to the graphic artist.

Following are some of these stylistic conventions that are very important when preparing a publication for print:

- The right-hand pages are given odd page numbers, and the left-hand pages are given even page numbers. These designations must be maintained even when blank pages are inserted within the text.
- The margins at the head, foot, face trim, and gutter should be consistent for every page. If you were to tear out individual pages of a book and hold them up to the light, the pages should "back up," meaning that the text from the front side of the page would fall in exactly the same position as the text from the back of the page.

- Repeating elements such as folios should also back up. This is true even in the case of magazine work, where different sections of the magazine may have very different layouts. In this case, the margins might change from one section into the next, but the folios (and any other elements which appear on every page, regardless of section) should remain in a consistent position throughout the entire publication.

Imposing Multiple Pages

Press Sheets

In practice, imposition determines how multiple pages should be placed on larger sheets of paper. These sheets of paper, onto which an image will be printed by a printing press, are called **press sheets.** The larger the press sheet, the greater the number of pages that can be printed on it. As long as press sheets are large enough to hold two or more pages, it is necessary to arrange the pages in a special order so that the resulting book will have its pages in the correct sequence. Here are some of the simple terms and phrases that apply to printing two pages on the same side of a single press sheet.

Spreads

Two pages that appear side by side on a sheet of paper are called a **two-page spread** or sometimes simply a **spread.** A large press sheet might hold four or even eight spreads, while a small sheet might hold only one spread (one pair of pages). These spreads can be one of two varieties: a reader's spread or a printer's spread. The **reader's spread** is a pair of pages whose order is the same as would be encountered by a person reading a book; for instance, if the left-hand page is the sixth page of the book, the right-hand page would be the seventh. The **printer's spread** is a pair of pages in the order necessary for printing, folding, and binding to yield the desired results. Pages in this order seldom appear in numerical order—in fact, the only pair of pages that would be in numerical order when shown as printer's spreads are the center two pages, such as pages four and five in an eight-page booklet.

Reader's spreads. Reader's spreads are a natural part of visualizing and creating a publication. In the traditional graphic arts workflow, before the days of personal computers and desktop publishing (DTP) software, artists would collect the type and artwork needed for each project and paste them onto heavy sheets on white cardboard. In most cases each

Graphic designer assembling an artboard as a two-page spread. This pair of pages will have a crossover, an image that will appear on both pages of a reader's spread.

board would carry the pasted-up artwork for two pages: the left and right pages from a reader's spread. This arrangement is such an integral part of the design process that the popular DTP software which has replaced the pasteup process can also show two pages at a time, in the reader's spread format.

Printer's spreads. Printer's spreads are necessary when pages will be folded before the binding process. As discussed in the chapter on binding methods, some specialized forms of binding (such as ***mechanical binding)*** do not require folding. As a result, imposing and printing these jobs will not require the pages to be arranged into printer's spreads. For the vast majority of work that is printed, however, the use of printer's spreads is essential.

Whether the origin of the project is artboards or floppy disks, an important common ingredient is converting the page order from the sequential page order characterizing reader's spreads into the less-familiar sequence of pages used to build the printer's spreads. Of course, imposition software will create the proper pairing of pages as part of ordering all pages on the press sheet, but knowing how to determine the printer's spreads manually can also be quite useful (see sidebar on facing page). If the project being imposed features so many pages that more than one press sheet will be printed, having this manual list of pages will allow verification that the pagination process has been successful.

Manually Determining Printer's Spreads

Regardless of how many pages appear in a book, it's easy to figure out which pages will appear together when the job is imposed into printer's spreads. Divide a sheet of paper into two columns. In the left column, write down the page number of the last page of the book. To the right of that number, write down the page number of the first page. On the next line, write down the number of the second page in the left column, and the next-to-last page in the right column. Continue on in this sequence, switching columns and advancing or subtracting by a single page, until all the pages are listed. Each row on your paper now shows the printer's spreads needed for successful imposition.

Here is an example of the printer's spreads for a 16-page signature:

16	1
2	15
14	3
4	13
12	5
6	11
10	7
8	9

Note that in the example above, the sum of the page numbers in each row is 17, which is one more than the number of pages in the signature. This is an easy way to double-check page sequence.

Printing Press Considerations

I have defined imposition as the process of arranging graphics (pages) into predetermined positions on a sheet of paper, and detailed how the building blocks of this strategy are the pairs of pages known as printer's spreads. Next, I will discuss a few more things that are fundamental to the imposition process, whether that imposition is done on a light table or a computer.

In determining how to impose the pages of your document, the type of printing press used to print the job plays a very important role. Different presses have a variety of different capabilities and can print a wide range of paper sizes. Some presses, such as web presses or perfecting sheetfed presses, can even print both sides of a sheet in one pass through the printing press. Although the impact of press choice on the imposition process is discussed in more depth in chapter 6, here's an introduction to the basics of press considerations.

Sheet size. The size of a sheetfed printing press (a press which prints cut sheets of paper) is typically expressed as two variables: the maximum width sheet of paper it can print, and the number of inks that the press can print in a single pass. Web presses, which print long rolls of paper that are cut into sheets after they are printed, are referred to by the number of colors that can be printed on the top of the sheet and then by the number of inks that can be printed on the bottom (these numbers are not always the same). Roll paper sizes for these presses come in a small variety, with roll widths of 26 in. (660 mm) or less being referred to as half-web sizes; a full-web press typically prints rolls from 32 in. (813 mm) to 44 in. (1,118 mm) in width. Using these strategies, one might refer to a "five-color 40-in. (1,016-mm) Heidelberg SpeedMaster sheetfed press" or a "six-over-six Miller half-web press." Although the paper for sheetfed presses is cut before it is printed, while the web press rolls are cut after printing, the imposition process for these two press categories is largely the same.

Forms and signatures. It seems simple enough to understand that the size of the press sheet limits the number of pages that can be printed on it simultaneously. A common sheet size such as 17.5×23 in. (444×584 mm) could be used to print four 8.5×11-in. (216×279-mm) pages on each side, for a total of eight pages. Each side of the sheet of paper is referred to as a *form*. Sheetfed forms are typically thought of as front and back forms, while web forms are usually called top and bottom forms. In the example just given, there are four pages involved in the front form and four pages in the back form. The combination of both front and back forms is called a *signature*. As yet another example of the industry's lack of semantic consensus, the term "form" might also be used in this way. Most often, signature is used when referring to an unspecified set of pages, such in "How many signatures have been plated so far?" Form is sometimes substituted for signature when referring to a particular group of pages, as in "We just finished printing the cover form."

The front and back forms of an eight-page signature.

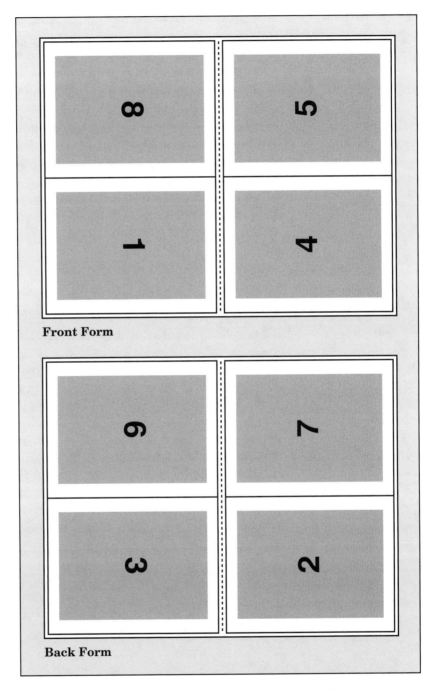

Front Form

Back Form

Throughout this book, I will attempt to avoid linguistic confusion by referring to a single side of an imposed press sheet as a form, while calling the two-sided imposed press sheet a signature (although the term signature can also apply to a smaller portion of the two-sided press sheet, as discussed in chapter 7). Keep this in mind when referring to the number of pages (and the number of repetitions of these pages) on each side of a sheet. In the job just mentioned, for instance, each form is said to be "1 up, 4 out" despite the fact that there are eight pages on the signature as a whole.

Signatures and forms are assigned a reference term, which varies widely throughout the printing industry. My personal preference is to name the signature after its contents, if this will result in a unique identifier for that signature (such as the *Cover Signature,* or the *Flyleaf Signature).* When referring to the text of a book or magazine, a letter designation is often used (such as *Signature A),* although the use of Arabic or Roman numerals is also common. The number of pages in a project helps determine how many signatures will be needed when imposing the job. Other factors that play a role include the size of the pages, the size of the press sheet to be used, and whether the cover pages should be printed on special stock or on paper that matches the rest of the book (this style of book is called a ***self-cover).***

Layouts. If a printed project has a large number of pages, a variety of different imposition styles may be required to complete the project. In such a project (comprising multiple forms), each form may have its own unique arrangement of pages. This grouping of pages is what makes up the imposition for each signature, and each specific arrangement can be referred to as a ***layout.*** Depending on the context and on the intent of the speaker, the term layout can mean the conceptual plan for arranging each signature's pages or it can refer to a hand-drawn guide used to position the film for each page.

For the next several chapters, I will use the second definition of layout as we embark on an overview of components essential to the print reproduction process.

3   Print Reproduction Basics

Many methods of printing information on paper depend on the use of printing plates. In most of these methods, an image can be created on the plates through a photomechanical process. The term "photomechanical" comes from a combination of two terms: ***photo,*** as in photographic, and ***mechanical,*** referring to control over exposure through the use of a physical object—in this case, high-contrast film.

In most printing plants around the world, plates are being created for printing presses through this method of selectively exposing the photosensitive printing plate emulsion through a film mask. Although there are alternatives to using film in the platemaking process, film-based plate preparation will be

A platemaker preparing to expose a metal lithographic printing plate through a high-contrast film negative in a vacuum frame.

with the industry for many years to come. Because offset lithographic plates are light-sensitive, they are exposed to light through the clear areas of high-contrast film. This means that a piece of film is used to control which portions of a plate will carry the printable image. The craft of arranging these films is called ***image assembly.***

The task of image assembly is carried out by a skilled craftsperson. In the past image assembly required a great deal of thought, as well as a talent for problem-solving. The widely used nickname for a person who does image assembly is a ***stripper,*** and the task of image assembly is more widely known as ***stripping.***

Image Assembly in Commercial Printing

Although any form of printing can make use of the process of imposition, not every print process utilizes stripping (the arrangement of film images for photomechanical plate exposure). Some types of printing do not require film, and therefore they do not need the services of a stripper. Let's review several of today's most common forms of commercial printing.

The many different types of printing processes in use throughout the world can be categorized as follows:

- *Planography,* which is printing created from a flat surface, such as offset lithography.
- *Intaglio,* a process in which a recessed surface controls the transfer of ink to substrate, such as rotogravure printing.
- *Relief printing,* which utilizes raised surfaces to create the printed image; examples of relief printing include letterpress and flexography.
- *Serigraphy,* a process that uses a stencil through which ink is forced to create an image; the most well-known example of this process is screen printing.
- *On-demand printing,* the newest category which encompasses a variety of processes including inkjet and electrostatic printing; it is also called nonimpact printing.

Most of these processes can employ some form of photomechanical exposure to prepare graphics for reproduction, the exception being on-demand printing.

Lithography. Lithography, a planographic printing process, requires an image carrier in the form of a plate on which image and nonimage areas are receptive to ink and water, respectively. After being mounted on the plate cylinder, the entire plate is first dampened with a water-based solution, which adheres to the nonimage areas of the plate. Next, the plate is brought into contact with an inked roller. The ink adheres only to the image areas. The inked image is then transferred to a rubber-like blanket and then "offset" from there to the paper. Lithography using such an indirect means of transferring the image from the plate to the paper is called ***offset lithography*** or, commonly, "offset."

The lithographic printing process.

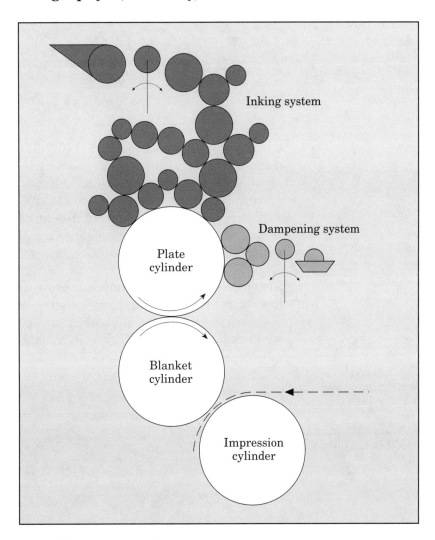

Inking system

Dampening system

Plate cylinder

Blanket cylinder

Impression cylinder

Rotogravure. Rotogravure is a printing process that relies on the use of engraved cylinders to transfer ink to paper. Originally, this engraving was done manually with a hand-engraving tool called a stylus. Alternative engraving methods utilize a photomechanical mask to control a chemical engraving process. For many years this engraving was done

The rotogravure printing process. *Adapted from* Understanding Digital Color, *by Phil Green* (GATF*Press,* 1998).

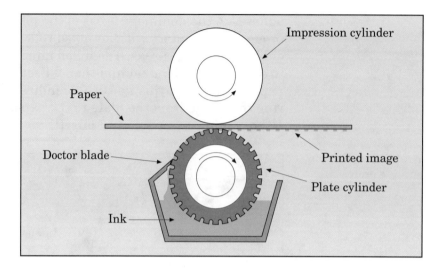

using a carbon tissue mask, but high-contrast film masks are more widely used today. Recent years have seen the development of electronic cylinder engraving, which is now in widespread use (as are both forms of the photomechanical exposure methods). The use of film or even electronic data to control cylinder engraving means that imposition is definitely a concern for printers with rotogravure presses.

Flexography. Flexography is a printing technique that is widely used in the packaging industry. A flexographic printing press uses a flexible plate with a raised image for transferring ink to paper or cardboard in a fashion not unlike a high-

The flexographic printing process. *Adapted from* Understanding Digital Color, *by Phil Green* (GATF*Press,* 1998).

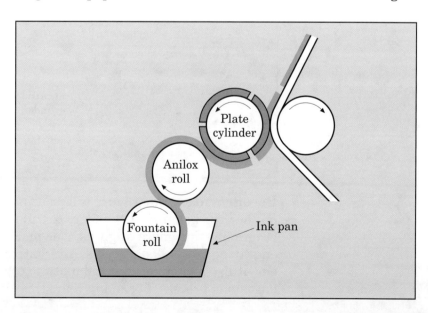

speed rubber stamp. Flexographic plates were originally made by heat vulcanization from metal forms. Today flexographic plates can be made photomechanically with the Cyrel photopolymer plate material introduced by DuPont as well as other similar products. These plates are imaged through exposure to light, using film positives. DuPont recently introduced a laser-imageable version of the Cyrel plate for the computer-to-plate process, which allows highly detailed flexo plates to be made without film.

Screen printing. Screen printing used to be known as "silkscreen" printing, because early screen printing equipment typically printed through silk mesh stretched over a wooden frame. When many think of screen printing, they might immediately think of Pittsburgh-born artist Andy Warhol's colorful portraits. Much of the packaging that we see and handle every day is screen-printed with industrial screen printing equipment.

Today's high-volume screen printer uses automated screen printing presses that employ automated squeegees, synthetic fiber screens, and metal frames. Images are printed by forcing colored screen printing inks through the holes in a stencil that has been chemically bonded to the screen. Positive films (black images on a clear background) are used to expose this stencil material. With one method of stencil preparation, immediately after development the wet stencil material is applied to the synthetic fiber screen; as the material dries it adheres to the screen. An alternative method involves coat-

The screen printing process.
Adapted from Understanding Digital Color, *by Phil Green* (GATF*Press,* 1998).

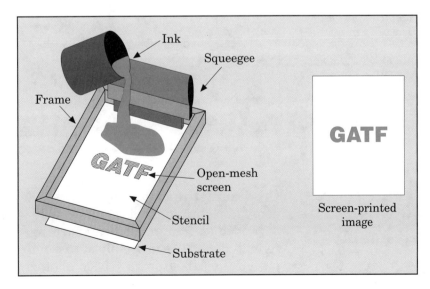

ing the screen itself with a photosensitive emulsion, reducing the number of steps in the stencil creation process.

The large screens used by industrial screen printers often carry multiple copies of the same image or combinations of several similar designs. The film assembly techniques necessary for arranging these images are nearly identical to methods used for producing flexographic and offset lithographic printing plates from film positives.

On-demand printing. On-demand printing is a catch-all phrase encompassing all of the popular forms of producing documents digitally, without the use of traditional pigmented printing inks. Some of the most well-known examples of this process are high-speed inkjet printers, electrostatic printers, and xerographic devices. Recent developments in this area have produced a wide variety of high-speed "digital presses"; these machines have been steadily increasing their share in the short-run printing market, formerly the domain of offset lithography. Although this is a filmless printing process, electronic imposition is an absolute necessity for the creation of booklets with on-demand equipment.

The Agfa Chromapress, an example of an on-demand printing press. It is based on the Xeikon engine, which uses the electrophotographic, or xerographic, imaging process. *Adapted from* On-Demand Printing, *by Howard M. Fenton and Frank J. Romano* (GATF*Press*, 1997).

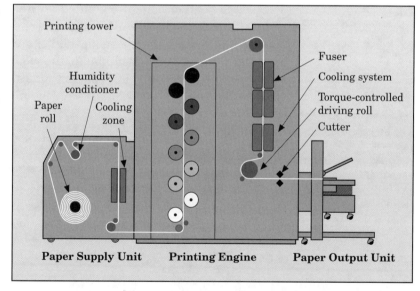

Printing tower

Fuser

Cooling system

Humidity conditioner

Torque-controlled driving roll

Paper roll

Cooling zone

Cutter

Paper Supply Unit   Printing Engine   Paper Output Unit

The Process of Image Assembly

Producing the film images. With the exception of on-demand printing, all of the previously listed categories have depended on film to create and arrange images intended for reproduction. The assembly of these film images occurs after pasted-up artboards have been photographed using large

A horizontal process camera, used to photograph pasted-up artboards.

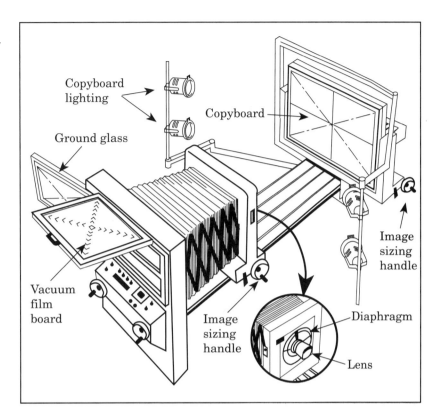

Copyboard lighting

Copyboard

Ground glass

Image sizing handle

Vacuum film board

Image sizing handle

Diaphragm

Lens

cameras and high-contrast film. This large camera is referred to by many names, including process camera, gallery camera, and graphic arts camera. Photographing the artboards results in large sheets of high-contrast film, also called orthographic ("ortho") film, lith film, or rapid-access film. This film makes a dramatic, abrupt transition between exposure and non-exposure, allowing the creation of film negatives that are either opaque (solid black) or transparent (clear areas). Negatives "shot" with the process camera are given to the stripper for use in the image assembly process.

The role of the stripper in image assembly. In a traditional workflow, the stripper's job is much more than imposing (positioning) the films. Before the widespread popularity of desktop publishing, the stripper's job included many other functions:

- *Properly arranging the individual films of each image or graphic relative to the position of that page's text.* When using traditional artboards, the pasteup merely indicates the position of a photograph or other graphic. Separate films—made from slides, prints, illustrations, or logo art-

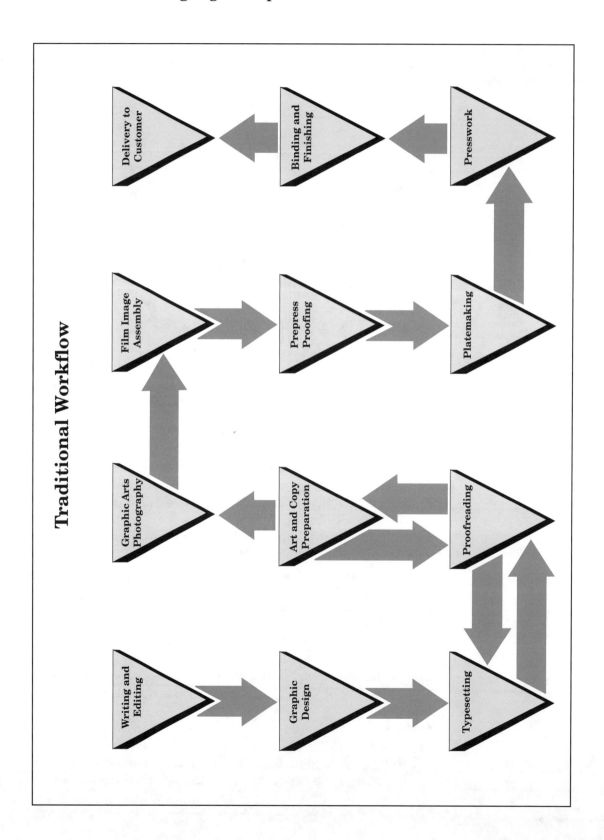

Traditional Workflow

work—must be stripped into the position indicated on the primary artboard. These films are taped to large sheets of clear plastic, typically polyester. A different sheet of polyester is used for each color to be printed. In the case of complex page designs, it is not unusual for a single press sheet to require a half-dozen or more polyester image carriers per color. In addition to these multiple sheets of polyester, the stripper uses materials such as Rubylith to reveal selected portions of images through a transparent window called a ***mask.***

- *Converting the black-and-white pasteups into areas of color* (a process known as creating ***color breaks).*** This involves using a variety of masking materials to control which areas of film will be exposed to each plate. Commonly used masking materials include goldenrod paper, orange vinyl, Rubylith, and Amberlith. After sheets of polyester or masking material have been used by the stripper, they are referred to as ***flats.***

- *Creating thin areas of overlap between adjoining colors.* This process is called ***trapping*** by prepress workers, but is often called "adding laps" or "building grips" by people in the pressroom. Trapping is needed to prevent small amounts of misregister in prepress and press operations from resulting in slivers of unprinted paper where colors would normally abut.

- *Compositing multiple layers of film for a single color by making the necessary exposures to a single, "final" film.* After processing, this single film is used to expose the plate—a process that is faster and more consistent than making multiple exposures from the original stack of films and masking materials.

Proofing. After the stripping process is complete, a ***proof*** is made from these films to assure that the stripping process has been done correctly. This proof might be in a single color (using photomechanical proofing materials such as DuPont's Dylux, which generates a type of proof called a "blueline"), or it might be in full color (using products such as Imation Matchprint, Fuji ColorArt, DuPont WaterProof, DuPont Cromalin, Enco PressMatch, AgfaProof, or others).

Platemaking. If the customer okays the proof, the stripped films are sent to the platemaking department. ***Platemaking*** is a term used to describe the process of exposing and processing the plate's emulsion to prepare it for mounting on the printing press. Printing plates for lithography are typically made from thin sheets of aluminum, coated with a layer of photosensitive emulsion. After exposure and processing, this emulsion remains attached to the plate in areas that produce a printed image.

This process is called plate*making* because many years ago the printer had to manufacture each plate from raw materials. Using a large sink (called a "plate whirler") and bottles of chemicals, the printer would manufacture the plate on the spot by swirling the emulsion onto a sheet of aluminum. Today, plates are purchased ready to expose—these plates are said to be "presensitized." Although creating plates from raw materials is no longer necessary, the worker responsible for exposing and processing these plates is still referred to as the ***platemaker.***

Plates can be separated into two categories: negative-working and positive-working. Commercial printers in North America typically use negative-working plates, while positive-working plates are more common in Europe. Each plate has its own advantages and disadvantages. The greatest advantage of negative plates lies in the simplicity of preparing films for plate exposure, while positive plates are favored for their ability to compensate for dot gain through overexposure.

On a *negative-working plate,* the negative films made by photographing the artboard (or output from a computer file via an imagesetter) are placed in tight contact with the plate surface and exposed with a high-intensity light. Light passes through the clear areas of the film (these clear areas correspond to the black portions of the original artwork, such as the type), and the energy of the light causes a reaction within the plate emulsion (a special chemical coating on the plate). In some cases, exposures from several different flats might be made to a single plate. After all exposures have been completed, the plate is ready to process. Plate processing used to be a manual task, performed in a sink with a cotton pad and a bottle of chemistry. Today, however, most printers possess automated plate processors.

The plate processor first bathes the plate in a chemical called a ***developer,*** which interacts with the plate's emulsion. The developer affects the plate differently depending on whether the plate is negative-working or positive-working. For negative plates, the light that passes through the clear portions of the film has caused the exposed portions of plate emulsion to harden; the developer then causes the unexposed areas of plate emulsion to detach from the plate. The plate is then transported to a second section within the plate processor where the plate's surface is rinsed with water to remove the unhardened emulsion from the plate. A third section "finishes" the plate by coating it with a thin layer of preservative, typically a gum arabic derivative, to prevent oxidization. Finally, the plate processor dries the plate, usually with hot air from electrical heating elements.

Positive-working plates require positive films instead of negative films for plate exposure. These positive films are clear in nonimage areas and contain black (opaque) areas where images are desired on the printing plate. Once again, the films are held in tight contact with the plate surface while a high-intensity light exposes the surface. In this case, however, the effect of light on the plate is to break up the long molecular chains of the emulsion. The destabilized emulsion is dissolved from the plate surface by the developer, leaving plate emulsion only in the unexposed areas. The remainder of the processing steps are the same as those for negative-working plates.

Both processes result in an aluminum plate that carries an image made from hardened areas of emulsion. These areas are oleophilic (meaning "oil-loving") and will attract the oily printing ink. The ink which is carried by these areas is then transferred to the rubber blanket of the printing press and finally to each sheet of paper that runs through the press. The background areas of the plate are hydrophilic (meaning "water-loving") and carry a film of water that prevents ink from sticking to the plate in the nonimage areas.

Image registration. Each color to be printed by the printing press requires a separate plate. Since multicolor images and graphics are reproduced using a combination of several inks, portions of these images appear on different plates. Therefore, it is extremely important that plates for multicolor printing be made using some form of register system. The most common register system involves punching small holes in film, polyester, and masking materials—holes that are just large enough to accommodate small metal or plastic posts, called *pins.* The punched materials are slipped over these pins and are held in a consistent, repeatable position. This process is known as *pin registration,* or *pin register.*

The use of pins on the light table to ensure that all images will properly register on press.

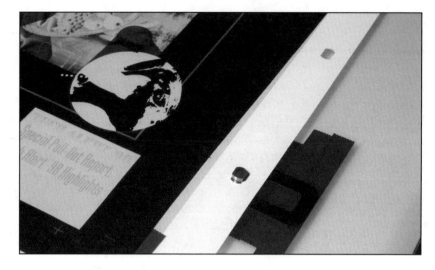

Although many forms of pin registration have been tried by printers, the majority of prepress work is now prepared by punching several holes simultaneously with a pin register punch. These punched materials are held in place by a long metal strip, known as a ***pinbar***, that contains several carefully spaced pins.

In the next chapter, we will see how all these elements are used together to strip a typical job for exposure to a negative-working printing plate.

4   The Art of Stripping

In 1983 a salesperson showed me a high-technology labor-saving device that he was sure would revolutionize modern image assembly. The device in question was a small block of clear Lucite with four wheels and a tiny knife blade. The principle was that this gadget could be set to a precise depth and pushed along the edge of a T-square, so as to create a perfect window in a sheet of Rubylith masking material. This salesman figured that, by avoiding the dreaded overcut, countless hours could be saved that would otherwise be spent burnishing the base side of the Rubylith mask to seal the overcuts. He was right about the advent of a powerful new labor-saving device that would revolutionize the process of image assembly—but we would have to wait for another year and the 1984 debut of the Apple Macintosh before the slow demise of the stripper became a certainty!

Only now, in the late 1990s, can such a statement be made without widespread condemnation. Many people take the diminishing role of conventional image assembly in today's print production workflow quite personally; I can assure you that, having been a stripper myself, it is not easy to contemplate a future without film and light tables. That day is already here for a select portion of the graphic arts industry; for the rest of us, it is an eventual certainty. The increased efficiencies of bypassing film in favor of direct laser exposure of printing plates with the computer-to-plate process are undeniable.

There is much to learn, however, from the fading process called conventional image assembly. Today's best electronic prepress workers are those with a solid background in the conventional processes. Their knowledge of how press, bindery, and finishing issues impact prepress functions makes them superior to workers who possess only computer knowledge. With this in mind, the rest of this chapter examines parts of the traditional image assembly process; later in the book, the impact of the printing press and postpress issues on the imposition process will be discussed. The goal for this chapter, however, will be to gain insight into the methods that traditional stripping utilizes to place graphics on a sheet, and perhaps to allow the reader to gain a renewed respect for the challenges inherent in the film-based imposition process. The work of an experienced, talented stripper elevates the process of image assembly beyond a craft into an art form—which is why this chapter is called "The Art of Stripping."

In this book, two common methods of stripping and imposing a job will be examined. The cover and interior (text) of a small 8.5×11-in. (216×279-mm) booklet will be used to illustrate these techniques. The text will be output from an imagesetter as single pages, while the cover will use artboards and traditional graphic arts camerawork. The inside front cover and inside back cover pages will be blank (unprinted).

Stripping a Sample Booklet Cover

I will start with the cover. (Stripping the interior of the booklet will be the discussed in the next chapter.) Although it is unusual in this day and age to actually receive a new job as pasteups (columns of black type on white photographic paper, glued to a white sheet of cardboard), it still happens on occasion. A more likely occurrence is the example illustrated here: a job that is to be reprinted from artwork created several years ago. For this particular job, the cover design has not changed; only a new photograph and a simple type change (replacing "1990" with the current year) is required to bring this artwork up to date.

The Artboards

An artist has prepared the pasteup in a typical fashion: the white cardboard is several inches larger than the booklet it represents, there are short black lines (***trim marks***) near every corner to designate the trim size of the job, it is a two-page spread, and the back cover is on the left while the front cover is on the right. There is a large amount of type, a few simple graphics, and a large red square indicating an area where a photographic image is to be positioned. Attached to the board with a long strip of tape is a sheet of clear plastic called an ***overlay;*** there are a few words glued to this overlay, above the red square. The artist has also attached a thin sheet of white paper (called a ***tissue***) to the board, and has

The graphic artist checking the clear plastic overlay attached to the artboard.

indicated that some of the type on the base art should be printed with cyan ink. The tissue also indicates that the type on the overlay should **_reverse_** out of the image, meaning that the area occupied by the type will contain no ink at all, allowing the paper to show through.

A tissue attached to the artboard providing the camera operator and stripper with important information about the job.

Shooting the Artboards

The pasteup (also called an ***artboard*** or simply a "board") is given to the camera operator, who will take photographs of both the board and the overlay with high-contrast film. Very few printing companies still retain a full-time camera operator; instead, a select group of strippers or platemakers (the "old-timers") will be pressed into service when camerawork is needed. At some printing companies, making camera "shots" has become so rare that they have actually sold (or discarded) their cameras, allowing darkroom space to be converted into a work area for more personal computers!

The camera operator makes an exposure with the large graphic arts camera onto a sheet of high-contrast ***orthochromatic*** film. The term orthochromatic means that this film is not sensitive to red light; therefore, red safelights are allowed in the camera darkroom. After exposure and development, the high-contrast film converts the white background areas of the artboard into solid black areas on the film. The type and other graphics that were rendered in black on the artwork can now be seen as clear areas on the film. Since the film now shows an image that is the opposite of the artboard, it is called a film ***negative.*** This high-contrast film is most appropriate for reproducing high-contrast subject matter such as text and lines; because of this, these negatives are also called ***line shots.***

In the case of the artboard for the booklet's cover, *two* negatives must be made—one from the artwork that is glued to the actual board (also called the ***base art),*** and another from the type attached to the clear plastic overlay which has been taped to the board. This overlay is clear for the convenience of the artist; it allows the artist to judge the position of the graphics on the overlay relative to the graphics on the base art. For the process of shooting negatives from this art, however, the overlay presents a challenge—how can the type on the overlay be photographed without photographing the base art graphics that can be seen through this clear acetate? This problem is solved by carefully cutting a sheet of white paper to the trim size of the document. Sliding a thin sheet of white paper underneath the overlay blocks out the graphics on the base art while still revealing the trim marks drawn on the artboard. Through this process, two separate negatives— one of the base art, another of the overlay—are made.

The negatives are usually not perfect, however, and must be touched-up in preparation for stripping. Flaws in the artwork (such as cutlines and overlapping layers of typesetting paper) can cause shadows, which appear as clear areas on the film. The film preparation process involves blocking out unwanted clear areas on the negative with a water-soluble paint called liquid opaque. Just as the name implies, opaque completely blocks the transmission of light through the film. This paint is applied with a small sable brush, although some strippers favor opaque markers that apply a similar fluid.

Opaque being applied to the film negative to block out unwanted clear areas.

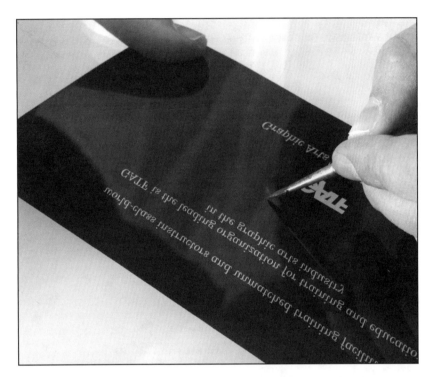

Squaring the Table

Once the films have been opaqued, the process of stripping (image assembly) can begin. The most important work surface for assembling these images is the *light table,* a large metal table with adjustable edges (called *rails*) and a removable glass top. Underneath this large sheet of thick glass are powerful fluorescent light bulbs, whose light is diffused through a sheet of white plastic. In order for stripping to be done accurately, the light table must create a perfect 90° angle where the front rail and left rail meet. Light tables can be adjusted in order to create this perpendicular alignment. The process of making these adjustments is called "squaring the table." Once the table is determined to be square, a pin-bar is taped to the glass, parallel to the front rail.

Squaring up a
light table.

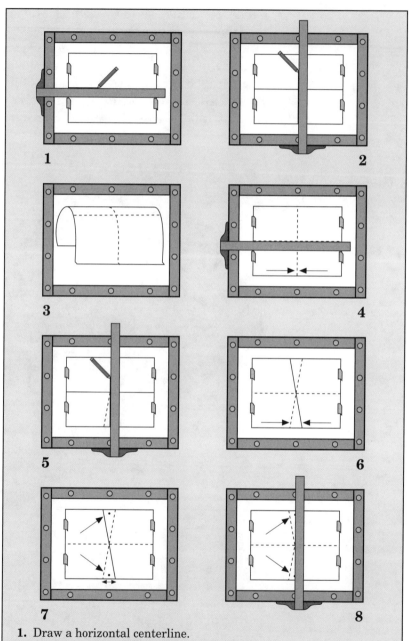

1. Draw a horizontal centerline.
2. Draw a vertical line bisecting the centerline.
3. Flop the sheet back-to-back.
4. Align the paper using the centerline.
5. Draw a vertical line through the original point of intersection.
6. Measure the distance between the ends of the two vertical lines.
7. Mark the halfway points between the vertical lines.
8. Adjust the front edge of the table so that the T-square's blade
   connects the two points.

A pinbar being taped to the glass of the light table so that it is parallel to the front rail.

Preparing the Layout

When the films are ready for image assembly, the stripper begins by preparing a *layout.* This layout will assist the stripper in positioning the films, so that each page will be printed in the desired location on the press sheet. The layout is often drawn on a large sheet of orange vinyl, although clear polyester or goldenrod paper can also be used. The material for the layout is punched before drawing begins, using the same pin registration system that will be employed for the rest of the stripping and platemaking process. Lines are then drawn on this material with an appropriate tool (ball-point pen for orange vinyl or goldenrod paper, or a

A sheet of orange vinyl attached to the register pins on the light table. The stripper is using a black ball-point pen to draw a horizontal line.

technical drawing pen and drafting ink for clear polyester). Straight lines are drawn with the aid of a tool called the T-square. In addition to serving as a straightedge, the T-square allows one to determine what is "square"—in other words, what is at a perpendicular angle relative to the front and left edges of the light table. The carefully drawn lines will guide the stripper in positioning the negatives during the stripping process. Many print shops have a number of "master" layouts stored in a drawer. When the shop needs to create a new layout that can be based on one of these masters, the stripper simply places the master on the pinbar and traces the lines onto a fresh sheet of the desired material.

Finding the horizontal center. As I navigate around the layout (and later, the press sheet), I will be referring to horizontal dimensions and vertical dimensions. These dimensions are always expressed relative to the pinbar on the light table or the gripper of the printing press (more on this in the next chapter). Horizontal lines are those that move from left to right across the sheet (in the same direction as the pinbar). Vertical lines are those that move from the front of the layout toward the back (perpendicular to the pinbar). Since some types of printing presses hold the stock by the short dimension while others grip the stock along its long edge, the paper-neutral terms "horizontal" and "vertical" will be used in this book, instead of the terms "width" and "length."

Although the layout for the booklet's cover will be extremely simple, it will still require most of the basic elements of any layout. The first task is to find the horizontal center of our layout relative to the punched holes. There are many ways to do this, and every stripper has a favorite. Mine is to position the T-square against the front rail of the table so that the stem of the T-square is pushed tightly against one side of the center pin of the pinbar. I then use a razor blade held against the T-square to make a tiny mark in the orange vinyl about an inch away from the center pin. Next I move the T-square to the other side of the center pin and repeat the process. Finally I measure the distance between the two marks with a ruler and use a pen to indicate the point in the middle. This is the center of the layout, relative to the pinbar.

Next, it is time to begin drawing the positioning lines. The first line to be drawn is the horizontal center of the sheet based on the preceding method. A problem quickly becomes apparent: the center pin is blocking the T-square from reach-

Finding the horizontal center of the layout: *(top)* positioning the T-square tightly against one side of the center register pin and using a razor blade to make a tiny mark on the orange vinyl layout sheet, *(middle)* positioning the T-square on the other side of the center pin and making another tiny mark on the layout, and *(bottom)* using a ruler to measure the distance between the two tiny marks.

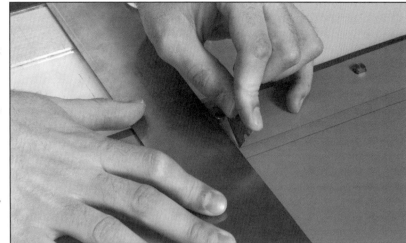

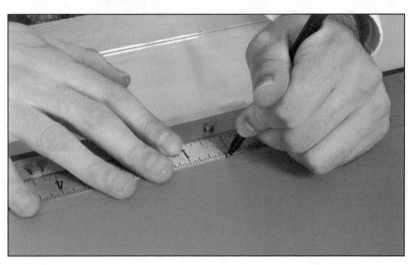

ing the center mark! For that reason, a large steel triangle with two perpendicular edges is used to draw this particular line. The triangle is placed against a horizontally positioned T-square and can now be moved into the correct position to draw the centerline.

Placing a triangle against the horizontally positioned T-square in order to draw the centerline.

Finding the plate bend allowance and vertical center. With the horizontal centerline drawn, it is time to determine where the image should be positioned vertically within the layout. An important concept to grasp at this point is that the material upon which the layout is being drawn is punched with the same pin register punch that will soon punch the printing plate. This means that any dimensions measured on the layout will correspond to the same dimensions of the plate. Most importantly, it means that the leading edge of the plate will exactly correspond with the leading edge of the material used for the layout. Because of this, the first line to be drawn on the layout sheet corresponds to the *plate bend* required by the intended printing press. This plate bend area includes the amount of metal that will be clamped into the plate mounting system of the press, as well as the additional area needed for the metal plate to bend from the gap where this mounting occurs onto the surface of the plate cylinder. The total distance that is considered the plate bend varies from press to press, but is always the distance from the edge of the plate to where the sheets of paper traveling through

The layout sheet after allowing for the plate bend.

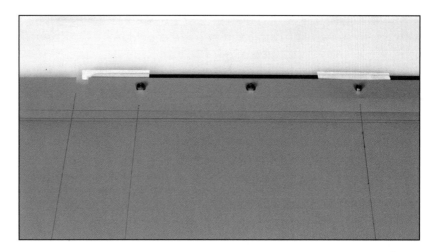

the press begin. For our example, the cover will be printed on a Heidelberg Speedmaster, which has a plate bend allowance of 1.6875 in. (43 mm).

Since this plate-bend line represents the edge of the press sheet, three more lines can be drawn to represent the back and sides of the stock. The cover is being printed on a press sheet (20×26 in., 508×660 mm) that is more than large enough to cover the 11-in. (279-mm) height and 17-in. (432-mm) width of our booklet's unfolded cover. At this time it is also useful to draw a line representing the *vertical center* of this press sheet (the purpose of this line is discussed in a few pages).

Determining gripper allowance. The next line is measured from the plate bend and will determine the placement of the cover pages on the press sheet. Typically the printed area is placed as close as possible to the leading edge of the sheet; the *leading edge* is the side of the press sheet that goes into the printing press first, which is also the same edge that has been punched for our pinbar. The press cannot print the first portion of paper at the leading edge because the paper is pulled through the press by strong metal clamps called gripper fingers. The paper clamped inside these grippers cannot be printed, and this gripper width allowance varies from press to press—for the Heidelberg Speedmaster, the gripper amount is 0.375 in. (10 mm). Instead of drawing the first line at this point, however, add the desired amount of bleed to this number and draw the line at the distance that includes them both. Allowing 0.125 in. (3 mm) of bleed for the cover, the line should be drawn 0.5 in. (13 mm) beyond the plate bend.

Outlining the image area. Once this line is drawn, the rest of the image area can be outlined. This task is as easy as measuring back another 11 in. (279 mm) to draw a horizontal line representing the top trim of the cover and measuring out from the center 8.5 in. (216 mm) in each direction to represent the left and right edges. In addition to the 0.5-in. (13-mm) margin between the edge of the sheet and the bottom trim of the cover, there is also a 7.3125-in. (183.5-mm) margin above the top trim and 3-in. margins to the left and right of the cover. Some of the margin above the top trim will be used for a process control device known as a color bar. The layout is now ready to be used in the image assembly process.

Stripping the "Base Art" Films

As stated earlier, the purpose of the layout is to assist the stripper in positioning the films so that each page will be printed in the desired location on the press sheet. This goal is accomplished by taping the individual films into the desired position on a sheet of clear polyester. Although there are several ways to do this, here is the method I prefer.

Starting with an empty light table, place a sheet of pre-punched clear polyester on the pinbar and lightly "fan it out." This means gently smoothing the polyester against the glass of the light table, in order to eliminate air pockets and ensure that all the material pulls against the pinbar with an equal amount of force. Once the material is fanned out, tape it down with a single piece of masking tape at the middle of the polyester's back edge—this serves to hold the polyester against the glass in the proper position. Finally, stack the completed layout onto the pinbar as well and repeat the fanning out process with the layout. Now one is able to slide the individual negatives underneath the layout sheet, with the emulsion side of the film up (away from the clear polyester).

Attaching the clear polyester to the registers pins and then fanning it out against the glass of the light table.

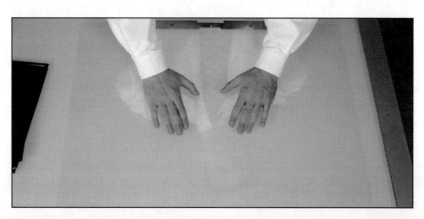

Sliding a film negative into position beneath the layout sheet.

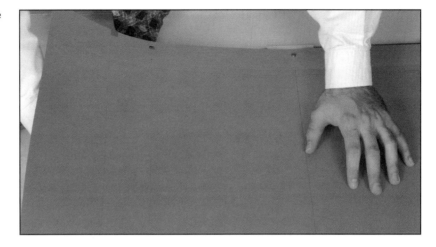

When the trim marks shown on the film are aligned underneath the trim marks drawn on the layout, press firmly down on the stack with one hand while removing a short piece of red stripper's tape from a dispenser with the other hand. Use several of these strips of tape to attach the film to the polyester in the desired position.

Using small pieces of red stripper's tape to attach the film to the polyester in the desired position.

Stripping the "Overlay" Films

The film negatives showing the base art images for both the outside back cover and outside front cover are now positioned on this sheet of polyester. This *completed* combination of stripping material (in this case, polyester) and film is referred to as a **flat.** The flat can now be removed by pulling both it and the layout off of the pinbar. There is more film to assemble, but this time a sheet of punched orange vinyl will be used, instead of clear polyester. Place the orange vinyl onto the pins, fan it out and tape it down before positioning the layout on top of the pins again. Now it is time to tape down the films created by photographing the overlay—position them using the very same method. One might be wondering why the line shot of the base art was taped to a sheet of clear polyester, but orange vinyl was used to hold the negative of the overlay. This is because an experienced stripper will read the instructions shown on the overlay, and notice that the base art must be used for more than one color while all the type on the overlay will be used only long enough to generate the knockout. Having the base art on clear polyester allows us the freedom to create a variety of different masks from materials such as orange vinyl, goldenrod paper, or even Rubylith, and Amberlith.

Creating Masks

Although both negatives have now been stripped into position, the job is not finished. Next, I will create a ***mask*** that will reveal the desired portion of the cover illustration—which just happens to be a photograph of GATF's Technical Center. As mentioned earlier, the artist placed a big red square on the base art to indicate the area that this image would occupy; since the film was not sensitive to the red light reflected from that square, an identical clear area resulted on the line shot. This square can be used as a mask, to reveal an image that has been converted into halftone dots. (See the sidebar on the next page for more information on converting photos into halftones.) If our cover photograph was only a halftone (printed in only one color of ink), it could be taped directly to the emulsion side of the line shot. The design, however, calls for a full-color image, which means that there will be four films for this image.

Because of the use of multiple films (also called ***separations),*** it will be easiest to recreate the clear area on the negative using a punched sheet of Rubylith or Amberlith masking material. Both of these commonly used products feature a colored gelatin coating over a polyester base; the gelatin can be cut with an X-Acto (artist's) knife, then peeled up with the corner of a piece of tape. The process is done in this fashion: with the flat carrying the base negative already fanned out and taped down to the glass, the masking material is fanned out and taped down on top of it. The gelatin side of the masking material is up, as is the emulsion side of the line shot. Using the T-square as a straightedge, carefully cut through the gelatin, using the clear square on the line shot

Converting Photographs into Halftones

Paintings, photographic prints, slides, and other forms of artwork are typically made up of continuous tones (areas of color that change smoothly from one shade to another). However, the printing press cannot deliver ink in varying shades. In fact, one of the goals of high-quality press operation is to print every job with a consistent ink density.

How, then, can one expect the press to simulate the continuous tones found in a photograph? By recreating the photo as a series of tiny dots—a process called *screening*. When the type of screening used employs equally spaced dots that vary in size, the resulting image is called a *halftone*.

As with so many other parts of the prepress process, this screening was once done with a camera and high-contrast film. During the photographic exposure, light reflected off the artwork and passed through a sheet of plastic (or glass) called a halftone screen. This halftone screen converted the original image into dots of varying size, with dot size corresponding to the tone values in the original image.

In today's digital workflow, images are scanned (or photographed with a digital camera) to create a computer file consisting of tiny colored squares known as *pixels*. Unlike the round halftone dots, these pixels are perfectly square. They also touch one another, so that every area of the image is covered by a pixel. When this digital image file contains information that is only black or white (and no gray values in between), it is referred to as a line art or bitmap image. Other digital images may have pixels that describe varying shades of only a single color; these files are called grayscale images. When image files are capable of describing varying shades of many different colors, we refer to them by the color channels used to describe the photo's color content, such as RGB images (containing red, green, and blue channels) or CMYK images (containing cyan, magenta, yellow, and black channels).

Due to the pre-digital tradition of calling all single-color images "halftones," many prepress workers make the mistake of using the term halftone to describe grayscale images contained in page layout documents. In reality these grayscale images do not become halftones until the image's pixels are converted into dots of varying sizes during the output process—a procedure that takes place inside the raster image processor (RIP).

Once a grayscale image file's pixels have been converted into appropriately sized halftone dots by the RIP, the imagesetter's laser beam is used to expose a raw sheet of film in the pattern of these halftone dots. After this film is processed, the resulting halftone is ready for image assembly. If the image being output is a full-color image, four pieces of film will be created—each containing a similar image made of halftone dots. Instead of halftones, however, these films are called the cyan, magenta, yellow, and black *separations.*

Positioning the masking material over the film flat carrying the base art negative.

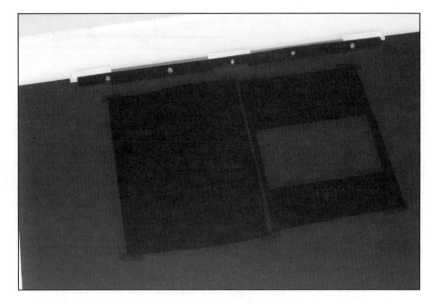

as a guide. A delicate touch and a careful hand are essential—if too much pressure is applied, the X-Acto knife will create a deep groove in the masking material's polyester base; if the cuts extend beyond the corners of the window, an overcut occurs (the short lines of the overcut may be visible as thin black marks on the printed sheet). If an overcut does occur, the stripper should flip the masking material over and burnish the corner gently but firmly with a smooth surface, such as the other end of the X-Acto knife. With all four sides of the window completely cut, use a piece of tape to loosen a corner of the gelatin from within the window. The remaining portion of the gelatin window can then be easily removed.

Using an artist's knife to cut through the thin membrane of the masking material.

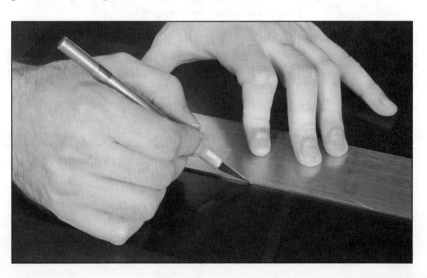

After using a piece of
tape to loosen a corner
of the window *(top)*,
the stripper removes
the masking material
from the window
(middle and bottom).

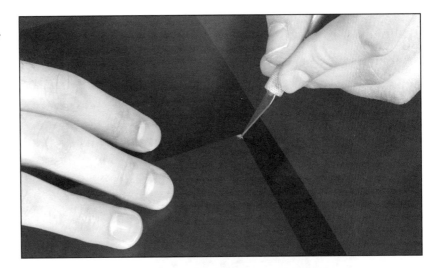

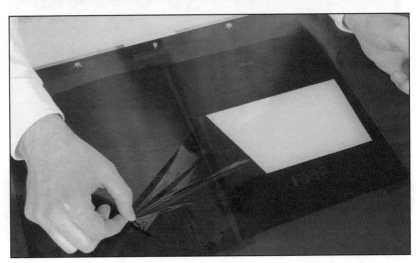

Stripping the Separations

Once the mask has been completed, the next step is to tape down the individual films for the photo; this process is often called "laying the separations." At this point, remove the flats from the pinbar and move the base negative flat aside. Place the mask back onto the pins (still emulsion up), fan it out, and tape it down. Next, place a punched sheet of clear polyester onto the pins and fasten it down as well. This polyester is the *carrier* upon which one of the color separation films of the cover illustration are fastened. This process will take some practice before it becomes natural because, first, the position of a negative image is being judged by referring to the cropping indications shown on a positive photograph, and second, because the emulsion-up separation is the mirror image of the photograph. With some practice, however, it becomes a natural process to look at a positive original as a guide to position films that are flopped negative images!

Although ideally the black negative should be positioned first, this is seldom possible because most black separations do not have adequate detail to allow for the careful positioning of the image. If this is indeed the case, begin by positioning the cyan film. (In some instances, magenta may be positioned before cyan; see the sidebar on the next page for an explanation of which to use first). While referring to the cropping instructions indicated on the original, carefully move the cyan separation into the correct position relative to the window in the masking material, then tape it down to

Stripper carefully positioning the cyan separation negative relative to the window in the masking material. After the negative is properly positioned, short pieces of stripper's tape are used to attach it to the polyester carrier sheet.

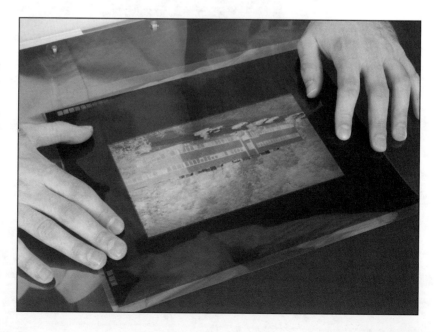

the polyester with a short piece of red stripper's tape on each corner. Be careful that the stripper's tape does not intrude into the window area, as this will prevent that portion of the image from exposing the plate. Once the film has been firmly taped into position, remove the stack of flats from the pinbar and place the mask flat aside. Replace the cyan carrier on the pinbar, fan it out, and tape it down.

Next, begin taping other separations in position based on this first color. Stripping color separations into perfect position on multiple carriers is called "registering the separations" and requires patience as well as a steady hand. Simply stacking another sheet of clear polyester and another color separation on top of this first carrier will not produce good results. Since both separations will appear to the stripper as black images on clear film, it is too difficult to tell which dots and marks are on which sheet of film. To provide a visual indication of which film is on the bottom, the stripper uses a sheet of material that will change the appearance of the bottom layer. Several different "tricks of the trade" can be employed to this effect. Most strippers use a thin sheet of white frosted acetate (usually called a *frosty*), while others use a sheet of yellow Color-Key proofing material. My personal preference is to use the thin sheet of waxy white paper that separates each sheet of clear polyester within the box! Although this flimsy material is difficult to control, its thinness makes it ideal for creating just enough softness to distinguish the bottom film without destroying the visual detail.

Incorporating whatever "frosty" you prefer, fan out and tape down another sheet of clear polyester, which will be used

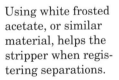

Using white frosted acetate, or similar material, helps the stripper when registering separations.

Determining Which Separation to Strip First

Each separation contains varying amounts of information; typically, the yellow separation contains the largest number of halftone dots, while a normal black separation contains very few halftone dots. As a result, a negative made from the yellow separation sometimes look like a clear window, while the black separation may contain so little detail that the outer edges of the image area can be hard to define. This information becomes important when one begins registering these negatives during the image assembly process. One probably would not begin by positioning the black negative over the intended window, since there probably will not be enough image on the negative to allow for exact image placement. The importance of positioning the first separation correctly cannot be overstated—making a mistake during this procedure would cause all the subsequent colors to be out of position as well. Most strippers begin the process of "registering the four-color" separations by positioning the cyan or magenta films over the intended window, since these negatives provide adequate image detail while allowing the perimeter of the window to be seen.

Although scanning software places tiny crosses (called register marks) at the corner of each image, it's important that we also check the internal register of the image itself. This was critically important prior to the widespread adoption of Adobe Photoshop, because the manual color correction process known as ***dot etching*** could cause misregister between the image and the registration marks. Even today, checking internal fit is important, since registering large-format film solely by the marks is difficult; the most common problem that one is trying to avoid, however, is stripping the yellow and/or black separations upside down! Since these two films often have very little useful information, it can be very easy to perfectly register the marks without realizing the image is emulsion-down instead of emulsion-up.

The key to checking internal fit is to look for highlights; the smaller and brighter, the better. Highlights are visible on the film negatives as black spots within the lighter image. On the black separation, these spots are relatively large in size. When another negative (such as the magenta) is positioned over the black negative, internal fit can be easily assured by centering the tight highlight patterns of the magenta negative directly on top of the larger highlights of the black separation. For this reason, one should always strip the black film first if possible, such as when the original image being registered is very dark, in which case the black negative will have a reasonable amount of detail. However, if one is unable to visually determine the edge of the window, it is hard to be certain that the image is positioned correctly. In that situation, begin by positioning a magenta or cyan negative first, and then registering the negatives according to the process described in this chapter.

(Sidebar continues on next page.)

Determining Which Separation to Strip First
(continued from previous page)

Positioning the black negative first is ideal, but what should the sequence be following this first step? Should the cyan negative be registered to the black, and then the magenta registered on top of the cyan (as is commonplace)? The answer depends on the screen angles used by the RIP during the screening process. The angles at which each row of dots in a separation are positioned is expressed in degrees; a typical angle set might be 45° for the black, 75° for the magenta, 90° for the yellow, and 105° for the cyan. When these rows of dots at different angles are seen together, the result is called a *rosette pattern*.

During the process of registering film negatives, this rosette pattern can make it difficult to ascertain whether or not internal image fit has been achieved. Therefore, when registering a set of four-color separations, use a sequence that allows you to be the best judge of internal fit. Look closely at the rosette formed when one negative is placed on top of another. If the resulting visual pattern obscures the highlight detail, try a different sequence.

for the black separation. Now one can see the use for the registration marks that appear along the outside of the image to help you register each new color on top of the existing separation. The shape and size of these register marks can vary, depending on how the color separation films were generated.

Two decades ago most color separations were done using a large gallery camera; in these separations, the register marks were actual targets applied to the edge of the photograph. Today the process for generating separations with a camera has been replaced by the use of digital scanners. Throughout the 1980s most print shops used scanners that had both input and output drums. The input drum used a beam of balanced white light to illuminate the subject, while the output drum used a laser beam to image halftone dots onto film. Separations made with this process have registration marks that look like parallel railroad tracks running along two sides. Today most printing companies and service bureaus use scanners only to input digital information into their computer systems. Once scanned, these images are color-corrected and retouched using programs such as Adobe Photoshop, and then output on a high-quality laser imagesetter. Separations that are output using this method will probably not have "railroad tracks"; instead the marks will likely appear as small cross hairs just outside each corner of each image.

As the black separation is brought into alignment with the cyan separation below, it becomes possible to align the registration marks of the top film exactly in position with the marks on the bottom film. This is done through the use of a small magnifying glass. Several common varieties of magnifiers are used in the graphic arts, but only collimating magnifiers that can control viewing parallax (such as the popular Beta ParaMag) are appropriate for this task. Once one feels that a perfect match has been achieved, press firmly on the separation with one hand while you tape each corner of the film down with short pieces of red stripper's tape. Then check again to make certain that the image has not shifted during the taping process.

Stripper using a collimating magnifier to ensure that register marks on the top film align exactly with the marks on the bottom film.

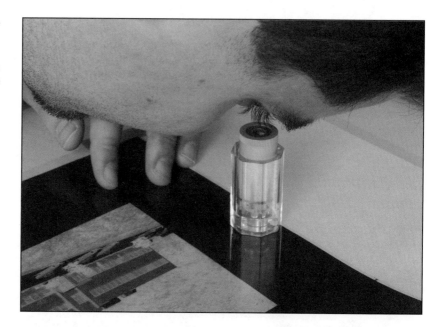

Remove all the flats, then restack all the same carriers so that the black is now on the bottom, the frosty in the middle, and the cyan carrier on top. If everything is fanned and taped properly, one should be able to use a magnifier to confirm that the register marks still fit. More importantly, now check the actual highlight details of the image itself to make sure that the registration of both images is correct. Highlights in the black film will appear as large areas of black spots; these same highlights will appear on the magenta film, but as smaller groups of spots. This characteristic will allow you to "check the work," to assure the true alignment of the images. This check can be important for several reasons:

- The output device may have a problem that causes the marks to be out of alignment
- The two colors may have been output at different times, causing the films to be of slightly differing sizes
- Some marks may have been trimmed off, to allow room for multiple images to be taped to the same carrier

Remember: the register marks serve only as an aid for positioning—what is most important is to verify that the actual images are in registration. If the highlight details do not fit, remove the tape from the cyan separation and register it again. Once one has verified that the cyan "fits" to the black, remove all the flats from the pinbar.

Only two more colors to go! Place the cyan carrier onto the pinbar, fan it out, and tape it down. Place the frosty on top of the cyan separation, then position a fresh sheet of clear polyester. Now the magenta separation can be registered on top of the cyan. Once registration is achieved, remove the magenta carrier and replace it with another sheet of clear polyester. Use the magnifier to register the yellow separation.

Creating Knockouts

Although a great deal of effort has been expended to assemble these elements, the stripping job is not over yet. The tissue attached to the artboard requested that the type on the overlay be reversed out of the cover photo. This is made possible by creating a ***knockout*** using high-contrast contact

The "overlay" line negative attached to a sheet of orange vinyl.

film. After attaching the overlay line shot to a sheet of orange vinyl, take that vinyl and place it on the empty light table with the emulsion of the film against the glass. Although one is now looking down onto the orange vinyl itself, the light from the light table allows one to see where the type is located on the negative. Using a razor blade, carefully cut a hole in the orange vinyl and remove it to reveal the type. The razor blade must be used with the lightest force possible, so that it cuts through the vinyl without cutting through the polyester base of the negative. It is helpful to hold the razor blade at a slant, so that any cuts which may occur can be hidden underneath the vinyl.

An opening cut into the orange vinyl to expose the type to be used to create a knockout.

Now that the type from the overlay is clearly visible through the hole in the vinyl, use this flat to expose a large, punched sheet of high-contrast film. For our purposes, use **contact** film, a type of film that creates an image opposite in tone of the film through which it was exposed. The exposure occurs in a vacuum frame. Although this frame may be large enough to look like a platemaking frame, the light source used for creating stripping films is different than the light used for exposing plates. The type of film preferred for stripping is called **bright-light** film, which means that it can be handled under lights that are much brighter than those found in the graphic arts darkroom. The important consideration is to reduce the amount of ultraviolet radiation present in the room lighting. In the past, this was done by placing a yellow sleeve over the fluorescent tubes in the light fixtures. Today, however, many printers use UV-filter sleeves that provide near-white illumination with greatly reduced ultra-violet content.

Punch the large sheet of contact film, and then place it emulsion-down on a pinbar inside the contact frame. This pinbar must be an exact match to the pinbar used on the light table. Next, place the overlay flat emulsion-down on top of the film so that the line shot is oriented **_right-reading emulsion-down._** This means that the film's image is positioned so that it is in the right direction to allow us to read it correctly (right-reading), and that the emulsion side of the film is facing down. Since the emulsion of the contact film is also facing down, the film is exposed through its polyester base to produce a contact that is also right-reading emulsion-down. Next lower the glass lid of the frame and turn on a vacuum pump to remove the air between the films and the glass for a very tight contact between all surfaces.

Finally, after allowing enough time for most of the air to be pumped out, press the exposure button, allowing a measured amount of light to be produced by the light bulb so that the film can be accurately exposed. After exposure, insert the film into an automatic film processor. A few minutes later the film will emerge developed and dry.

The resulting film will be completely clear across its entirety, with the exception of the type—the words from the overlay will now be in black on this clear background. As mentioned earlier, this film is called a knockout because the opaque black type will prevent light from exposing the printing plate, causing the type to reverse itself from the image when printed. What happens to the orange vinyl with the overlay line shot? Although it should not be needed again, write **_prework_** on it and keep it with the rest of the flats.

Masking Type

There are still a few more things to do before the work is finished. The tissue indicates that the type on the base art is to be more than one color. By default, any type whose color is not indicated is assumed to print in black ink; the only markings on the tissue ask that the year of the booklet and the headline on the back cover be printed in cyan ink. This can be easily done by first employing a method similar to that used in preparing the knockout to expose the cyan type. As with the overlay line shot, begin by placing the flat carrying the base art negative face down on an otherwise empty light table. Once again, use a sheet of orange vinyl and a razor blade to cut a hole that reveals the type to be printed in cyan. This sheet of orange vinyl can now be used as a mask to expose the type to the cyan plate.

Stripper creating openings in the orange vinyl to expose type that will print in cyan.

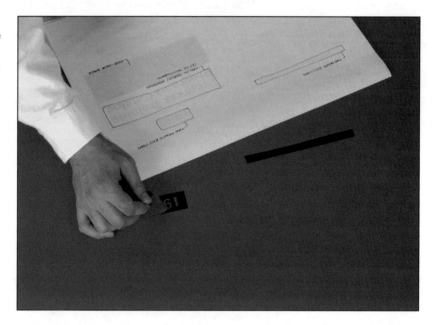

The black type is trickier. Because of the way in which the type appears in several different areas, several holes will have to be cut in the orange vinyl to properly mask them all. Of course, the more holes that are cut into the sheet of orange vinyl, the flimsier and more difficult it becomes to handle. Therefore a more expensive masking material such as Ruby-lith or Amberlith will be used to create a mask for the black type. The process for doing this is similar to that by which the image mask was created. Begin by placing the flat carrying the base art negative emulsion-up on the light table. Next place a sheet of masking material on top of the pinbar with its gelatin side up and use an X-Acto knife to carefully create a series of windows that reveal all the type (except for the year and headline on the back cover). Once the gelatin material is peeled up, we have the mask needed to expose the type for the black plate.

Labeling the Flats

At this point it looks as if the stripping of the cover is finished. I now have a variety of flats that can be used to expose the type and images as needed for the cyan, magenta, yellow, and black plates. All of this work, however, has been completed without providing adequate instructions for others in the pre-press area about how all these pieces can be used together to create printing plates. The solution is to label each flat with enough information that any other prepress worker could pick up this job and know what to do with it. There are many ways to label flats. Some printers prepare self-adhesive stickers that specify what information should be documented on each flat, but most strippers simply write directly

Labeling the film flats and masks.

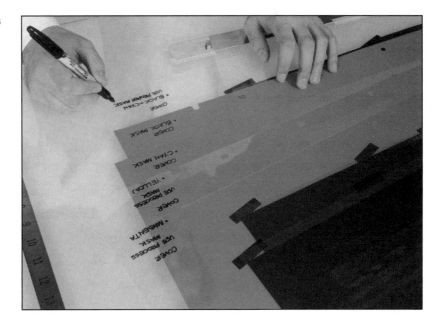

on each flat with a permanent marker. At a minimum, each flat should be labeled with the job number, form, side, and stacking order (the color can be shown in the stacking order diagram). If the flat can be used for several different purposes, more than one stacking order diagram can be drawn on the flat. In addition, label all the flats with information about the form (front or back), the signature (such as "Cover") and the job number.

Exposing the Marks

Done yet? Not quite! The final piece of the puzzle is to provide a method of exposing the marks that will help the press-room and bindery personnel to properly print and fold the sheet. The simplest way to accomplish this for the booklet cover is to use a small film scribe to scrape thin lines through the orange vinyl used as a layout. Some strippers do not like this method because the scribe used to cut the marks into the orange vinyl will immediately become unusable for scribing film; in fact, after a few months the scribe itself will be worn out and require replacement. I like this method, however, because it is fast and allows excellent control over the placement of the marks. As an alternative, some strippers will attach films imaged with thin lines to the back of the layout sheet, then open holes in the layout sheet with a razor blade to expose these lines to the plate.

Using a scriber to cut marks into the orange vinyl.

The important marks to include in the layout include the horizontal trims, the vertical trims at the back of the sheet, all folds, a side guide mark, and short lines depicting the center of the sheet in both the horizontal and vertical directions. These short lines should actually extend slightly beyond the edge of the sheet so that a skid of printed paper will show the center mark as a line drawn down the stack. If these marks are for a layout that will be used again and again, expose the marks to a sheet of punched duplicating film; in that way, one will have a *master marks flat* that saves the trouble of cutting marks into subsequent layout sheets.

Congratulations! You've just walked through all the steps necessary to strip a *very* simple job from an artboard using traditional methods. This workflow is very slow, tedious, and labor-intensive. More importantly, the complexity of most jobs accomplished by this method becomes so great that some sort of error (whether on the part of the stripper, the platemaker, or some other person involved in the process) is practically guaranteed. This scenario set the stage for the relatively rapid adoption of desktop publishing hardware and software throughout the publishing industry.

The workflow that early proponents of desktop publishing used to output and impose jobs is discussed in the next chapter.

5 Desktop Publishing with Manual Imposition

Desktop publishing (DTP) is a catch-all term that describes the many functions involving a personal computer (an affordable computer that is small enough to fit on a desktop) and document creation software utilizing the PostScript page description computer language. In the decade between 1984 and 1994, nearly every printing company in the world added computers and output devices in order to join the DTP revolution.

The profound influence that Adobe's PostScript has had on every facet of the printer's business is discussed later in this book; for now, suffice it to say that the influence of DTP and PostScript was minimal until the widespread adoption of internal drum imagesetters in the late 1980s and early 1990s. These high-quality devices finally allowed desktop publishers to realize the dream they had been chasing for several years: to output digital files containing accurate halftone dots directly to film, on the same page and at the same time as text and other graphics.

Designing Pages with DTP

The last chapter discussed how to strip a sample booklet cover starting from artboards. This chapter discusses how to strip the interior of the sample booklet using films output by an imagesetter from digital files. Using a popular page layout software program (in this case, QuarkXPress), the designer has built eight pages worth of text, graphics, and images. Looking at the computer monitor, the designer specified the size of the booklet and the margins within each page; then, columns of text were created and positioned next to logos and other graphics. The full-color photographs were scanned in by the same method as in our previous example, but instead of the images being output to film directly after scanning, the electronic information for each photo was com-

A screen capture showing a two-page reader's spread of the QuarkXPress document used to create the interior for the booklet.

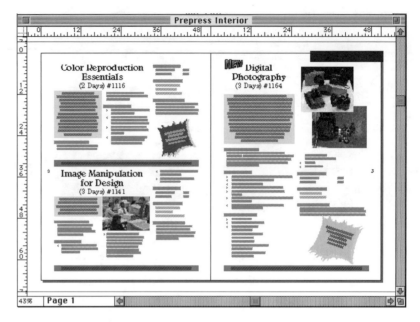

bined with the text and other graphics within the page layout document. Because colored text and reverse text have all been specified within the desktop publishing software, there will be no need to cut windows, to make type masks, or to even generate knockouts with contact film.

During the design phase, the designer was able to make low-resolution printouts of these pages by outputting the QuarkXPress document on a black-and-white laser printer. This process was repeated when the electronic files for the job were received by the printing company. The printer, however, used a more sophisticated device called a ***digital color proofer*** in order to output the document in full-color. In both cases, the intent was the same: to verify that the output from the file was correct and that it matched the look of the document as seen on the computer screen. This color output created at the printing company is called a ***proof*** and is typically sent to the designer for approval before film is created.

Outputting Film on an Imagesetter

Our booklet is no exception to this rule. The designer has seen and approved the color proofs, so film can now be output using the digital files of this DTP document. The PostScript output process is discussed in more detail in a later chapter; but for now, let me simply say that choosing the Print command in QuarkXPress allows PostScript information describing the pages in the booklet to be received by the imagesetter. A few minutes later the imagesetter uses a laser beam to transfer the information about the document to film. Since it does not take long for each page to be completely imaged by the laser beam, all of the pages are exposed and the film is ready to process in a relatively short time.

In some printing companies the film from the imagesetter automatically travels directly into an adjacent film processor. This method, known as ***online processing,*** produces the fastest film output with the least human intervention. Due to cost considerations and machine interface problems, however, many prepress managers opt to manually unload film from the imagesetter (either as a short roll or as multiple sheets) and then insert this film into a film processor under the appropriate darkroom conditions. Since most imagesetters use panchromatic film that is sensitive to red light (unlike the orthochromatic camera film mentioned earlier, which was safe to handle under red light), the darkroom can only have a dim green light to work under.

When the film for our booklet has emerged from the processor, one can see that each page is complete. Using scissors, trim each page to a size slightly larger than the finished size of the booklet. These pages have trim marks and register marks created by the page layout program, which has also identified each page by page number and plate color. Since each different color output to film should result in a different printing plate, page layout software typically identifies these films as the black plate, magenta plate, etc.

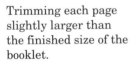

Trimming each page slightly larger than the finished size of the booklet.

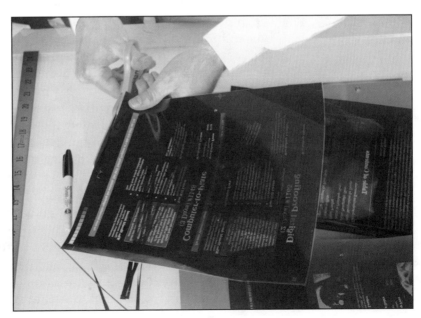

Creating the Stripping Layout

Now that the film has been exposed and developed, the next step is to create a layout for stripping these films. This time I'll be preparing plates for a smaller format printing press: the Komori Lithrone 28 SAPC. Using the same basic method as described for the cover, punch a sheet of orange vinyl and determine its center mark. After using the T-square and triangle to draw the vertical center, measure from the lead edge of the masking sheet and draw lines representing the plate bend (in this case, 1.675 in., 42.5 mm) and gripper margin (0.375 in., 10 mm). Checking the job jacket (information about the job supplied from the salesperson or customer service representative), indicates that the text of our booklet is to be printed on 17.5×23-in. (444×584-mm) paper. Measuring out from the vertical center, it is simple to determine the left and right edges of the sheet and draw them on the layout. Working back from the plate bend, locate and draw the 17.5-in. line representing the back of the sheet.

Horizontal positioning. Now it is time to draw the lines for positioning each page on this sheet. Using simple math, it is easy to figure that if the booklet is 8.5×11 in. (216×279 mm) and our sheet is 17.5×23 in. (444×584 mm), only four pages can be printed on each side of the sheet. That will work perfectly for this example: since there are only eight pages to the text of the booklet, four pages can be printed on the front of the sheet, and the remaining four pages on the back. A more substantial challenge is fitting these pages on the sheet, when the impact of the plate bend and gripper margin are taken into account. As you may have already realized, subtracting the 17-in. width of the printer's spread from the 17.5-in. width of the press sheet leaves only 0.5 in., which is not enough paper to accommodate the gripper margin and normal bleed allowances. As a result, I will be forced to "grip into the work," meaning that the line I'll draw will be closer to the edge of the masking material than the plate bend and gripper margin would normally allow. Gripping into the work also means that I will be prevented from printing any bleed images near the face trim of two of this form's pages. Begin the layout by drawing a horizontal line 0.375 in. (9 mm) back from the plate bend; this line represents the face trim of two pages on the sheet. Next draw another horizontal line 8.5 in. back from this face trim; this line is where the folds between all pages will occur. Measure back another 8.5 in. from the fold, and draw a line representing the face trim of the other two pages. Finally, measure back another 0.125 in. and draw a line, indicating where any bleed images from these two pages should end. In this case this final line falls in the same position as our previously drawn line representing the back edge of the press sheet.

Vertical positioning. With the horizontal lines complete, it is time to draw the remaining vertical lines on the layout. Starting from the vertical centerline, measure to the left 0.125 in. (3 mm) and draw another vertical line indicating the *head trim* for two pages on the sheet. Continue measuring to the left another 11 in. (279 mm), and draw the vertical line representing the *foot trim* of these same two pages. Next draw another line 0.125 in. beyond the foot trim; just as with the horizontal lines, this will represent the point at which bleed graphics should end. Finally, we can draw a line to represent the left edge of the press sheet. The distance to measure can be calculated by dividing the press sheet size by 2, then subtracting the measurements we have already made: $23 \div 2 = 11.5$; and $11.5 - (0.125 + 11 + 0.125) = 0.25$ in. Now repeat this process, drawing the same four lines to the right of the vertical center.

Positioning the Films

The process of stripping the text pages to this layout can now begin. As in the cover example, begin by removing the layout from the pins and putting a punched sheet of clear polyester on the pins. After fanning out and taping down the polyester, place the layout back down onto the pins and fasten it down as well. Find the black negative for page one, and slide it wrong-reading emulsion-up under the right side of the orange vinyl, with the head towards the center of the layout. Align the trim marks on this page so that they match the layout's 8.5×11-in. (216×279-mm) area near the gripper. (The reason that page one is positioned in that spot will be explained later.) If there is any discrepancy between the position indicated by the layout and the trim marks on the film, make certain that the gutter marks on the page perfectly match the fold line on the layout. Then position the head trim mark on the gutter side of the negative to perfectly match the head trim line on the layout. If there's more than just a tiny difference between the marks on the film and the lines on the layout, double-check your layout measurements and redraw the layout, if necessary. Tape down this negative using the same technique explained earlier for stripping film separations;

Stripping a form in a checkerboard pattern (seen right-reading emulsion down). With the booklet described in this chapter, pages 1 and 5 will be stripped on one flat, and pages 4 and 8 of the same form will be stripped on a complementary flat.

but only tape the corners at the foot and the face, leaving the corner of the page in the center of the layout untaped.

Next find the black negative for page five and slide it under the left side of the orange vinyl, wrong-reading emulsion-up, with its head towards the center of the layout. Position this film as the back page, then tape down the three corners at the face and foot.

Trimming Corners

The corners of each page overlap in the center of the layout. The live areas of the pages do not overlap, rather it is the portion of the film containing the trim and register marks that are piled up on top of one another. You can resolve this problem by carefully trimming away the conflicting corners of each page. If the films do not contain any text or images near these corners, they can be quickly trimmed away using scissors; if the films contain image information right out to the corner, however, you will have to be much more careful.

My favorite method of trimming back the corners is to first remove the layout from the pins, then slide a very thick square of clear polyester (at least 0.012 in., 0.3 mm) beneath both negatives where they overlap. It is handy to keep some 12-mil (0.012-in.) polyester sheets on hand for this use; experienced strippers call these squares *cutting sheets.* If one is unable to find a piece of 12-mil polyester, glue together three squares cut from the 4-mil polyester that you are probably using for stripping. Use a short piece of masking tape to roll back and secure the top negative. Place the T-square horizontally across the center of the bottom page, then position your steel triangle so that the 45° angle just touches the edge of the bleed area. Use a sharp razor blade against the edge of the triangle to trim off the corner of this negative. If everything was positioned properly (and pressure was not excessive), the cutting sheet will have protected the polyester that carries the negatives from being cut by the razor blade. Remove the T-square and triangle. Place the layout back on

Trimming and taping corners of film negatives: (1) Cut the corner of the first negative at a 45° angle.

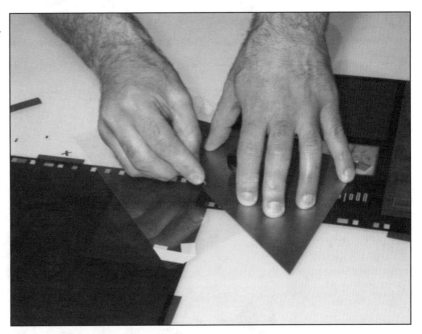

the pins just long enough to verify that the trimmed edge falls exactly at the intersection of the fold and the vertical centerline. Be careful not to press down on the layout, which might crease the rolled-back film for the other page. Remove the layout and trim off additional film, if necessary.

Next slide the 12-mil cutting sheet out from under the trimmed page and place it on top. Remove the tape from the other negative, allowing it to unroll on top of the cutting sheet. Place the T-square horizontally across the center of this page and position the triangle at the intersection of the two pages. Carefully trim the negative to come as close to the first film as possible, without actually allowing the negatives to touch. Remove the cutting sheet, which allows you to tape down the negatives where they meet, being careful to avoid covering any of the image areas on either film with tape.

Trimming and taping corners of film negatives: (2) Also cut the corner of second negative at a 45° angle but leave a small gap between the two films so that they do not overlap.

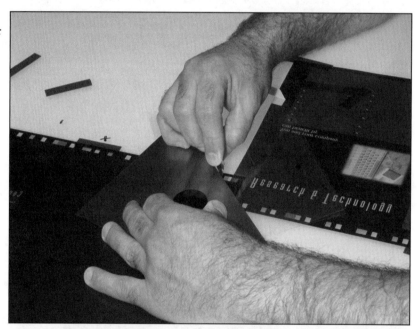

Trimming and taping corners of film negatives: (3) Apply a strip of red tape where the trimmed corners meet.

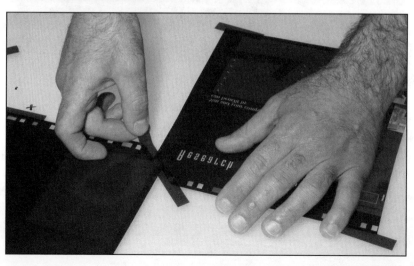

Registering the Colors

At this point the light table should contain nothing but a sheet of clear polyester with two pages firmly taped down in opposite corners. Now one is ready to register the other colors of these two pages, using the same techniques described for registering separations in chapter 4. Cut away the overlapping corners on every flat; even if there is no image in either corner, the double thickness of film that will occur if the corners are left untrimmed will affect image register and possibly damage the mask that you will be creating later. Follow

Using a collimating magnifier to ensure that the colors register properly.

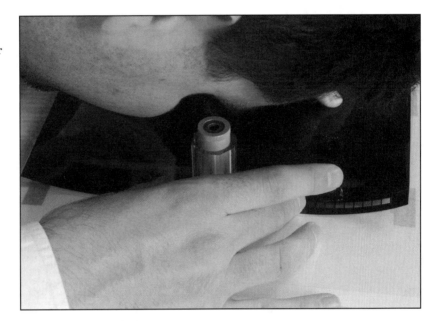

the same sequence one would use to strip separations; lay the cyan to the black, remove both flats and the frosty, then put the cyan on the light table. Replace the frosty, and lay the magenta to the cyan. Follow the same method to lay the yellow to the cyan. In every case, pay close attention not only to aligning the register marks, but also to the highlight content of the images. Also look for type that shows up on more than one negative—for example, red type will appear on both the yellow and magenta negatives—and use the frosty to make certain these letters register perfectly in both colors.

Now that all the colors for pages one and five have been registered, begin the process again. Tape a fresh sheet of clear polyester to the light table and tape the orange vinyl layout sheet down on top of it. Slide the black negative for page four under the left side of the orange vinyl, with its head toward the center, and tape it into position near the pinbar. Tape down three corners, and then slide the black negative for page eight under the right side of the orange vinyl to the position at the back of the sheet. Tape it down, trim both sheets to avoid any overlap, and register the other colors for these two pages in sequence.

Creating Masks

Now that all sixteen pieces of film for the front of the sheet are taped down (four colors × four pages), the next step is creating masks for exposing these films to the printing plate. Begin by taping the layout onto the empty light table, and then taping a sheet of Rubylith to it. Using a T-square, triangle, and X-Acto knife, carefully cut the gelatin of the masking material to expose page one. Whenever possible (and especially at the fold), position the straightedge (the T-square or the triangle) on the side of the line that does not cover the page; also be sure to hold the X-Acto knife at a very slight angle, so that the handle of the knife tilts toward the center of the page. Using this method will cause the groove made by the knife blade to be hidden by the edge of the masking material, allowing the mask to create a clean edge when exposing the image. First trim the fold, and then the bleed line at the pinbar. Next use the triangle to cut the center line and then the bleed line at the foot. Finally move the T-square to the other side of the fold and cut the window for page five. Once both windows are cut, use a short strip of masking tape to peel up the masking material.

Holding the X-Acto knife at a slight angle toward the center of the page when cutting a mask, so the groove made by the knife blade is hidden by the masking material.

Now the mask for pages one and five is finished. Repeat the process for pages four and eight—with one important exception: cut all the lines, except for the folds, by following the layout sheet. Clear the light table and tape the completed mask for pages one and five down to the glass, gelatin side up. Tape down the mask-in-progress, and use the already-completed mask as your guide when cutting the folds. The reason for this is simple: many pages may contain images or graphics that "run to the fold." If the fold lines are not cut accurately, the result may be thin white gaps between adjoining pages with bleed images, or dark lines created by two bleed images overlapping—so be careful when cutting windows that meet at the fold. Seeing both masks on the light table at once, you may notice that all those rectangular windows look somewhat reminiscent of the game board on which you might play checkers—that is why strippers sometimes refer to making the masks for this method of stripping as "opening up the checkerboards."

Labeling Flats

Everything is now stripped for the front side of the text form, but we are not done yet. It is time to label the flats so that the platemaker will understand how the pieces work together. Typically the first Rubylith flat is called "Mask A," and flats carrying the negatives to be exposed through this mask are marked as "magenta+A," "cyan+A," etc. Follow the same sequence with the remaining flats, calling the second sheet of Rubylith "Mask B." Label all the flats with information about the form (front or back), the signature (in this case, call it "Text"), and the job number.

Front/Back Considerations

Now comes the task that separates the good strippers from the bad and tells the world whether or not one knows how to square a light table (and if your T-square is bent)! Flip the orange vinyl layout over, and tape it down to the light table with the lines facing the glass. Place Mask A on top of the pins and look carefully to see if the mask lines up exactly on top of the folds and bleeds. If it does, congratulations—everything about the work is perfectly square. For the majority of strippers, however, the mask and the layout will disagree in some manner, making it necessary to distinguish between the front side of the layout and the back side. It is also advisable to create one set of masks for the front side and a separate set for the back. Some strippers create this second set by making a pin-registered emulsion-to-emulsion copy of each mask on a large sheet of duplicating film (often called *dupe film).*

Of course, distinguishing between the front and back of layouts and making separate masks for each side is also essential when using layouts whose left and right sides are intentionally dissimilar. Typical situations involving this kind of layout include pocket folders and other work that will later be diecut, as well as six-page forms and combinations of packages or labels of differing sizes.

It is best to make a habit of beginning work on the second side of any form in this manner: fan out and tape down a sheet of clear polyester to the empty light table, then tape down the orange vinyl layout with its lines facing the polyester. Next carefully retrace all the lines from the first side onto this second side. If the folds diverge more than 0.063 in. (2 mm) from each other, throw the layout away, and then resquare the light table, and start over. Once one has drawn the lines on both sides of the orange vinyl, repeat all the steps used to strip the flats and cut the masks for the front side. When these flats are stripped, label the orange vinyl layout itself. Be sure that the side of the layout just used to position the back films (negatives that were wrong-reading emulsion-up) is labeled "Front," since this information will be important during the platemaking process when the flats will be exposed right-reading emulsion-down.

Cutting the Marks

Finally, it's time to cut the marks into the layout, as previously described. Once these thin lines are cut in, many strippers and platemakers refer to the layout as the *marks flat.* On very large jobs involving numerous forms with identical layouts, it is not uncommon for multiple layouts to be traced from the original (so that several strippers can work on the job simultaneously). In that situation, however, it is likely that there will still be only one marks flat for all the forms with identical layouts.

From Stripping to Digital Imposition

In chapters 4 and 5 stripping has been demonstrated in two ways: the cover was stripped in the traditional, time-honored method of image assembly from artboards, while the interior text was stripped from multiple negatives created using desktop publishing software and output in single-page format from an imagesetter. Most strippers could have stripped all eight pages of the text form in about the same time it would have taken to assemble the cover spread. By outputting fully assembled pages, page layout software has revolutionized the printing industry and ended the challenge of manually converting single-color pasteups into multicolor printing. Instead, since the early 1990s, the job performed by most strippers has become a stale, monotonous series of layouts and checkerboard masks.

Even that basic process is quickly becoming obsolete. As discussed throughout the remainder of this book, printing companies everywhere are discovering the advantages of using imposition software to increase the number of pages that can be stripped from a single sheet of film. Many companies today use large-format imagesetters and imposition software to create fully imposed output. This process uses sheets of film as large as a printing plate so that each plate can be exposed with a single exposure. Still other printing companies are making the most of digital imposition by arranging pages and exposing plates digitally with the latest computer-to-plate technology.

As adoption of these methods spreads, the end of traditional stripping is in sight. Strippers who want to remain employed in tomorrow's printing industry must learn to use the tools of digital imposition to accomplish the same tasks for which they once used X-Acto knives and T-squares. The good news for this dying breed is that a background in the traditional graphic arts is the best education for learning the finer points of digital imposition. For those readers who might not have spent the last ten years on a light table, however, the critical basics of paper, press, binding, and finishing are discussed in the following two chapters.

6　Paper and the Printing Press

In the last two chapters we reviewed the ways in which individual pages can be stripped into position for press. Now let's consider how the proper position is determined and what factors influence the sequence of pages on the sheet. In this chapter we will cover basic information about paper, examine the major printing press configurations in use today, and determine the impact of the printing process on imposition.

Basics of Paper

Paper size and paper handling methods account for most of the variables in the imposition process. Although the importance of understanding the basics of paper manufacturing cannot be stressed enough, many of today's electronic prepress workers are totally unfamiliar with these issues. This chapter highlights the important attributes and considerations of this essential part of the printing process.

Paper Manufacture

Paper is manufactured from refined cellulose fiber, and the leading source of this cellulose is wood pulp. During this manufacturing process, the paper gains several attributes that will affect how it is used in the pressroom. After wood pulp is obtained (through chipping trees, sawmill residue, recycling wastepaper or several other methods), the pulp is highly diluted with water (to approximately one part wood fiber to 200 parts water) before flowing into the *headbox.* The wood pulp slurry exits the headbox through a rectangular nozzle called the *slice*, which deposits the pulp across a moving wire belt. As the pulp passes through the slice, the fibers become aligned in the same direction as the water flow. The moving wire belt (which might actually be made of a plastic mesh or bronze) is part of the *fourdrinier paper machine.* As water and fine particulate matter drains through holes in the wire, more layers of wood pulp slurry are deposited on the belt. The

A fourdrinier paper-making machine. *Adapted from* The GATF Encyclopedia of Graphic Communications, *by Frank J. Romano and Richard M. Romano* (GATFPress, 1998).

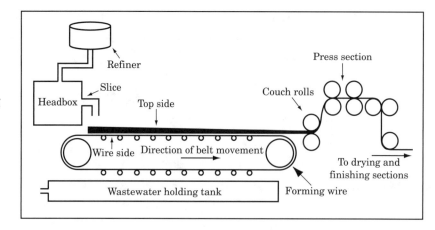

side of the paper that is not in contact with the belt is called the "felt" side and has a visibly smoother surface than the wire side, which has a tighter structure. Unfortunately, this two-sided nature is an undesirable effect that reduces the versatility of paper stocks; modern improvements in paper manufacturing have reduced the visible difference between felt and wire sides of paper. Additional stages in the paper-making process include the couch roll, which vacuums additional water from the paper before it is lifted from the wire via suction and transferred to the press section. The press section features rollers that compact and smooth the paper, as well as even out moisture levels across the width of the paper roll. Finally, the paper passes through the drying section; here, the paper rolls around heated cylinders that reduce the moisture content to as low as 2–8%.

Types of Paper Stock

The paper may also receive a coating, resulting in a bright, extremely smooth surface that is ideal for high-quality image reproduction. Common surface treatments for creating **coated stock** include highly refined clay. The clay is used as a pigment, which is adhered to the base stock through the use of an adhesive (also called a binder). Paper is available with coatings on a single side, or on both sides. Although there are a variety of ways in which these coatings can be applied to the sheet (such as blade coaters or cast coating), all coating application is done either in-line or off-line. In-line (also called on-machine) coating is applied on the actual papermaking machine, so that the process of forming, drying, and coating the paper is done in direct succession. Off-line (or off-machine) coating occurs on free-standing equipment after the papermaking process has been completed. This allows greater flexibility and higher speed than in-line coating, as well as permitting coating to continue even when papermaking production lines are shut down.

Despite the image reproduction advantages of these smooth-surfaced stocks, uncoated paper (also called ***offset stock***) is in more widespread use. Although this is due in large part to the lower cost of offset papers, there is another important factor—ink applied to uncoated stock by a printing press will be absorbed more readily by the stock, hastening drying of the printed sheet. This allows for high-speed printing without the use of extra equipment to help dry the ink, a description that applies to newspaper presses and other forms of "cold-set" printing.

Paper Thickness   In addition to being available in a choice of coated or uncoated stocks, paper also comes in a variety of thicknesses. Most of the paper we handle on a daily basis is the thin variety called ***text stock;*** items such as perfect-bound book covers, business cards, or response cards, however, are typically printed on a thicker grade of paper known as ***cover stock.*** The specific thickness of paper is usually expressed in terms of the weight of a standard size and quantity of the paper in question. This is known as the paper's ***basis weight.*** For book papers, the unit of measure is one ream (500 sheets) of 25×38-in. (635×965-mm) paper. The basis weight of cover stocks is measured as the same quantity of a smaller sheet: 500 sheets of 20×26-in. (508×660-mm) paper. Using this standard can be a little confusing at first; a sheet of 80-lb. (often written as 80#) book weight stock is thinner than a sheet of 60-lb. cover stock! Book stocks are usually specified between 30 lb. and 120 lb., while cover stocks are often chosen in the 50-lb. to 100-lb. range.

An alternative (and less confusing) method of specifying paper weight is the metric measure known as ***grammage,*** which specifies the weight of one square meter of a single sheet of paper. (The unit of measurement of grammage is grams/square meter, usually abbreviated *gsm* or g/m^2.) This simplifies the specification of paper weight, since the unit of measure is the same regardless of the category of paper being ordered. To use the previous example, the grammage of 80-lb. book stock is 118; clearly, this is a lighter stock than 60-lb. cover, which has a grammage of 162.

Comparing sheet size, basis weight, and grammage of four common types of paper.

Paper Type	Sheet Size	Basis Weight	Grammage
Bond and writing	17×22 in. (432×559 mm)	16	60
		20	75
		24	90
Cover	20×26 in. (508×660 mm)	50	135
		60	162
		80	216
		100	270
Book	25×38 in. (635×965 mm)	40	59
		50	74
		60	89
		70	104
		80	118
Index	25.5×30.5 in. (648×775 mm)	90	163
		110	199
		140	253

Grain Direction

The attribute of paper that most greatly affects the imposition process is grain direction. All papers have a grain pattern, and knowing the direction of this grain pattern is essential in designing the most effective folding order. As wood pulp flows through the slice, all the long cellulose fibers tend to run in the same direction. This arrangement of fibers occurs predictably, and we refer to the direction of these fibers as the ***grain*** of the paper.

The cellulose fibers provide a stiffening effect within the paper that makes it more difficult to fold. It is very important, therefore, to know the direction of these fibers before folding the stock—folds made "with the grain" (in the same direction as the cellulose fibers) occur cleanly and easily, while folds made ***across the grain*** (perpendicular to the direction of the cellulose fibers) can cause the paper to crack and fold unevenly. Although not correct in terms of traditional usage, the phrase ***against the grain*** is also commonly used to refer to this predicament. The grain direction of a sheet of paper is referred to as either ***grain short*** or ***grain long;*** generally, the grain direction of the paper should favor the last fold that will be made in the folding machine, since that fold will be fighting against the greatest total paper thickness. Large sheets of paper that will be used to print eight pages on each side should be ordered as grain short, meaning that the cellulose fibers run in the same direction as the short dimension of the sheet.

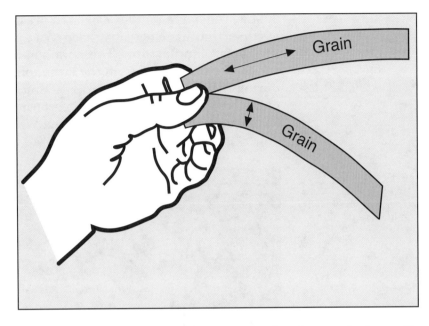

Paper cut in the direction of the paper grain *(top)* and across it. Paper is stiffer in the direction of the grain than across the grain, and folds are cleanest when made parallel to the grain direction.

Paper for Sheetfed Presses

Despite the wide variety of print reproduction methods available (including offset lithography, rotogravure, flexography, screen printing, and on-demand printing), most work that is to be printed will utilize either a **sheetfed** printing press or a **web** printing press. The most common forms of both of these presses can be found in the offset lithography print market,

A four-color sheetfed lithographic printing press.

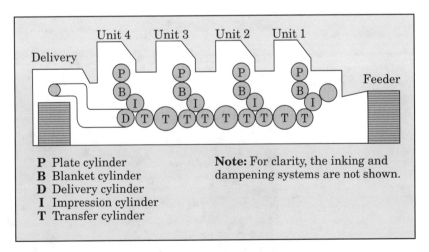

P Plate cylinder
B Blanket cylinder
D Delivery cylinder
I Impression cylinder
T Transfer cylinder

Note: For clarity, the inking and dampening systems are not shown.

but the attributes separating these two types of presses and the effect that these configurations have on imposition methods are usually quite similar, regardless of the actual print reproduction method involved.

Cutting Paper into Sheets

Just as the name implies, sheetfed presses use precut sheets of paper that have been trimmed to a predetermined size by the paper manufacturer. These individual sheets are trimmed or "sheeted" from the large rolls of paper created during the manufacturing process. Since the paper is still quite fresh when these cuts are performed, significant shrinkage can occur after trimming. When printers call this paper "green," they are not referring to the color of the stock.

A six-color sheetfed lithographic printing press, as viewed from the feeder end of the press.

Press operator loading a pile of paper into the feeder of a sheetfed press.

A close-up of the sheet-separation unit on a sheetfed printing press.

When requirements mandate that paper be of an *exact* size, it is necessary to pretrim the paper before running it through the press. This is done in the printing plant with a large guillotine paper cutter. The cutter operator grabs a few inches of paper from the top of a stack of untrimmed paper (this handful of paper is called a "lift," because it should never be more than can be comfortably lifted without back injury) and shoves it against the back stop of the paper cutter. The cutter is set to a depth that is just slightly smaller than the requested size of the stock, at which point the inconsistent nature of the paper size becomes apparent. The uneven edge of the lift of paper is called the **wild side,** and the "clean-up" cut made to equalize the sheet size is called a **back trim.**

Standard Sheet Sizes

Most paper is sold in standard sizes, but it is also possible to order an unusual "custom-cut" sheet size. Paper mills manufacture paper rolls in widths that are multiples of the most common sizes, making these sheets the most economical to purchase. The standard sizes are popular because they allow for a usable number of pages to be printed simultaneously, with just enough extra paper left over for process control marks (such as trim marks, fold marks, and color bars). As mentioned earlier in this chapter, standard sizes are slightly different for cover stocks versus text stocks. The most commonly used standard text size is 23×35 in. (584×889 mm), while cover stocks tend to come as 25×38-in. (635×965-mm) sheets.

A few standard sizes do not include any extra paper, the most common examples being precut 8.5×11-in. (216×279-mm) paper for photocopiers, duplicator presses, and on-demand printing methods. In addition, single-sheet jobs such as letterheads and invoices are typically printed on 17×22-in. (432×559-mm) stock. As shown in the following illustration, this standard size allows for four letterheads to be printed at once, and then separated with only two cuts—a very efficient workflow, but one suitable for only the simplest of jobs.

An 11×17-in. (432×559-mm) sheet size allows four 8.5×11-in. (216×279-mm) letterheads to be cut out of one sheet of paper with no trim waste.

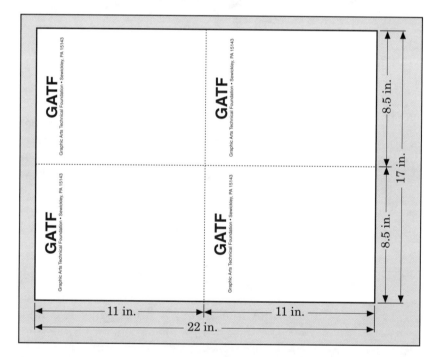

Sheet Allowances

The bleed. This previous example of printing letterheads is inadequate for most print jobs because it does not allow for graphics to *bleed* off the edge of the trimmed page. In order to achieve a consistent and attractive look in graphics that run off the edge of a trimmed document, the untrimmed press sheet must allow enough room for the image to extend beyond the trim, creating some margin for error. As mentioned in chapter 2, this extended image is called the bleed, and is typically 0.125 in. (3 mm) beyond the trim.

People unfamiliar with this aspect of print reproduction often try to run the graphic off the edge of the sheet. This causes the ink not transferred to the paper to build up on the rubber blanket of the printing press, from where it is transferred onto the edge and back of the paper. By the same token, one may attempt to print a bleed graphic within a larger press sheet containing several pages but with no gutter (waste area) between the pages. Inevitably the single ***bust cut*** made to separate the pages will stray from the intended spot and the bleed image will fail to reach the edge of the single page or will be seen as an unwanted mark on the edge of other pages.

The gripper margin. Another reason why the 17×22-in. (432×559-mm) press sheet is inadequate for most jobs is that no allowance has been made for the unprintable area where the press must grab the edge of the sheet. In order for the paper to travel through the printing press, small metal claws called ***gripper fingers*** must clamp down on the paper and pull it through the series of rollers within each inking unit. Since the gripper covers the leading edge of the sheet as it makes its way through the press, this area, called the ***gripper margin,*** or often simply the ***gripper,*** cannot be printed upon during the pressrun. Moreover the printing process leaves small indentations called ***gripper marks*** in the paper, flaws that can be avoided by making certain that the press sheet is large enough to avoid "gripping into the work."

The overfeed infeed on a sheetfed press, showing why the stripper must compensate for the grippers on the impression cylinder.

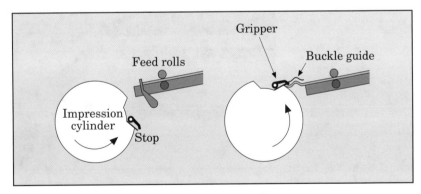

The guide side. Understanding the importance of the press gripper is a key to grasping the concepts about to be discussed, but it is not the only important aspect of how paper travels through the press. In order to consistently print the image in the same spot on every sheet, it is necessary to control the position of each sheet within the width of the press (perpendicular to the direction the paper travels through the press). As each sheet of unprinted paper is picked up from a large stack of paper at the feed end of the printing press, some form of mechanical process attempts to align every sheet so it will be gripped in the same spot.

Although there are several ways in which presses can accomplish this, anything that serves this purpose is typically referred to as a ***side guide.*** Some presses use a small bar to push the sheet into position, while others pull the sheet to the desired spot using vacuum suction. Whatever the method, the side guide creates a consistent, repeatable "margin" from the edge of the sheet to the edge of the image being printed. The printing press has two side guides, but only uses one side guide at a time. Since these guides can be moved into position for use or slid out of the way when not in use, it is important to know which side of the sheet was being guided during the printing process. This edge of the sheet is typically called the ***guide side,*** or simply the ***guide.***

Press operator adjusting the side guide mechanism on a sheetfed press.

Gripper and guide designation. Every sheet that passes through a printing press has both a gripper and a guide. As stacks of paper are unloaded from the delivery end of the printing press, the press operator is likely to mark the top sheet of the pile with several **X** marks—two along the gripper, and two along the guide. This identification allows the workers involved in the binding and finishing processes to measure from this reference edge when trimming, folding, diecutting, or embossing the job.

Press operator putting X marks on the guide side of the printed press sheet.

For example, a cutter operator working on a press sheet full of business cards would insert the guide side of each lift of printed sheets into the cutter. The guide would be ***jogged*** (pushed repeatedly) against the back stop of the cutter, while the gripper edge of the stack is jogged against the side of the cutter. The longest cut in this direction is made first, so that the wild side of the paper is eliminated. The next cut will be to insert the gripper into the cutter, jog it against the back stop, and take the longest cut in this direction, removing the wild side of the paper in this short direction.

In the same way, folder operators need to know the guide and gripper of each job; typically, the guide would enter the folder first while the gripper jogs against the folder's guide. The folding process is discussed in much greater detail in chapter 7. For now, suffice it to say that the gripper and guide have a tremendous impact on how the job will be paginated, folded, and trimmed.

Backup Impositions for Sheetfed Presses

Very few printed jobs requiring imposition are single-sided. More often sheets are printed on both sides. ***Backing up*** the sheet (printing the second side) can be done in a variety of ways, each having its own rationale. The remainder of this chapter addresses the four basic methods through which this backup can occur: sheetwise, work-and-turn, work-and-roll, and perfecting.

Folder operator checking press sheet to verify gripper and guide edges.

Sheetwise Imposition

Sheetwise imposition, the simplest backup method, will be discussed first. The sheetwise method prints a completely new set of pages on the second side of the sheet; none of the pages that appeared on the front side are repeated on the back. Knowing that the side guide may be activated on either side of the press, it is easy to understand that the sheet's guide side can be maintained even when the sheet is printed on both sides. In other words the front side of a sheetwise form is typically printed first, with the sheet guided on the right side, as seen from the gripper. After the front is completely printed, a member of the press crew called the *feeder operator* moves the pile of press sheets back to the feed end of the press. The sheets are then flipped over before being inserted into the press, but the edge of the sheet that was gripped on the first pass is the same edge that will be gripped during the second pass through the press. While this paper is being reloaded, another member of the press crew moves the first side guide out of position, and activates the side guide found on the opposite side of the press; in this way, the edge of the sheet that was guided during the first pass is the same edge that will be guided during the backup. As the sheets emerge from the press after the second pass, they are oriented correctly for insertion into the folding machine.

One should be aware that some paper folding machines actually invert the stack of press sheets before folding; using

Paper and the Printing Press   87

this sort of folder means that the preferred workflow will be to print the back side of the sheet first (with its guide side on the left, as seen from the gripper) and deliver the sheets to the folder with the front of the sheet facing up. Check with the bindery to be sure which orientation is preferred when sheets are delivered; if not, the result may be delays and additional charges, as every lift of paper might have to be flipped over by hand before loading onto the folder. All of the examples throughout the remainder of this book assume the use of a simple folder that does not invert the sheets; if the folder does flip the sheet before folding, one will have to make adjustments as needed to assure that the completed sheets leave the press with the side guide to the right of the gripper (fronts facing up).

Sheetwise is the most common form of imposition because it allows the maximum number of different pages to be printed in the shortest period of time. Let me illustrate the usefulness of sheetwise imposition by examining a sample job: a 30-page saddle-stitched booklet composed of 8.5×11-in. (216×279-mm) pages, with an extra flap of paper attached to the back cover for use as a reply card. As is typical with magazines, this project will use an uncoated paper for the text pages and a heavier, coated stock for the cover. Since the cover comprises six pages (outside front cover, inside front cover, inside back cover, inside flap, outside flap, and outside back cover), the ***page count*** (number of pages) could also be referred to as "24 plus cover."

For the text, start by selecting a very large sheet of paper. This is typically the most cost-effective way to print a job, since the larger sheet carries more pages, thereby reducing the number of different signatures that have to be printed and keeping the amount of time needed to print the job as low as possible. For this example, the job will be printed on a 40-in. (1016-mm) press; this allows us to use a 23×35-in. (584×889-mm) press sheet. This is a very common size press sheet to use for 8.5×11-in. (216×279-mm) work, since the amount of waste (paper that will not be used in the final project) is kept to a minimum. Just enough extra paper would be available, however, to print the trim marks, color bars, and other types of process control devices. The 23×35-in. press sheet has room for eight pages on the front form and eight pages on the back form, for a total of sixteen pages. Identify this first sheet as "Signature A."

Signature A for the interior of the sample 30-page (including cover) saddle-stitched booklet. This signature contains pages 1–8 and 17–24.

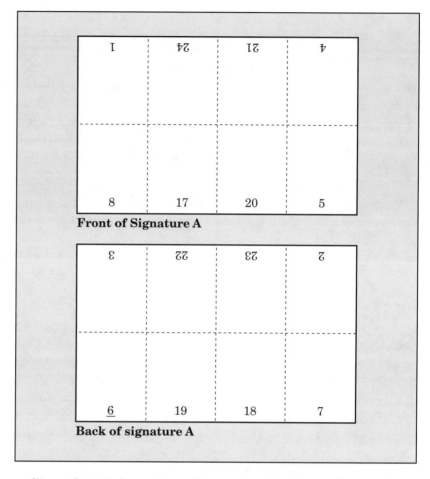

Front of Signature A

Back of signature A

Since the total number of text pages is 24, another eight pages still need to be imposed. Although it would certainly be possible to print the remaining pages on a sheet of paper only half the size of the previous press sheet (to print four pages on the front and four pages on the back, for a total of eight pages), we have decided not to do this. Instead the same 23×35-in. (584×889-mm) sheet will be used to print the remaining eight pages. There are several reasons why this is desirable:

- Using only one text sheet size allows us to order a large quantity of paper in a single size, lowering the price
- The large sheets will not have to be cut down to a smaller size before they are printed
- Most importantly, the press operators will not have to **break down the press** (make adjustments required to run a smaller-size press sheet) between signatures

Anyone in print management will claim the real money is made in the pressroom. This makes it essential to plan wisely in order to conserve as much press time as possible. In keeping with the previous naming convention, identify this second text sheet "Signature B."

Work-and-Turn Imposition

How should the remaining eight text pages be arranged on a sheet large enough to hold sixteen? A different type of imposition will be used. Instead of the sheetwise imposition used for Signature A, the eight pages of signature B will be imposed in a style called ***work-and-turn.*** Unlike the first signature (which used one set of printing plates for the front, and a second set of printing plates for the back), the imposition style known as work-and-turn allows us to print both sides of the sheet using only a single set of plates. All eight pages of this signature are arranged in the proper order on this sheet (page order will be discussed in the next chapter), and the sheet is printed on one side.

Signature B as a work-and-turn imposition. Signature B will print pages 9–16, which form the center signature of our sample booklet.

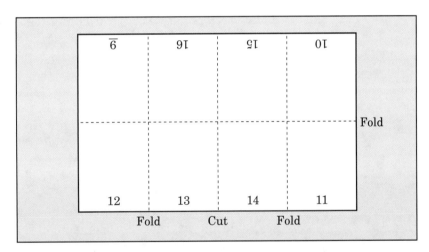

After one side of all the sheets has been printed, the press operator must wait a short time for the ink to dry. The amount of time necessary varies according to the amount of ink coverage and the drying capabilities of the press. Once the sheets are dry, the feeder operator turns them over and reinserts them into the press. As in the sheetwise style, the gripper edge from the first pressrun will be maintained for the printing of the second side, and the side guide on the opposite side of the feedboard will be used to maintain the same guide edge for both pressruns. Now it is apparent where the name of this style comes from: first we "work" to print the first side of the sheet, then we "turn" the sheets over and print the same images on the second side. In some printing plants, this imposition style also goes by the less graceful name of ***work-and-flop.***

After the work-and-turn signature has been printed on both sides (and given more time to dry), the sheet is cut in half before folding. The cutter operator inserts the lifts into the guillotine and jogs the guide against the back stop; the gripper is jogged against the side of the cutter, and then the entire pile is given a cleanup trim to eliminate the wild side. Finally, the sheets are split in two with a second cut. Each half of the sheet is now identical in page order and content to the other half, with the exception that half the stack is ready to go directly into the folder while the other half needs to be turned over before being folded.

Two-Out Sheet-wise Imposition

An alternative to using the work-and-turn imposition style for Signature B—printing both sides of the sheet with a single set of plates—would be to impose the sheet in the ***two-out sheetwise*** style. With this method, the same four pages would be printed in two locations on the front of the signature. After the first side was printed, the sheets would be reinserted with the same gripper edge, and a second set of plates would be mounted on the press to print two copies of the remaining four pages. From a prepress viewpoint, this would be rather wasteful. Although the same number of sheets would have to be printed and the same drying time issues come into play as with a work-and-turn imposition, two sets of printing plates will be required, instead of one set with work-and-turn imposition.

Although work-and-turn is more economical from a prepress viewpoint, there are some good reasons why two-out sheetwise might be the preferred imposition method. Press operators prefer two-out sheetwise because both copies of each page are printed at the same time on the same side of the sheet, making it easier for the press operators to assure a consistent appearance between these two images. It is not uncommon for signatures that are printed work-and-turn to differ noticeably when the front of the sheet is compared to what should be identical images on the back. Of even greater importance is the impact of additional finishing operations on the press sheet. Processes such as lamination, foil stamping, and diecutting can sometimes be performed on the full-size press sheet. Having both copies of the pages requiring

Signature B as a two-out sheetwise imposition. Signature B will print pages 9–16, which form the center signature of our sample booklet.

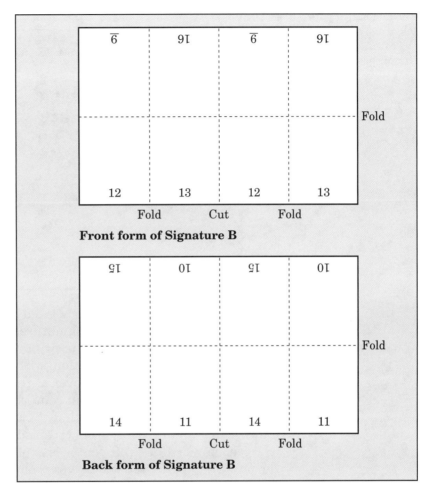

| 6̄ | 9I | 6̄ | 9I |

Fold

| 12 | 13 | 12 | 13 |

Fold   Cut   Fold

Front form of Signature B

| SI | 0I | SI | 0I |

Fold

| 14 | 11 | 14 | 11 |

Fold   Cut   Fold

Back form of Signature B

finishing operations on the same side of the sheet cuts the finishing time in half, making two-out sheetwise imposition less time-consuming than work-and-turn.

Work-and-Roll Imposition

So far, for the sample project, the imposition style of two signatures has been designated. Between the sixteen pages that will print on Signature A (sheetwise) and the eight pages that will print on Signature B (work-and-turn), twenty-four pages have been imposed. All that remains is the cover, which will be printed on a heavier sheet of coated paper— a type of paper usually referred to as ***coated cover***. The standard size for the coated cover is 25×38-in. (635×965-mm). On a typical job, this sheet size would allow us to print eight pages; our job, however, has the unusual attribute of an extra 5.75×11-in. (146×279-mm) panel that folds out from the back cover. This sort of fold-out configuration, called a

The fold-out, or gate-fold, configuration of the cover for the sample booklet.

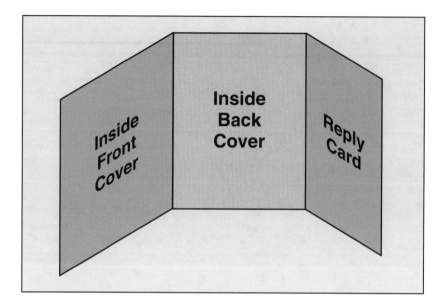

gatefold, will cause us to incur a great deal of **waste** (unprinted area) on our cover signature.

The best that can be done is to print the cover pages as shown in the following illustration, with the flap, outside back cover, and outside front cover at the gripper. You can also see that these pages are not centered on the sheet, but instead have been slid over so that the Outside Back Flap is only 0.5 in. (13 mm) away from the guide side of the sheet (the reason why this is off-center is explained near the end of the next chapter). That still leaves room on the same side of the sheet to print another set of pages, which presents two choices: either repeat the same three pages again, with the foot of the second set near the head of the first set (separated by a wide margin) or print the three inside pages at the back of the sheet, with the head of these three pages near the head of the first set (separated by a much smaller margin, typically 0.5 in., or 6 mm). The first possibility is called a **head-to-foot** arrangement, while the second possibility is a **head-to-head** arrangement.

One should now also be able to recognize the first possibility as a two-out sheetwise imposition (the second side of the sheet would require a completely different set of plates). For this example, however, the cover will be printed using the second imposition style, known as **work-and-roll** (also called **work-and-tumble**). Similar to a work-and-turn imposition, work-and-roll allows us to print both sides of the press sheet from a single set of printing plates. Once the first side

The outside back cover, outside front cover, and outside back flap printed "two-up" on a 25×38-in. press sheet with the foot of the second set near the head of the first set.

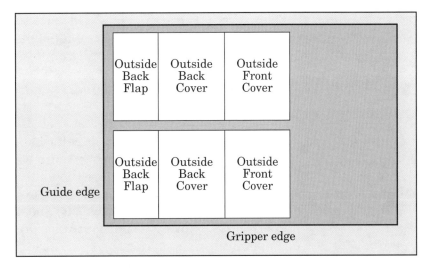

The cover to the sample booklet printed as a "work-and-roll" on a 25×38-in. press sheet. Note the head-to-head arrangement of the pages. Once the first side is printed, the sheets will be flipped so that the back edge of the sheet will be used as the gripper edge when the sheets are backed up.

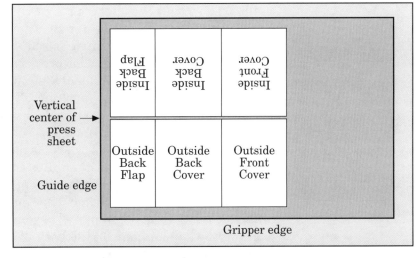

is printed, however, the sheets are flipped so that the back of the sheet is now used as the gripper edge. The advantage of this method, for the press operators, is that the side guide of the press remains in the same location.

Work-and-roll signatures place some unique restrictions on the printing process. To make it simple for the press crew, pages must be stripped in the vertical center of the press sheet. The stock must also be back-trimmed carefully before printing so that every sheet is exactly the same size, since variations in paper size will cause the image on the second side to move in relation to the image on the first side.

This sample cover is another situation where the prepress supervisor prefers one style of imposition (work-and-roll) while the pressroom supervisor prefers another style (two-out sheetwise). The strippers would want to run the cover as a work-and-roll, so that only one set of plates is required. However, if the run length (quantity of press sheets to be printed) is long enough, printing the job as a two-out sheetwise would avoid the labor of back-trimming hundreds of lifts of unprinted stock.

Perfecting Imposition

In this example the cutter operator has agreed to back-trim all of the stock before printing, so we will be able to strip the job as a work-and-roll. Before the plates are made, however, a sharp-eyed stripper realizes that the cover form requires only two colors of ink on each side, meaning that the job is perfect for printing on our four-color press with ***perfecting*** capabilities. The perfecting press has the interesting ability to either print all its inks on one side of the sheet, or to be configured so that the sheet is rolled while traveling between two printing units. This creates the same result as the work-and-roll method, but in a single pass through the printing press. Eight- and even ten-color presses that ***perfect*** are now available, but the most commonly found perfecting presses are still two- and four-color machines. The stripper's discovery allows us to make two identical sets of plates for the press, both stripped in the work-and-roll imposition style. The first set of plates prints the required two colors on the front of the sheet; the press then flips the sheet in the direction of paper travel and grips it at what had been the back of the sheet only moments earlier. The remaining two printing units use the second set of plates to complete the job by printing the same image on the back of the sheet. This style of imposition is called ***perfecting work-and-roll.***

Although the advantages of printing both sides of the sheet on a single trip through the printing press are considerable, so too is the amount of work required to set the press for perfecting. Since it takes the same amount of work to put it back to normal, you may find that once this adjustment is made you will be asked to prepare jobs that would normally be printed sheetwise as ***perfecting*** signatures. The only caveat with imposing for a perfecting press is that the number of colors to be printed on each side of the sheet must be appropriate for the location of the reversing cylinders; check with your pressroom supervisor. In other words, you cannot perfect a sheet with two colors on each side using a five-color press with reversing cylinders located between the fourth and fifth units; that style of perfector is designed to print

A sheetfed perfecting press.

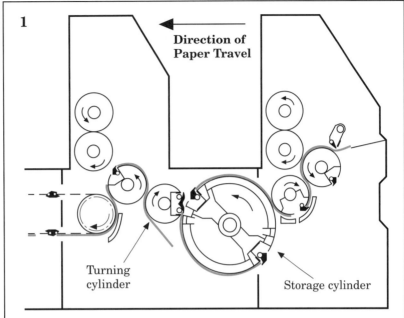

1

Direction of Paper Travel

Turning cylinder

Storage cylinder

Two straight-forward sheets are on the large-diameter (storage) cylinder. The tail edge of the lower sheet is taken by the grippers of the turning cylinder; at the same time, the grippers of the storage cylinder open.

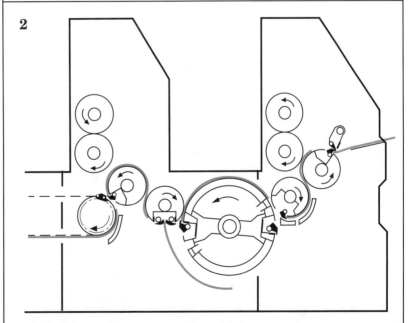

2

The sheet is held by the grippers of the turning cylinder. The tail edge of the sheet becomes the leading edge.

four-color process on the front of the sheet and black ink only on the back side.

Setting up a sixteen-page signature to perfect is only slightly trickier than imposing a sheetwise signature. A properly done imposition of a perfecting form will lead to the same gripper, guide, and page sequence that would have been employed had the signature been stripped sheetwise. The distinguishing part of the process is the front of the sheet. Since the sheet changes grippers between sides, the entire page sequence will be rotated 180° from what would have appeared on the front of the sheetwise signature. As long as the pages are stripped to the vertical center of the press sheet, you need only turn the normal page sequence on its head for the front of a perfecting sheet. It is important to consider the back trim when determining the vertical center of the sheet and check with the cutter operator about how much the size of the sheet was reduced. If necessary, impose the job based on 22.75×35-in. (578×889-mm) stock, rather than on the original 23×35-in. (584×889-mm) sheet size.

Perfecting Work-and-Turn Imposition

The remaining sheetfed press imposition style that needs to be addressed is really just a combination of several styles already discussed. Suppose that one wants to print eight pages of a standard 8.5×11-in. (216×279-mm) format on 23×35-in. (584×889-mm) sheets of 70-lb. offset text, and the one-color nature of the job makes it a good fit for your perfecting two-color press. How to strip the job? As a ***perfecting work-and-turn.*** The only difference between this imposition style and a standard work-and-turn is that care must be taken to strip the job in the vertical center of the sheet, as well as in the horizontal center. In perfecting work-and-turn, two identical sets of plates are made for the press, with the stipulation that one completed set of plates will be rotated 180° and punched again at the tail. This tail-punched set of plates is mounted on the press units that will print the back of the sheet. This method, however, requires the press crew to roll the cylinders that hold the plates (the adjustment will be roughly equal to the difference between the stock size and the plate size).

Imposition for Web Presses

Now that the major imposition styles for sheetfed presses have been covered, what about web presses? A web offset lithographic press is a press that prints on a continuous web, or ribbon, of paper fed from a roll and threaded through the

A four-unit blanket-to-blanket web offset press with optional delivery to a folder or sheeter.

The press configuration shown here is the most common, but variations are possible. For example, with some presses having more than six units, the folder(s) is placed in the middle of the total press configuration and the infeeds are placed at each end.

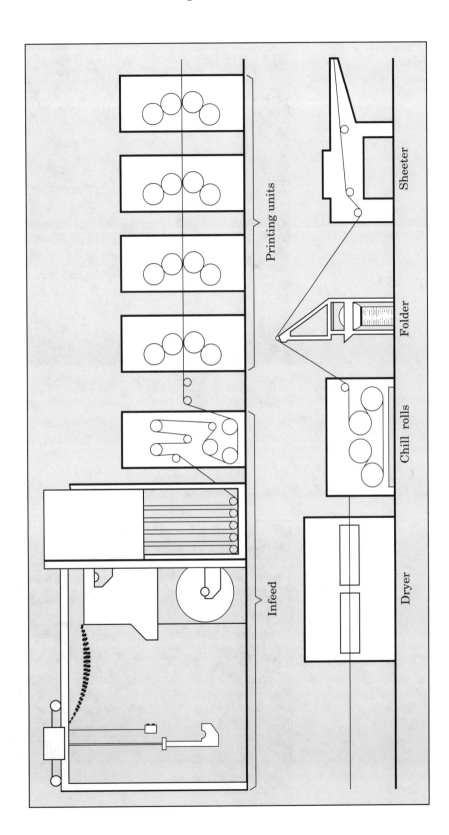

Infeed   Printing units

Dryer   Chill rolls   Folder   Sheeter

A four-color blanket-to-blanket web offset press, as viewed from the roll stand.

press. Since this press handles the paper only once, it must print both sides of the paper web simultaneously. Even though the roll of paper is continuous, the amount of information that can be printed on this roll is limited by the size of the press's printing plate.

The continuous nature of the paper web means that there is no "gripper" as we know it from the sheetfed press. Instead,

The "web" of paper passing between two printing units of a four-color blanket-to-blanket web offset press.

when imposing jobs for a web press, we refer to the ***leading edge*** of the image. Since this leading edge never changes, web presses have no means of printing a web that corresponds to the work-and-turn, work-and-roll, or perfecting imposition styles. Instead, every form on a web press uses a sheetwise imposition style; variations such as two-out and four-out sheetwise are quite common. The major difference between imposing sheetwise forms for a sheetfed press and imposing for web presses is that the forms for the two sides of the web are called the *top form* and the *bottom form;* they are never referred to as "front" and "back," the terms used for sheetfed press impositions.

After the printed web passes through the drying equipment (if the press is so equipped), a high-speed device called a ***sheeter*** cuts the roll into individual sheets of paper. At this point, these flat press sheets may be collected and sent to the bindery for ***off-line*** folding and/or trimming. These off-line functions, however, eliminate many of the high-speed advantages that a web press has over its sheetfed counterparts. Instead of off-line folding, it is much more likely that this web press will be equipped with ***in-line folding*** capabilities.

The stripper needs to know a lot about folding and binding. The choices and restrictions inherent in these tasks will determine the page order of every sheet that is imposed. The next chapters discusses this topic in depth.

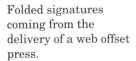

Folded signatures coming from the delivery of a web offset press.

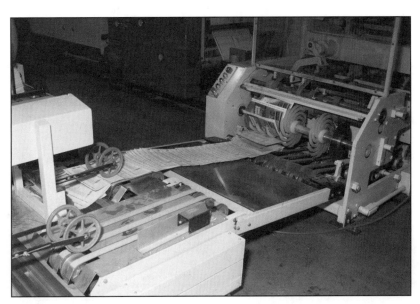

7 Folding, Binding, and Finishing

The previous chapters discussed the basics of paper and how the size and style of a sheet affects the printing process, as well as the options available for handling paper in a printing press, in terms of our ability to print both sides of the sheet simultaneously or separately. Whether printing occurs on sheets of precut stock or on long web rolls, paper and presses obviously have a lot to do with the imposition process. Their influence is easy to see. What is not easy to grasp is the enormous effect that folding and binding methods have on imposition. This chapter considers how paper is folded, as well as what methods are in widespread use for binding pages into books.

We have all folded pages from our notebooks into paper airplanes; perhaps you have entertained yourself with the Japanese art of origami. I once watched one of my students turn a sheet of paper into a beautiful swan that doubled as his business card! Paper folding is an ancient tradition, but one that is also alive and well in the printing plants of today. In the area known as the bindery, sheets of paper are not only folded, but also trimmed, drilled, saddle-stitched (stapled), and perfect-bound. Although many other functions may occur in the bindery, these areas are of great concern for the stripper during the imposition process. Later in this chapter, a few of the many options available in the finishing department will be discussed.

Basics of Folding

On the surface folding seems like a relatively simple, straightforward concept. Take a sheet of paper, roll one end back to meet the other, and flatten it down. Try folding a sheet of cardboard, however, and one will immediately see the effect that paper grain has on folding. Folds made parallel to that direction ("with the grain") are executed more easily and produce a cleaner, sharper crease. Once the first fold is made, try to fold the cardboard at a right angle to the first fold. It is doubly difficult not only because you are now folding against the grain, but also because you are folding through two sheets instead of one! When possible the grain direction should match the direction of the final (and most difficult) fold within the sheet.

Folders

Buckle folders. Most people have had the opportunity to use a small, tabletop folding machine. In principle these small devices are very much like the large folders that are found in the bindery. Place a stack of paper into the feed end of the folder, where a conveyor belt and a rubber roller combine to feed single sheets of paper from the bottom of the stack into the business end of the folder. The conveyors transport the paper forward at high speed, until the sheet slams into a metal stop. Because the front of the sheet has come to a complete stop while the back of the sheet is still moving at a high speed, the sheet buckles near its middle. If the place where the fold occurs is not correct, the position of the stop can be adjusted. This simple principle is also used in large folders. All folders operating under this principle are called *buckle folders.*

Operating principle of a buckle folder.

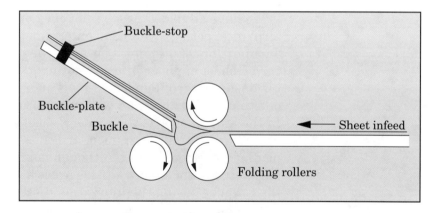

The accompanying series of photographs shows the process of a sheet being folded three times using a large buckle folder. Flat sheets are propelled onto a high-speed conveyor belt; at the first buckle, the sheet travels upwards into the metal cage until it encounters the stop. The sheet is folded at the location of the pinch rollers and then continues its forward motion from these rollers back onto the conveyor belt. The first belt comes to an end, and the sheet is delivered to a

Small bindery with large buckle folder at the right.

The press sheet entering the first buckle plate on the buckle folder.

second belt, which is traveling at a right angle to the first belt. The folded sheet is driven up into another cage where a new set of pinch rollers puts the second fold in the sheet, perpendicular to the previous fold. The paper exits these rollers and slips off the second belt onto the third belt, which is traveling in the same direction as the first belt. The folded

Folded paper leaving
the first buckle plate
and being transported
on a conveyor to the
second buckle plate.

edge of the sheet travels up to meet the stop, and a knife is
employed to cleanly fold the sheet a third time. After this
fold occurs, the sheet is pushed out by the pinch rollers and
delivered to the end of the folder by the third conveyor belt.
At this point bindery workers pick up handfuls of these

Folded sheet of paper
entering second buckle
plate.

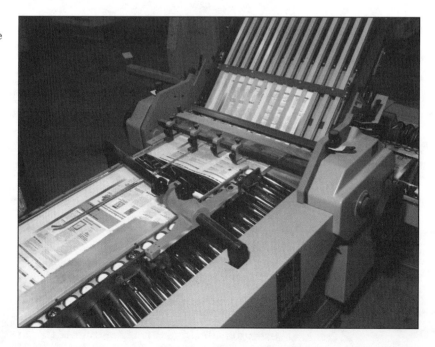

folded signatures and take them to the area where they will be turned into books or booklets. The units that make the second and third folds are usually removable so that only the required amount of equipment need be set up.

Bindery operator removing folded signatures from delivery of buckle folder.

Knife folders. An alternative to the buckle folder is the knife folder. The operation is similar, except that the fold is created by pushing a thin metal blade against the sheet at just the right moment. Knife folders are often required when stock is heavy, or when folds are being made against the grain. There are additional methods by which paper can be "convinced" to fold where desired. For example, coated cover stock can be scored by impact from a thin strip of metal rule before folding; this metal rule breaks the surface fibers, lowering the resistance of the paper to folding. Another method (often employed by in-line folding equipment for web presses) involves spraying a thin stream of water onto the paper exactly where the fold will be attempted. The dampened fibers become more supple, making the paper easier to fold.

Combination folders. Many of the large folders used in printing plants incorporate both buckle and knife folding mechanisms. These machines are often called ***combination folders.*** Combination folders require less floor space than all-buckle machines that fold the same sheet size. Change-

Operating principle of a knife folder.

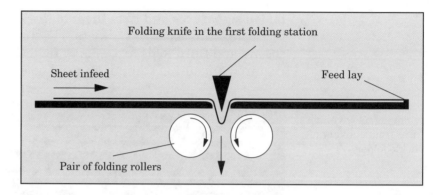

Folding knife in the first folding station

Sheet infeed

Feed lay

Pair of folding rollers

over from eight-page to sixteen-page or thirty-two-page signatures on a combination folder is quicker than on an all-buckle machine because it is not necessary to move the various sections into position.

Types of Folds

The folds in the previous example were all ***right-angle*** folds, that is, each new fold was perpendicular to the previous fold. Although these are the most common folds in a publishing environment, it is sometimes necessary to create folds that

A variety of folds.

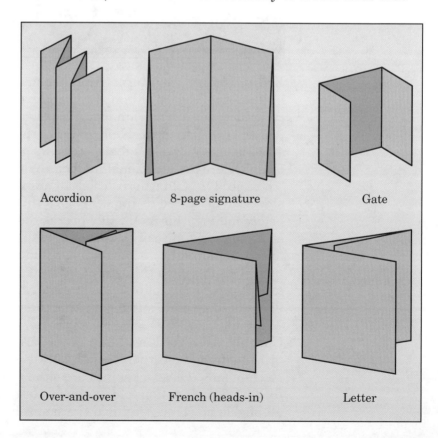

Accordion   8-page signature   Gate

Over-and-over   French (heads-in)   Letter

are parallel to the previous fold. This type of fold includes the *letter fold,* which allows a standard 8.5×11-in. (216×279-mm) sheet to be inserted into a #10 business envelope, and the *accordion fold,* which is often used for invitations or announcements.

Signatures

A flat sheet has two large surfaces (front and back); fold that sheet in half, and four pages are created. Folding the paper a second time makes an eight-page signature, while folding a sheet of paper three times produces a sixteen-page signature. The sixteen page signature is the most common for sheetfed printing of magazines and books; a great deal of publication printing on full-size web presses is also in a sixteen-page format. Although it is possible to add a fourth fold, allowing the imposition of thirty-two pages (each roughly 5.5×8.5 in., 140×216 mm), this is seldom done in commercial printing. The difficulty of producing an accurate fold through all that paper and the need to send the signature through the folder a second time (since most printers own three-buckle folders) is sufficient to discourage most bindery supervisors. Instead, these half-size books will typically be imposed as a pair of sixteen-page signatures running side by side (the choice of work-and-turn versus sheetwise will likely be determined by run length). When printing is completed, the signatures are first cut in half, and then folded as individual sixteen-pagers. However the fourth fold is no hindrance to book publishers; paperback books typically *do* utilize a fourth fold, since the alignment of these folded pages need not be as exacting as the standards typically applied to commercial printing.

This step-by-step look at the folding process included a very important detail that is so subtle it easily goes unnoticed. Every time the sheet went into the cage on the all-buckle machine to meet the headstop, it went up. In the rough shorthand of the imposition process, the folding sequence portrayed was "up, up and up." With most three-buckle folders, it is possible to change any fold to a "down" fold; this adjustment, however, will incur extra setup time in the bindery (or might be completely overlooked!) and should be avoided.

Folding Dummies

Now that I have explained the process by which sheets are folded, it is time to examine how the sequence of pages on each signature is determined. To do this, the *folding dummy,* a very old-fashioned tool, will be used. The folding

A buckle folder with a "down" cage.

dummy is created manually, by folding up a number of small sheets of paper in the same order that the printed signature will be folded. The imposition software available today automates the imposition process, making the creation of folding dummies unnecessary; however, most prepress department supervisors still insist on the creation of folding dummies to verify that the software has imposed the job as anticipated. These small sheets of paper also serve as a guide for the bindery foreman on how the folder should be set up, and how each signature is to be folded. It seems that even with today's digital imposition options, the old adage still holds true: "If you print the job without a dummy, then *you* are the dummy!"

Designating the gripper and guide edges. The first step in creating the folding dummy is to obtain a blank, rectangular sheet of paper for every signature to be dummied. In most cases, a blank sheet of 8.5×11-in. (216×279-mm) paper will suffice for the folding dummy. Next, jot down the form information in the center of the sheet; for instance, "Form A— Front." Also mark the gripper and guide side of the sheet by writing "grip" or "gripper" along the appropriate long edge, and "guide" along the appropriate short edge (typically the right side, as seen from the gripper). Mark an "X" on each side of these words, as shown in the following illustrations. Flip the sheet in the direction appropriate for the printing

Marking the guide side on the sheet to be used for the folding dummy.

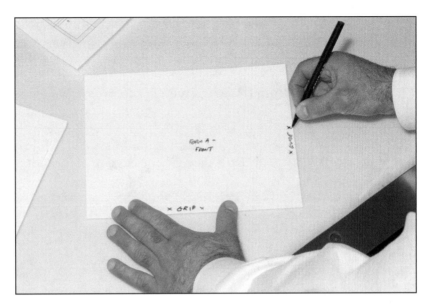

Marking the gripper edge on the sheet to be used for the folding dummy.

method (for this example, assume the form is to be printed sheetwise), and make the appropriate pair of X marks on this side as well. Regardless of how you plan to print and impose the sheet, you should now have the gripper edge of the sheet close to you, with the guide side of the sheet on the left. This is ideally how the sheet should deliver from the press after its last pass; otherwise, someone will have to flip the sheets in small lifts until this final orientation is achieved.

Folding the dummy. Make the folding dummy in the style of a sixteen-page signature. Picture the folding machine in your mind as you create the dummy. This simulates the actual process of using a three-buckle folder. Begin by sending the guide side of the press sheet into the folder, with the back of the sheet facing upwards. Fold the sheet by lifting the guide side up and folding it over to meet the opposite edge of the sheet, giving it an "up" fold. Make the second fold by lifting the gripper edge of the sheet, then folding it over to

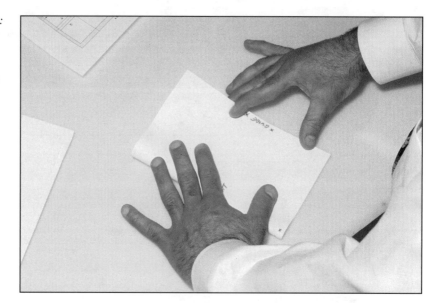

1. Folding the dummy: Make the first fold by lifting the guide edge of the sheet and folding it over to meet the opposite edge of the sheet.

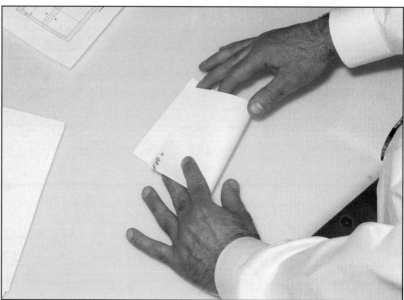

2. Folding the dummy: Make the second fold by lifting the gripper edge of the sheet and then folding it to meet the opposite edge.

meet the opposite edge. The second fold was made using this method because the three-buckle folder would also use the gripper edge of the sheet to make its second fold. Finally lift the folding edge of the sheet created in the first step and fold it over to meet the opposite edge of the sheet.

3. Folding the dummy: Make the third fold by lifting the folding edge of the sheet created in the first step and folding it over to meet the opposite edge of the sheet.

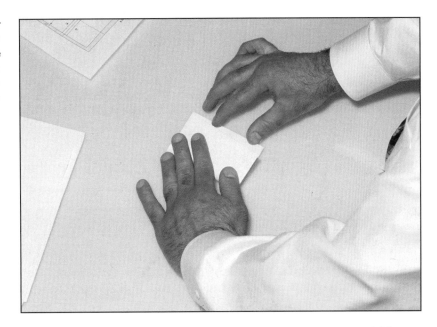

Adding page numbers. The next step in creating a folding dummy is to mark the correct page number on every folded panel of the dummy. Start by orienting the folded paper so that it looks like the first page of a booklet (throughout most of the world, that means the folds will be at the left and the top, while the open edges will be at the right and the bottom). Then use a pen or pencil to mark down the page number near the bottom of every page. The page numbers written down depends on the nature of the project. For example, if a book begins with an introduction, the opening pages might be numbered "i", "ii," "iii," and so on. Other common examples could include the cover pages of a self-cover booklet (OFC, IFC) or the table of contents (TOC). Collectively, items like the introduction, preface, and table of contents are called the ***front matter.*** There is also the ***back matter*** at the end of the book, which might include a glossary, index, appendix, or other content. Occasionally, the back matter will require special page numbers, but it is usually numbered with Arabic page numbers, like the main body of the book.

1. Adding page numbers: Orient the folding dummy so that the folds are at the left and the top.

2. Adding page numbers: Use a pen or pencil to mark the page number at the bottom of every page.

Many find it difficult to mark down the page numbers of some pages near the end of the folded dummy because the pages will not have an open edge at the face. In this situation, lift the paper at the foot, and sneak the pen up onto the page to scribble the number. Other tricks of the trade include notching the entire dummy at the foot, resulting in triangular flaps that can be opened to allow for easy page numbering. Make certain that you always underline numbers containing a "6" or a "9," to eliminate confusion when these page numbers are viewed upside down. Now that every page has been

A folding dummy for a sixteen-page sheetwise layout *(top)* and the dummy opened up showing imposition for front and back forms.

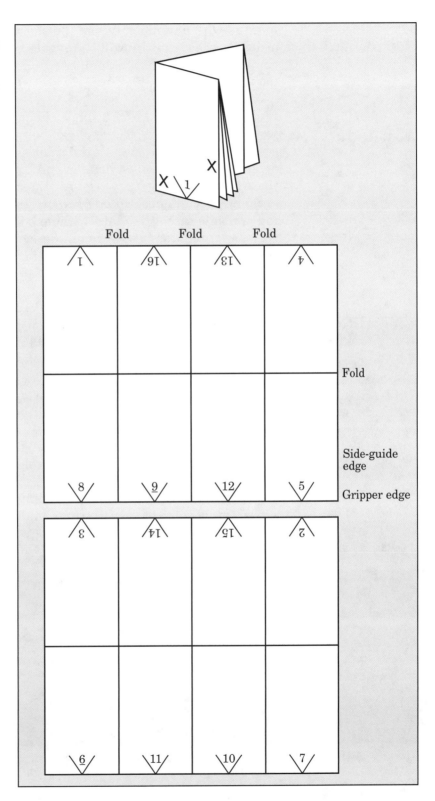

marked with a number, unfold the sheet; the proper page order for the signature will be revealed. The process remains the same whether one is dummying up a sixteen-page, eight-page, or four-page signature.

Binding Methods

If all projects could fit on a single sheet of paper, this chapter would end right here. That seldom being the case, many projects will include a variety of different signatures, often with a variety of imposition styles. The problem will be to bring these signatures together to create the completed book. There are many techniques, called ***binding methods,*** for combining multiple signatures into a single book. Although the options for binding books are numerous, our discussion will be restricted to the four methods that comprise the majority of work printed today: saddle-stitching, perfect binding, case binding, and mechanical binding.

Saddle-Stitching

Saddle-stitch binding, probably the most popular form of combining signatures, is widely used for everything from magazines and catalogs to church bulletins and programs for public events. In this process, one or more signatures are stacked on top of an angled metal surface called a ***saddle.*** The folds in the signatures are carefully centered on top of the saddle, and then staples are driven through the stack of paper to bind the signatures together. These staples are aligned in the same direction as the fold and should pierce the fold itself. Saddle-stitch binding can be done in small quantities with a modified stapler, using standard office-variety staples. Most saddle-stitch binding, however, is

A saddle-stitched booklet.

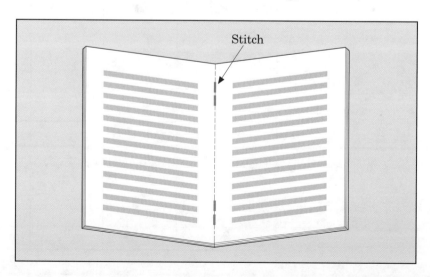

Stitch

The signatures for a booklet stacked on the saddle of a saddle-stitcher.

performed with an automated binding machine using a conveyor chain and a high-speed stitching head. Like a massive needle and thread, this high-speed method uses rolls of thin wire that are cut, bent, and inserted as needed. When staples are created from a roll of wire (as opposed to being premanufactured), the process is called *stitching* instead of stapling.

A close-up of the stitcher head on a saddle-stitcher.

Semiautomatic and automatic saddle-stitching. When multiple signatures are saddle-stitched together, the book grows from the center towards the front and back simultaneously. This outward growth can be seen by observing a team of bindery workers operate a semiautomatic saddle-stitcher. The process involves several workers, with each person standing next to a pile of identical folded signatures. The maximum number of workers that can be employed at the saddle-stitcher simultaneously is determined by the number of *stations* available on that particular machine. The conveyor chain carries a large number of metal saddles. As each saddle passes a station, the bindery worker grabs a folded signature off the top of the pile and places it onto the saddle. Opening the folded signature so that the interior's folded crease can be thrown over the saddle is made easier by providing a lip (an area of the paper margin which is greater on one side of the folded signature than the other). How to incorporate a lip into an imposition plan is explained in the next chapter.

The piles of folded signatures are distributed in order, with the center signature located the farthest away from the stitcher head and the outermost signature piled up closest to the stitcher head. Before being placed on the conveyor chain, the first signature is opened in the middle so that half the pages are on one side of the saddle while the remaining pages are on the other side. The signature is oriented so that its head (the folded edge along the top of each page) is point-

With an automatic saddle-stitcher, the operator places signatures into hoppers, and then the signatures are automatically fed onto the conveyor.

ing down the chain towards the stitcher. As this saddle passes the next station, the worker opens another signature and places it on top of the first. Like a cowboy riding a horse, half the signature goes on one side of the saddle and the remainder goes on the other side. This process continues at every station until the complete stack of signatures enters the stitcher head. At this point the signatures are abruptly halted by a metal stop and quickly stitched. Because the head of each signature comes in contact with the stop, these signatures are said to have been "jogged to the head." The above, again, was an example of a semiautomatic saddle-stitcher. With automatic saddle-stitchers, which are also quite common, an operator places signatures into hoppers that automatically feed the signatures onto the conveyor, eliminating the need for a human at every station.

Trimming saddle-stitched booklets. In some cases the stitched booklets are now trimmed without human intervention by a ***three-knife cutter.*** In many cases, however, bindery workers transport large piles of the untrimmed booklets to the guillotine cutter. The cutter operator picks up small handfuls of these booklets and inserts them head first, with the stitched side (called the ***binding edge)*** against the side wall of the cutter. After the booklets are jogged to assure correct positioning, a large clamp comes down on the stack to hold it steady. Next the huge knife trims the unneeded margin of the press sheet from the foot of this pile of booklets. After the trim is complete, the cutter operator flips the books over so that the freshly trimmed foot is jogged against the backstop, while the binding edge remains against the edge of the cutter. The extra paper at the head of each book is then trimmed, and the books are turned 90° so that the binding edge is jogged against the backstop. Finally, the third trim cuts the face of the book, eliminating the unwanted face margin and creating a clean, straight edge.

Page sequences with saddle-stitched booklets. The first page of the signature thrown on the conveyor chain at the last station is now the first page of this booklet. Since that signature straddled all of the previous forms, the same holds true about the final page in the booklet. In fact, if the last signature to be thrown on the chain was a sixteen-pager, then the first eight and last eight pages of this booklet came from that signature.

Drawbacks of saddle-stitching. Since saddle-stitching is so simple and easy, one might wonder why it is not used for all binding needs. That is because saddle-stitching has numerous limitations that prevent it from being used for certain projects. Perhaps the most important limitation is that the number of signatures being stitched should not exceed the number of stations available on your automated saddle-stitcher. In the event that this should happen, one would be forced to first gather and pre-stitch two or more signatures together. These "combined" signatures are then placed back on the chain, and additional signatures are placed on top. The stitcher head must be adjusted so that the second set of staples does not interfere with the first set. Even though this method can allow a greater number of signatures to be bound together, one will probably avoid this technique due to the effects of our next restriction. When too many pages are saddle-stitched at once, the booklet refuses to lay flat; instead, the book will attempt to open to the center spread of pages. Another restriction limiting the size of saddle-stitched booklets is the effect called **creep,** which is also referred to as **push-out.** Creep and how to compensate for it is discussed in the next chapter.

Perfect Binding

If saddle-stitching is only appropriate for a limited number of pages (which you may have inferred by my use of the term "booklet" throughout our discussion), how are larger projects bound? The answer is called **perfect binding,** not to be confused with the **perfecting** imposition style discussed in the previous chapter (another example of the linguistic torture that printers inflict upon themselves). The text pages of a perfect-bound book are glued to a cover; in order for the cover to hold these pages in place through repeated opening and closing, a small amount of glue must be absorbed into the binding edges of the text pages. The resulting effect is that the text pages are glued not only to the cover, but to each other as well. Because of the importance of glue in this binding method, it is sometimes referred to as **adhesive binding.** In order to aid the absorption of glue into the binding edge of each signature, the folded edges of each signature are trimmed off and roughened at the binding edge before gluing. Another notable difference between perfect binding and saddle-stitching is that multiple signatures in the perfect-binding process are simply added to the stack: the second signature follows the first, with the third signature following the second, etc.

Automated perfect binding. Perfect binding can be auto-mated for creating perfect-bound books in much the same way an automated saddle-stitcher eases the production of saddle-stitched booklets. The perfect-binding process typi-cally involves several discrete pieces of equipment. The first operation is called *gathering,* with the gathering machine using a conveyor chain similar to that described previously. Once again, bindery workers are positioned at individual stations, with each worker responsible for adding another signature to the *pocket* (also called a *hopper)* as it travels towards the binding area. Instead of the signatures being opened, they are truly stacked—each one on top of the previ-ous one. If sixteen-page signatures have been printed, this means that the first signature on the chain will contain the first sixteen pages of the book, the next signature contains pages 17 through 32, and so on.

Once all the signatures are gathered together, they undergo the process that prepares the binding edge for gluing. Whether done in-line by a perfect binder or in a separate operation by a *backbone cutter,* the procedure is the same. The gathered collection of signatures (also called a *book block)* is clamped and rotated, so that the binding edge is down. Next a knife or saw *mills* off the first 0.125 in. (3 mm) of paper from the bind-ing edge; the paper being removed is known as the *grind-off.* This prepares the book block for the application of adhesive in the *gluer.* Following this process, the *cover feeder* scores the cover stock to prepare it for attachment to the book block. The cover feeder wraps this scored cover around the glue edge of the book, then the *nipping station* pushes the book block against the spine of the cover while clamps hold everything together. Finally the book exits the perfect binder, ready to be trimmed by a three-knife trimmer (or in the manual process previously described for saddle-stitched booklet production).

Notch binding. A popular variation on perfect binding is known as *notch binding.* This method relies on notches that remove about half of the paper at the point of each fold. These notches allow the paper to fold more completely, providing a nearly flat surface for cover adhesion, without milling. It is common for the operator of the perfect binder to give the notch-folded signatures a slight cleanup grind of 0.063 in. (2 mm) or less, in order to make the binding edge perfectly square. *Burst binding* and *punch perforation binding* are procedures that are very similar to notch binding.

Perfect binding line.
*Courtesy of Muller
Martini, Inc.*

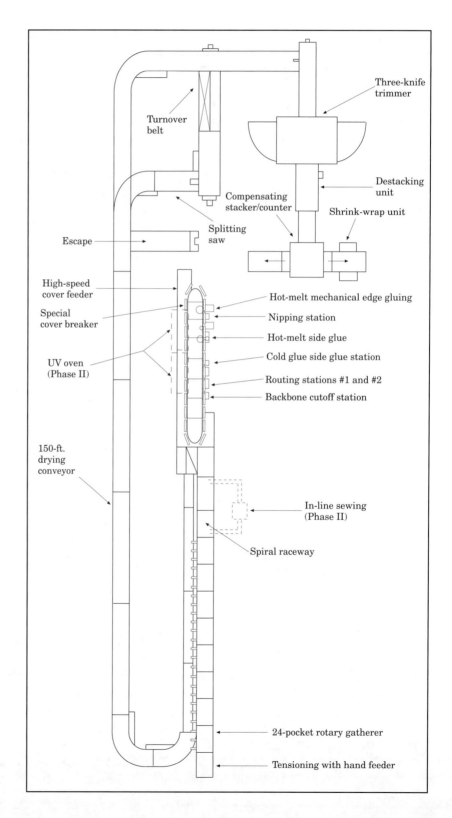

Turnover belt

Three-knife trimmer

Destacking unit

Compensating stacker/counter

Shrink-wrap unit

Splitting saw

Escape

High-speed cover feeder

Special cover breaker

UV oven (Phase II)

Hot-melt mechanical edge gluing

Nipping station

Hot-melt side glue

Cold glue side glue station

Routing stations #1 and #2

Backbone cutoff station

150-ft. drying conveyor

In-line sewing (Phase II)

Spiral raceway

24-pocket rotary gatherer

Tensioning with hand feeder

Imposing for perfect binding. It has already been mentioned that imposing for perfect binding is different from imposing for saddle-stitch binding because of the way in which page order is affected. Perfect-bound signatures each contain a contiguous range of pages, while this is true only for the center signature of a saddle-stitched booklet. Other signatures in a saddle-stitched booklet would have a contiguous range of pages for the first half of the signature, then jump a number of pages before beginning a new contiguous range of page numbers for the remainder of the signature. Another major difference between perfect binding and saddle-stitching is the presence of a ***binding edge gutter*** with perfect binding.

In imposition for saddle-stitching, two pages making up a single printer's spread touch at the fold. If a job is imposed for perfect binding, it may contain extra space between each pair of pages. This gutter at the binding edge is double the amount of paper that will be removed by the backbone cutter. Typically grind-off during the perfect-binding process is 0.125 in. (3 mm); therefore, the binding edge gutter is 0.125 in. on each side of the fold, for a total of 0.25 in. (6 mm) between printer's spreads. If a notch-fold will be employed, you might plan ahead for a 0.06 in. (2 mm) cleanup grind—requiring a binding edge gutter totaling 0.125 in. In the case of burst binding or punch perforation binding, you might

An imposition for perfect binding showing the binding edge gutter.

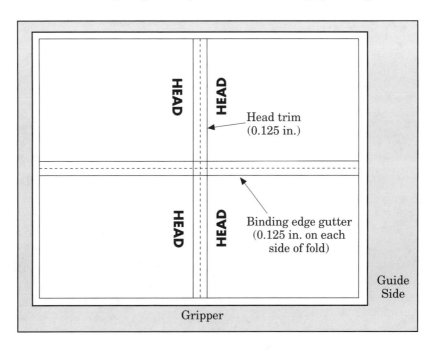

forego the grinding process completely, resulting in an imposition without a binding edge gutter, which differs from a saddle-stitching layout in page order only.

Case Binding

Case binding is a process similar to perfect binding in that text signatures are gathered sequentially and then bound inside a cover. In case binding, however, the signatures are typically sewn together instead of being glued. Imposing signatures for this binding method is the same as for burst binding or punch-perforation binding, in that no binding edge gutter is required. Although it is possible to have perfect-bound books that are sewn together or to perform case binding on books with adhesive-bound text, both of these instances are less common. Work closely with the book binder to achieve a workable layout in either of these unusual situations.

Mechanical Binding

The final binding process to be discussed is actually a broad category of different binding methods. *Mechanical binding* is a catch-all term that includes any method of joining single sheets through the use of some sort of mechanical device. Methods utilizing plastic or metal rings, coils, and spirals are among the most common because they require very little specialized binding equipment. More substantial methods such

A comb-bound publication.

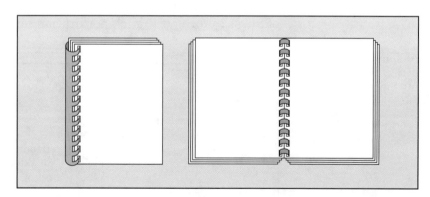

as three-ring binders may be preferred in certain situations because they allow the contents of a book to be changed or added to at a later date. The common factor in all of these binding methods is that they employ individual pages, trimmed to final size. In most cases these pages will be printed *one-up,* which is to say they will have been printed on a press sheet no larger than the final size of the page. This method of printing is ordinarily used for on-demand printers, photocopiers, and small duplicator printing presses.

When pages utilizing a mechanical binding process are to be printed on a large press sheet, imposition is required. Since these pages will go directly from the printing press to the cutter, however, there is no need to take the usual precautions regarding the folding process. Typically, this sort of job is printed on the front side of the sheet last (the opposite of most sheets that will later be folded) and the pages are arranged in sequential page order. This is done so that the cutter operator can make individual piles for each page in the actual page order of the booklet, for insertion into a collating machine.

Before imposing these jobs, the printer must determine whether or not the pages have graphics that bleed off the edge of the page. If this is the case, the pages on the press sheet must be separated with gutters to allow for bleeds. If there are no bleeds, the pages can safely be printed without gutters, allowing the cutter operator to make ***bust cuts*** between pages. This method can reduce the time required to cut down the job by more than 50%.

Basic Finishing Processes

In addition to folding and binding, another postpress process that can have an impact on imposition is finishing. The list of finishing operations is seemingly endless; in fact, each facet of the printing industry has its own group of finishing processes that are unique to that market. Rather than provide an in-depth discussion of these finishing techniques in this book, a few of the most common procedures and how they affect the imposition process will be discussed.

Lamination

Lamination, a popular process for creating a lustrous glow on printed sheets, is especially popular for magazine and paperback book covers. The effect of lamination on the imposition process is purely economic. The imposition style must allow for the maximum number of pages to be laminated in the least amount of time, with minimal effort expended by the laminator. Since many printing plants do not have in-house capabilities for lamination, they must send out printed sheets to be laminated. This process can be rather expensive. It's cheaper to laminate a small number of large sheets rather than a large number of small sheets; therefore, covers that are to be laminated should be printed on the largest feasible press sheet. Moreover, since most covers are laminated on the outside front and outside back pages only, it would be a waste of money to print these jobs in a work-and-turn imposition style. Most printers strive to keep their lamination costs as low as possible by running pages to be laminated as four-up sheetwise forms on large press sheets.

Another important consideration is print sequence. In a normal workflow, the front of the sheet would be printed first so that the completed press sheets have the back side up, ready for insertion into the folding machine. If the lamination is to appear on the front side of the sheet, however, the press sheets will have to be flipped before lamination. For this reason, sheets to be laminated should have the side to be laminated printed last.

Foil Stamping, Diecutting, and Embossing

Foil stamping, diecutting, and embossing are all operations performed by letterpress machines. Many printers still have these machines, left over from the days when all printing was done by the letterpress process. In most cases, these presses are relatively small and are unable to print (or finish) an area larger than 20×26 in. (508×660 mm). Fortunately, the nature of a letterpress can allow it to handle a sheet that is much larger than its image area. To maximize the portion of the sheet that can be foil-stamped, diecut, or embossed, the work should be located near the gripper and moved close to the guide side of the sheet. Letterpresses do not have a plate cylinder, so we do not refer to its "plate bend"; instead, the entire unprintable space at the edge of the sheet is called the gripper margin. The typical gripper margin for a letterpress is 0.5 in. (13 mm). When planning the imposition for a pocket folder, diploma, or other printed piece requiring finishing, locate these items near the intersection of the guide and gripper.

Diecutting. For an example, recall the cover form in chapter 6. The cover was comprised of six pages (outside front cover, inside front cover, inside back cover, inside flap, outside flap, and outside back cover). The cover was printed as a work-and-roll, with the entire image slid off-center to the left so that the location of the outside back flap was only 0.5 in. (13 mm) away from the guide side of the sheet. This was done intentionally so that the lines requiring perforation and scoring would be located close to the guide side. With the cover printed, we are now interested in how best to perform this diecutting operation on the covers.

The most important consideration is that the cover signature was printed as a work-and-roll, meaning that when one

A printed sheet can be seen entering the platen area of this diecutting machine.

Operator adjusting die on a diecutting machine.

set of covers had its outside pages up, the other cover on the same sheet had its inside pages up. Since scoring and perforating should be performed on the top of the sheet, the press sheets must be cut in half lengthwise before being sent through the diecutter. Once this is done, the back half of the sheet is flipped over, so that all sheets now have their front sides facing up. Now every sheet can be gripped by the guide side, which places the flap close to the letterpress gripper, making it easy to fit the work within the limited image area of the letterpress. Had the letterpress been large enough to diecut two covers simultaneously, it would have been of great benefit to print the covers sheetwise or perfecting, so that both covers would have had their fronts on the same side of the press sheet.

Embossing and foil stamping. The same principles of bringing work close to the gripper/guide side intersection and diecutting the proper side of the sheet also apply to the common finishing operations of embossing and foil stamping. By their nature, these operations must be performed on the correct side of the sheet. Just as with lamination, it pays to think ahead and print the side of the sheet requiring the finishing *last*—that way, the sheets will not have to be manually flipped before finishing can begin.

A sheet of paper being foil-stamped.

Converting envelopes. Irregularly shaped objects such as envelopes are entirely diecut from the sheet by a process called **converting.** Many of the same precautions that apply to diecutting also apply to converting. In most cases, binderies that offer converting services will have a specific layout they want you to follow. Deviating from this layout can seriously increase the price of converting. In order to fit the maximum number of envelopes on the press sheet, odd angles and nested arrangements are used. After the envelopes are diecut from the press sheet using a single, large die, the resulting envelopes are folded and glued into the familiar product.

Nesting five #6¾ commercial envelopes on a 17×22-in. sheet of paper, as shown in the illustration, allows all envelopes to be cut diagonal to the grain. *Courtesy Williamhouse, a division of American Pad and Paper.*

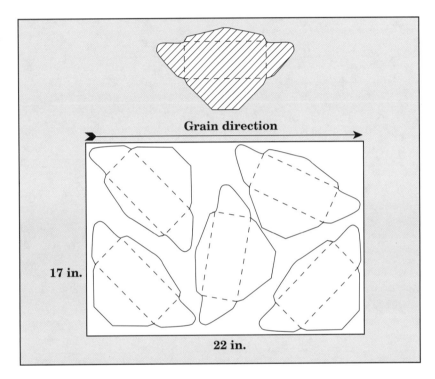

Grain direction

17 in.

22 in.

Keep these special considerations in mind when imposing a pocket folder or envelope. It is common for prepress workers to center pocket folders on the press sheet, which leads to great consternation in the finishing department when the press sheets have to be trimmed several times before the pocket folder will fall into the image area of the letterpress.

This chapter provided an overview of folding, binding, and finishing considerations. In the next chapter I will plan a complex job from start to finish, applying the principles covered to this point.

8 Planning the Imposition

This chapter takes a look at some of the choices available to the printer when it is time to plan the imposition of a print job.

Preliminaries to Planning

First determine who typically makes the choices that shape each job. In most cases commercial printers receive work as the result of a meeting or a phone call between a customer and the printer's salesperson. In addition to the actual requirements of the job (size and number of pages, number of colors, binding and finishing options), these two people will likely begin to theorize about the best plan for printing the job. This sort of speculation usually ends at the choice of press ("For 50,000 copies, the new half-web will have to be used"), but it is not unheard of for these armchair quarterbacks to say things like "run the cover on a small sheet, for the best control" or "run the cover as a four-up work-and-turn so I only have to pay for one set of plates."

Estimating the Job

After the salesperson has concluded this discussion with the customer and called in the job information to the printing plant, a staff person known as the ***estimator*** picks up the project and begins to work on a price quotation for the job. Not having been a party to the conversation between the salesperson and customer, the estimator will believe they had a compelling reason to use a small sheet or to plate the cover for a work-and-turn. Unfortunately, the decisions often reached by the salesperson and customer may be ill-formed or based on incomplete knowledge of the process. These incorrect notions of how to impose and print the job may then be used by the estimator in preparing the quote.

Entering the Work Order

Once the customer has approved the quoted price, all components of the job (disks, photos, laser proofs, even the occasional artboard) are delivered to the printer. The customer service representative (CSR) who is assigned to that salesperson is responsible for entering the work order and filling out the paperwork that will accompany the job through the production process. Among these items is the ***job jacket*** (sometimes called a job ticket or job docket), a large printed sheet that carries most of the particulars about how the job will be printed—how many forms, which press, what size sheet of paper, how many colors, what binding method, etc. (This information is often printed on the face of a large envelope, hence the term "jacket.") In some printing plants the CSR actually is responsible for filling in all this information, in which case, the CSR "plans" the job. In many cases, however, the CSR only fills out a portion of the information before passing the job jacket along to another person called the ***planner.***

A selection of job jackets.

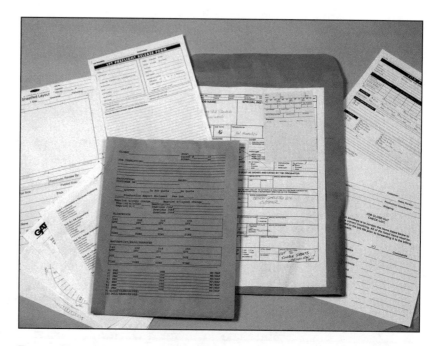

Planning

Regardless of who is responsible for this function, the planning stage of any job is of critical importance. The decisions made at this point will impact not only how the job is to be printed but also how the folding and binding will be performed and the cost of finishing services. An important aspect of this function is determining the size and quantity of paper needed

A customer service representative (CSR) completing a layout sheet.

for the job because, in many cases, the person who plans the job also orders the paper. Another primary function of planning is the creation of ***layout sheets.*** (These are not to be confused with folding dummies or the full-size orange vinyl stripping guides discussed earlier in the book.) Layout sheets are documents that provide instructions on how the form will be imposed, along with additional information regarding the stock to be used, the number of inks, the imposition style, etc. Once again the completion of these layout sheets typically falls to either the CSR or the planner.

Role of the Planner

What are the steps for taking a customer's job and moving it through the printing plant? When are the plans for a job made, and by whom? The purpose of this chapter is to answer all these questions, because even if you are working as an output technician in the electronic prepress department, it is in your best interest to understand the secrets of job planning. Since job planning is still primarily a manual process, anyone responsible for imposition will either be planning work or carrying out the plans of others. In either case be on the alert for plans that are incorrect or inefficient.

Let me illustrate the process of planning for imposition by working with another example. In this case the customer has requested 20,000 copies of an 8.5×11-in. (216×279-mm) paperback book that has 92 pages plus a cover. The cover features four-color process and lamination, while the majority of the text is black only. There are, however, a few full-color illustrations scattered throughout. Although it might be possible to saddle-stitch 92 pages if extremely light stock were used, the customer wants the more prestigious look and feel of a perfect-bound book. All the computer disks for the digital files have been delivered, as well as a number of slides that are to be scanned for reproduction on both the cover and on selected text pages.

Steps in the Planning Process

For the purpose of this example, assume that you work as a CSR in a printing plant where the customer service representatives are responsible for doing their own planning. That means it is up to you to determine the answers to all the little (and big) questions surrounding this job. Let us walk through the decision-making process, in the most logical order:

1. Determine which printing presses to use. Although the size of the pages and the type of paper to be printed are important considerations, the main factor determining the choice of press will be run length. In this case, the customer has requested 20,000 copies. Our printing plant has high-speed web presses that could run 20,000 copies of a single signature in less than an hour's time, but this particular printshop considers the minimum quantity for such a press to be 40,000 impressions. Although exceptions can be made to this rule, the longer setup time and greater paper waste incurred while the press is starting up (also called **run-up** or **makeready)** make it unlikely that we would be able to justify printing this job on a web press. Instead, consider using one of the sheetfed presses. With top speeds of 10,000 to 12,000 impressions per hour, these machines can also churn out the paper. This particular printing plant has sheetfed presses that can print on stock as wide as 40 in. (1016 mm); a width that allows sixteen-page signatures to be printed, if desired.

2. Choose the paper size, weight, and type. At this early stage we will select one standard sheet for the text and a different standard sheet for the cover. A preliminary goal is to try to keep costs low by using these sheets for all signatures. In many cases, however, stock for certain signatures may have to be trimmed down, or a paper with a specific size or grain direction may have to be ordered for special situations.

The steps in the
planning process.

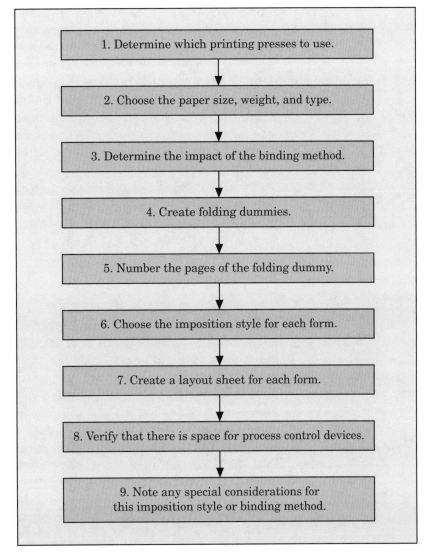

In the case of the text, choose a large sheet in a standard
size and weight; in this example, *23×35-in. (584×889-mm)
grain-short 70-lb. offset white*. Since the customer does not
typically have a preference for any specific paper manufacturer, use a local distributor that gives great service and
good prices. This standard size is routinely used for printing
sixteen-page signatures on sheetfed presses, so use this size
unless you are presented with a compelling reason to
change.

Choosing stock for the book cover is a little more complex.
Although selecting a small sheet for book covers allows the
press operators to concentrate on a single image, this cus-

tomer is concerned about price. Since running more images on a larger sheet is more cost-effective, consider selecting a press sheet that is large enough to print two or four covers simultaneously. Looking over the job specifications for more detail, notice that the outside front and outside back covers are to be laminated. This clinches the decision in favor of 25×38-in. (635×965-mm) stock because, first, it is a standard size used when four-out imposition of cover spreads is desired and, second, the outside supplier that will be doing the lamination can handle sheets as large as 30×40 in. (762×1016 mm). The customer is also interested in a heavy sheet that will make the cover of the paperback book more durable. In the fashion typical of these softcover books, however, the customer will accept the use of less expensive paper that is coated on one side only; the inside front and inside back cover pages will be printed on the uncoated back side of the stock.

After taking all these factors into consideration, you can order "25×38-in. (635×965-mm) grain-short 80-lb. white cover, coated one side" from your local paper house. But how much paper should be ordered? For the cover that decision can be made right now: knowing that four covers fit on the 25×38-in. sheet, order a minimum of 5,000 sheets (20,000 ÷ 4). However, a typical practice is to include 10% more paper to cover run-up and spoilage (sheets with defects). This brings the total cover stock order to 5,500 sheets. The quantity of text stock to order cannot be fully determined, however, until more of the following questions are answered.

3. Determine the impact of the binding method. We already know that this project will be perfect-bound, because the customer has specifically requested it. This choice will affect both the cover and the text forms. The cover must now contain a *spine* (extra paper added between the front and back covers to accommodate the thickness of the book block), and the text signatures will be stacked one on top of another, instead of being gathered, as in saddle-stitching.

4. Create folding dummies. As you may already have guessed, this book cannot be evenly divided into *sixteen-page* signatures. Begin, however, by creating five identical sixteen-page folding dummies. These five dummies represent eighty pages, which leaves twelve pages. There is a common signature style for *twelve-page* signatures, but this method is only suitable for jobs featuring gatefolds. Since there are no gate-folds in this book, we'll make up the remaining text pages by printing one signature as a *two-out eight-pager* and the other as a *four-out four-pager*.

As discussed in chapter 7, begin the sixteen-page dummies by marking the gripper and side guides of each of the five blank sheets; you should also label the front and back of each sheet. During this early planning stage, however, we'll forego marking the form name and page numbers—that informa-tion has yet to be determined. It is important, obviously, that the correct folding sequence is used to create the sixteen-page dummies: "up, up, and up" (three "up" folds). Push the five folded sixteen-page dummies off to the side, so that we have room to create a dummy for the eight-page signature.

Since all of the folded dummies for the job should be of the same size when folded, create this next dummy by obtaining a fresh sheet of the same paper that was used for the sixteen-page dummies and cutting it in half. Push one half of the sheet off to the side for later use; the remaining half-sheet will be our eight-page dummy. First, mark two Xs along the long edge of the sheet closest to you but do not write the word "grip," as you did on the sixteen-page dummies. Next, make two X marks along the short side of the sheet appear-ing to the left of the previous marks. Now fold the sheet by bringing up the left edge and folding it over to meet the right edge. Now lift the side of the sheet closest to you and fold it back to meet the tail of the sheet.

1. Folding the dummy for the eight-page signature: Make the first fold by lifting the left edge of the sheet and folding it over to meet the opposite edge of the sheet.

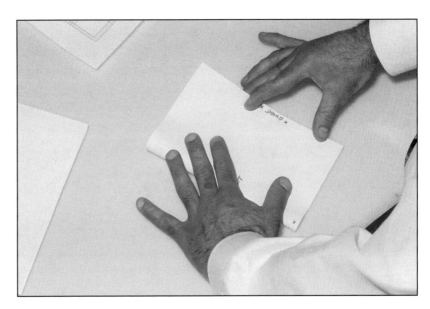

2. Folding the dummy for the eight-page signature: Make the second fold by lifting the edge of the sheet closest to you and then folding it to meet the tail of the sheet.

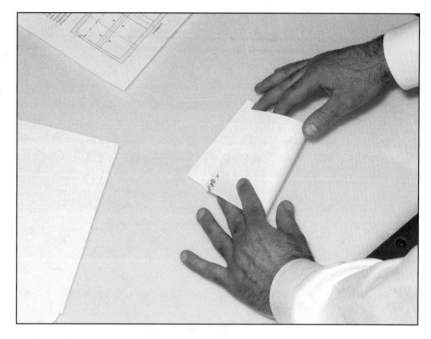

Cut the remaining paper in half again and put aside one of the resulting sheets; the sheet still in front of you represents the final four pages of text. Orient this small sheet so that a long side is closest to you. Mark two Xs along that side, then make two more X marks along the short side of the sheet that appears to the left of these first marks. Lift that side of the sheet, folding it over to meet the right edge.

To fold the dummy for the four-page signature, (1) orient a long side of the sheet toward you and (2) then lift the left side of the sheet so that it meets the right side.

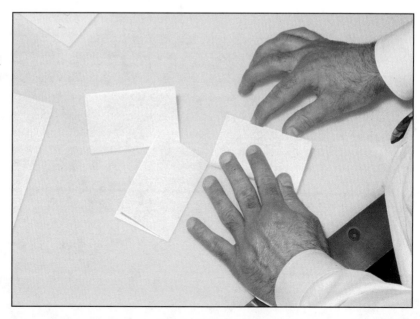

Finally, pick up the remaining scrap of paper; this will become the dummy for the four-page cover. Just as you did for the four-page text dummy, draw pairs of X marks along two sides and fold the sheet in half, making certain that your X marks appear along the face of the inside front cover and along the foot of the inside front and back cover pages. You now have all the folding dummies needed to *paginate* (determine page order) the sample book; seven dummies for the text and one for the cover.

5. Number the pages of the folding dummies. It is time to mark down the actual page numbers on each folding dummy so that you will be assured of the correct imposition later. Start with the cover, since it is the simplest to number. Orient the folded piece of paper as you would hold a magazine; when you turn the page, does a pair of X marks appear along the left face edge? If not, rotate the sheet 180°. Return

Putting page numbers on the folding dummy for the cover ("cover form") of the project booklet. In this example, the first page will be marked "OFC" for outside front cover.

the sheet to its folded state, write "Cover Form" in the center of the first page, then begin writing down the page numbers in sequence. The first page should be marked "OFC" (for *outside front cover),* the second page is marked "IFC," the third page is marked "IBC," and the final page is the "OBC."

Pick up a sixteen-page folding dummy and hold it so that the open sides appear on the right and at the bottom; then write "Form A" in the center of the first page. Pay close attention to the next step! To avoid a potential disaster, mark each folding dummy with the actual page number that will be printed as part of the folio. If the first page of the book's text was page 1, this would be no problem. Unfortunately, this is seldom the case; most books have unnumbered front matter (i.e., title page, copyright page, foreword, etc.) or front matter numbered using roman numerals (e.g., i, ii, iii). Our example is a typical paperback book, with a number of pages contained in the front matter. Following along with the printout supplied by the customer, indicate the actual content of these front matter pages directly onto the folding dummy: title page, copyright page, TOC (table of contents),

Putting page numbers on the first sixteen-page folding dummy. Since this is a book, the front matter will be numbered using roman numerals. Thus, the first page of the book will be page i.

TOC2, and three pages for the preface. Also indicate the preface pages by the numbers that appear as part of the folio: i, ii, and iii. Finally, there is a blank page (which is indicated by writing "blank" on the folding dummy) and then the actual page 1 appears. The eight pages of front matter have taken up half of this first signature. Continue by marking the actual page numbers on every page until you reach the end of this folding dummy.

Hopefully you are aware of the impact that perfect-binding will have on the pagination of our book! This choice of binding method is important because it determines that the page numbers will move sequentially through one form and on to the next. A saddle-stitched book would be numbered differently, as discussed in the previous chapter. If there were no reason to do otherwise, the numbering process for our current project would continue on by numbering the four remaining sixteen-page dummies, then the eight-pager and finally the four-pager until all five sixteen-page folding dummies have been given page numbers.

There are instances, however, when these rules should be broken—our example is one of them. In referring to the customer's notes, we might notice that the pages carrying four-color process images are 42, 43, and 64 through 68. This brings up some important considerations. Ideally, these color pages should be concentrated onto as few forms as possible. In this example, the most economical plan would be to have the four-color process images appear on the eight-page or four-page signatures. Since these signatures will probably be printed two- or four-out on a large sheet size, press time for these forms will be reduced, meaning less time is spent on the four-color press. In addition, since the remaining forms can be printed on a less expensive (in terms of billed cost per hour) one- or two-color press, the cost of producing the job is reduced. If the job was quoted with all text signatures running on a four-color press, any money saved by moving most of the work to less expensive presses adds up to increased profits for the printer.

By carefully examining which pages will need to print on the four-color press, you may reach the following decision: Form A will be followed by two more sixteen-page signatures, Form B and Form C. The fourth text folding dummy will represent the four-page signature; that form will be followed by another sixteen-pager and then the eight-page signature. In this way, pages 42 and 43 (located on Form D, the four-pager) can be printed on the four-color press, as can pages 64 through 68 (printing on Form F, the eight-pager). With the addition of the final 16-page signature (Form G), the order of the signatures has been finalized.

6. Choose the imposition style for each form. By default, every signature can be arranged in a sheetwise imposition style. Your job during this planning process is to look for any clues that may indicate why something might not work and how it should be altered. Base your judgments on the size and variety of presses available, as well as on the capacities and capabilities of the folding, binding, and finishing equipment that will be used. In the case of our example, we have already discussed the imposition style for the cover: it will be printed four-out sheetwise, so that the front covers are on the same side of the paper. This will allow the press operators to see all the front covers simultaneously, increasing the likelihood of a color match across the sheet. More importantly, it will allow the entire sheet to be laminated in a single pass, reducing the price our supplier will charge to perform the lamination process. Our folding dummy only represents one of these four covers. The full imposition of the cover form is illustrated in the next section, when a layout sheet is created for each form.

But what about the text pages? With the exception of forms D and F, the remainder of the text has only a single color (black) on each side; these ***one-over-one*** forms are perfect for our two-color perfecting press. It might take some convincing to persuade the press crew to make the necessary adjustments to permit the press to perfect, but with five perfecting signatures printing 20,000 copies each, that should be an easy argument to win. Mark up the folding dummies for forms A, B, C, E, and G clearly so that the perfecting process is obvious. Open the dummy up to a flat sheet and position the dummy so that the gripper is towards you with the guide side on the left. Since this is how the sheet should look when it delivers from the printing press, write "second gripper" along the gripper edge. Next, roll the sheet backwards so

Writing "second gripper" on the folding dummy for a perfecting signature.

that the guide side is still on the left, with the second gripper at the back edge of the sheet, facing down. Write "first gripper," surrounded by a pair of X marks along the edge of the sheet closest to you, then make an additional pair of X marks along the guide side, which will still be on your left (the terms *first gripper* and *second gripper* always signify a

Writing "first gripper" on the folding dummy for a perfecting signature.

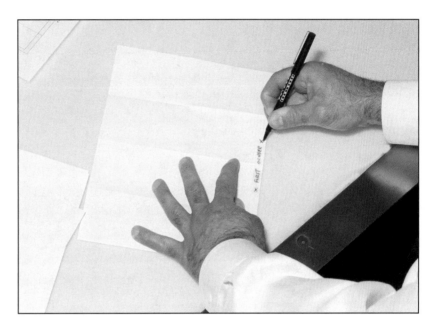

perfecting signature). As with the cover form, the remaining folding dummies (D and F) do not constitute the full press sheet. The layout for each of these forms will be diagrammed in the next step.

7. Create a layout sheet for each form. In addition to creating folding dummies, the person planning a print job usually completes a document called the *layout sheet.* Each form gets a separate layout sheet, and these layout sheets are two-sided. An example of a typical layout sheet is shown in the following illustration. Spaces are provided where the job planner can note detailed information about every form, including the inks, sheet size, and imposition style. As you can see, the major feature of this form is a rectangle that represents the press sheet. Using a straightedge and a pen, lines can be drawn on this sheet to represent the folds and trims of the press sheet. These are the measurements that the stripper will use if a hand-drawn layout sheet is created for conventional image assembly. Likewise, these same mea-

A sample master layout sheet. (See Appendix A for additional master layout sheets.)

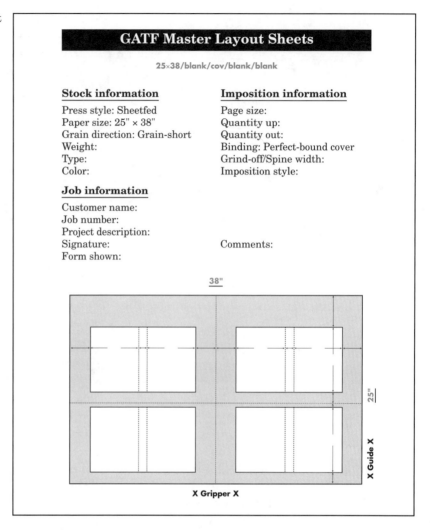

GATF Master Layout Sheets

25×38/blank/cov/blank/blank

Stock information
Press style: Sheetfed
Paper size: 25" × 38"
Grain direction: Grain-short
Weight:
Type:
Color:

Imposition information
Page size:
Quantity up:
Quantity out:
Binding: Perfect-bound cover
Grind-off/Spine width:
Imposition style:

Job information
Customer name:
Job number:
Project description:
Signature: Comments:
Form shown:

38"

2.5"

X Guide X

X Gripper X

surements will guide the output technician in creating a digital imposition style.

Most printing plants using layout sheets will have a small number of "masters," a collection of commonly drawn layouts that can be photocopied as needed. Fortunately for you, our example also makes use of this *master layout sheet* concept. (Appendix A includes a collection of layout masters.)

The master whose imposition style is "25×38/blank/cov/blank/blank" is the starting point for the first layout sheet. Simply photocopy this page from the book, and fill in the blanks and write in the missing dimensions. We already know the press sheet size (25×38 in., 635×965 mm) and the size of the front and back covers (8.5×11 in., 216×279 mm), but what about the width of the spine? This dimension can be obtained by measuring the thickness of a single sheet, and referencing that measurement against a chart that reveals the number of pages per inch this paper will create. Paper vendors can usually supply these measurements for their popular text sheets. If the correct number cannot be easily located, measure the thickness of four sheets at once, using a very precise instrument called a micrometer. Experienced job planners judge the width obtained from these measurements against their experiences in creating perfect-bound books, sometimes opting to use a spine width slightly smaller (or larger) than the measurements indicate. For this example, select a spine dimension of 0.1875 in. (5 mm) based on experience.

Number of pages per inch, based on the thickness of four sheets of paper as measured with a micrometer.

Micrometer Reading*	Pages per Inch	Micrometer Reading*	Pages per Inch	Micrometer Reading*	Pages per Inch
0.007	1142	0.019	420	0.031	258
0.0075	1066	0.0195	410	0.0315	254
0.008	1000	0.020	400	0.032	250
0.0085	942	0.0205	390	0.0325	246
0.009	888	0.021	380	0.033	242
0.0095	842	0.0215	372	0.0335	238
0.010	800	0.022	364	0.034	234
0.0105	762	0.0225	356	0.0345	232
0.011	726	0.023	348	0.035	228
0.0115	696	0.0235	340	0.0355	224
0.012	666	0.024	332	0.036	222
0.0125	640	0.0245	326	0.0365	218
0.013	614	0.025	320	0.037	216
0.0135	592	0.0255	314	0.0375	212
0.014	570	0.026	308	0.038	210
0.0145	552	0.0265	302	0.0385	208
0.015	532	0.027	296	0.039	204
0.0155	516	0.0275	290	0.0395	202
0.016	500	0.028	286	0.040	200
0.0165	484	0.0285	280	0.0405	198
0.017	470	0.029	276	0.041	194
0.0175	456	0.0295	272	0.0415	192
0.018	444	0.030	266	0.042	190
0.0185	432	0.0305	262	0.0425	188

*Thickness of four sheets of paper.

With the actual page dimensions figured, it is time to determine the allocation of the paper that will *not* be part of the finished product—the margins. Begin at the gripper edge (also called the ***lead edge)*** of the sheet, and work our way back. For our example, assume that the printing press requires a gripper margin of 0.375 in. (10 mm). Add to this the bleed margin of 0.125 in. (3 mm), and the total distance from the edge of the sheet to our first trim will be 0.5 in. (13 mm). The next line has already been defined as the top trim of the cover; it occurs 11.5 in. (292 mm) from the lead edge.

The next line defines the ***head trim,*** which is drawn 0.125 in. (3 mm) back from our previous line. This is a very important measurement, and one that must be consistent throughout the entire project. The head trim for a cover form must be identical to the head trim used throughout the text. Regardless of how much extra room there is on this cover press sheet, the amount of extra paper in the head trim must be limited to the same 0.125 in. about to be used in the text. (Although head trim amounts of 0.25 in. (6 mm) and 0.063 (1.6 mm) are also widely used, 0.125 in. is by far the most common measurement.) The reason why this amount must be kept equal throughout the entire project is easy to see: at some point, the cover and several text forms will be brought together for binding. This collection of folded signatures will be jogged against two surfaces: the binding edge and the head of the sheet. In the case of covers and other four- or six-page sheets, the head will be a trimmed edge, which is a set distance beyond the location of the book's final trim. More importantly, for eight- or sixteen-page signatures, the head of the sheet will be created by a fold that occurs exactly halfway between two opposing pages. As you will discover when creating the layout sheets for the text forms, the amount of paper between the tops of two opposing pages is usually 0.25 in. (6 mm), resulting in 0.125 in. (3 mm) of head trim for the finished book. If the amount of head trim is not kept equal for all components of the project, the finished book will not trim properly.

Next, draw a new line 0.375 in. (10 mm) back from the head trim, following that with another line 0.125 in. away, to define the foot of our next set of pages. These lines duplicate the same dimensions found at the foot of this press sheet, so that when the covers at the front of the sheet are separated from the covers at the back of the sheet, the margins at the foot will be equal. Since we are defining this new line as the foot of the second set of pages, you can tell that the cover will be imposed in a head-to-foot imposition style. Press operators typically prefer this configuration, because running one front cover directly behind another front cover helps the press crew achieve an identical appearance on both images.

Measuring back another 11 in. (279 mm), draw a line for the top trim of the second set of covers. As an aid in determining bleed position, draw another line 0.125 in. (3 mm) away (some planners do not indicate bleed lines on the layout sheets, leaving these measurements up to the stripper or output technician). This completes the horizontal lines on our layout sheet diagram. Next, the spacing of the vertical lines will be discussed.

Unless there is a contributing factor (such as foil-stamping or diecutting), perfect-bound pages are generally centered from left to right: the margins between the edge of the paper and the face trim of the pages will be equal on both the left and right sides of the sheet. Furthermore, if these margins are added together, the result will equal the amount of space between face trims in the vertical center of the sheet. To figure this amount, simply add up the width of all pages and spines (8.5 + 0.1875 + 8.5 + 8.5 + 0.1875 + 8.5 = 34.375 in.), and subtract that number from the width of the press sheet (38 − 34.375 = 3.625 in.). Now divide that number by four (3.625/4 = 0.90625 in.), and you will have the calculated the margin at each face trim, 0.90625 in. or 23 mm. (If you are defining the imposition for traditional image assembly, try to express these dimensions using fractions, which can be located on a ruler. For instance, 0.90625 in. equals $^{29}\!/_{32}$ in. With digital imposition, you will be using decimal numbers.)

Using these calculations, indicate the measurements on the layout sheet. Since you have been indicating bleed areas, continue to do so, making the face margin 0.78125 in. (20 mm) plus 0.125 in. (3 mm) for bleed. Once you have written down all the dimensions, use a calculator to total all the dimensions in the vertical direction, to make certain this number falls within the short dimension of the press sheet. Next, do the same for the horizontal direction, verifying the result against the long dimension of the press sheet.

As you begin to plan the text forms for the job, you will need to obtain new master layout sheets that are appropriate for each form. (See Appendix A for similar master layout sheets.) Beginning with the perfecting text forms, make a copy of the master whose imposition style is "23×35/blank/pb/blank/blank."

The perfecting text forms will be stripped in nearly the same way as the four-out cover, with a few important differences. Most noticeably, the imposition style will no longer be head-to-foot; pages will now run head-to-head, so that the completed press sheet can be folded as a sixteen-page signature. In order to maintain the standard 0.125 in. (3 mm) head trim after these signatures have been folded, the total space between heads will now total 0.25 in. (0.125 in. × 2) or 6 mm (3 mm × 2).

The most interesting consideration is the effect of back-trimming the sheet. As you may recall from chapter 6, printing jobs with the perfecting method requires that the short dimension of the sheet be consistent throughout the run, which will not be the case when the carton of paper arrives from the paper house. This consistent depth is assured by backtrimming all sheets before they are run through the press—often as much as 0.125 in. (3 mm). In our current example—involving five perfecting forms, each with a run length of 20,000 impressions—we are looking at backtrimming more than 100 cartons of paper. Although in some printing plants that factor alone might cause the job to run sheetwise, we will assume that our printing plant has the latest in cutter technology and that the ability to run these five forms in half the time required to print them sheetwise will be worth the effort.

If the stock was 23×35 in. (584×889 mm) before backtrimming, it will now be 22.875×35 in. (581×889 mm). Imposing jobs for perfecting means centering the vertical dimensions on the sheet. Adding up the two 11-in. (279-mm) pages and the 0.25-in. (6-mm) margin between the heads gives us 22.25 (565 mm). Subtracting this number from 22.875 in. leaves only 0.625 in. (16 mm). Half of that amount must go at the tail of the sheet, leaving only 0.3125 in. (8 mm). That might work for some perfecting jobs, but the text of this job features numerous halftone images that bleed off the head, face, and foot. It would be impossible to print these images correctly on this sheet size because the grippers are reaching into image areas. Instead, you must weigh the cost of changing to a 25×38-in. (635×965-mm) sheet against the quick-turnaround benefits of perfecting that the 25×38-in. sheet allows. Once again you will have to side with the perfecting method; this means you can discard the master layout sheet selected earlier, in favor of the master "25×38/blank/pb/blank/blank."

After being backtrimmed, the new text stock size will be 24.875×38 in. (632×965 mm). Using the same method previously discussed, you can determine that the margin along the gripper edge of the sheet will total 1.3125 in. (33 mm), or 1.1875 in. + 0.125 in. (30 mm + 3 mm). Do not forget to revise the horizontal margins as well on the new master layout sheet.

8. Verify that there is space for process control devices. Now that you have decided to order a larger sheet size for the text of the book, you can utilize another important tool: ***color bars***. Color bars are usually located horizontally across the tail of press sheets. This series of colored squares is among the tools called ***process control devices*** because they provide information about the density of ink being applied by the printing press, as well as many other useful features. Including these bars on every set of plates you impose is very important. Your bars should run to within 0.5 in. (13 mm) of each edge of the sheet. Depending on the manufacturer and the purpose, color bars vary in size across the vertical dimension. GATF color bars, for example, fit into a 0.375-in. (10-mm) window, while some variations of the SWOP color bars occupy a much larger space. To use color bars, therefore, leave a minimum of 0.5 in. of stock beyond the final trim— 0.125 in. (3 mm) for image bleed and 0.375 in. (10 mm) for color bars. Though there may be times, as in our example, where you may be tempted to run a sheet that does not have room for color bars, do your best to resist this idea. The sav-

Press operator using a densitometer to read the color control bar on the press sheet. The bar provides information on ink density, trapping, and dot gain.

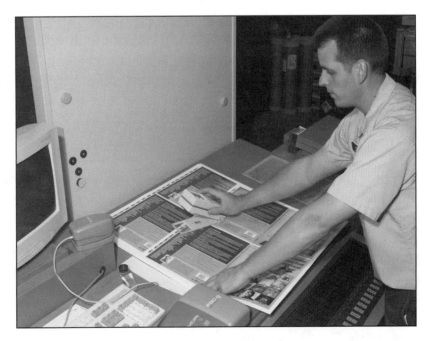

Press operator measuring ink density on three press sheets that have different types of color control bars.

GATF/SWOP Proofing Bar

Six-Color Control Bar (Two-Tiered)

Six-Color Control Bar (Single-Tiered)

ings realized by running a smaller sheet without color bars will be more than offset by additional costs if the customer rejects the run because of inconsistencies in the print quality.

In traditional image assembly, color bars are made from long strips of film. Printing companies purchase enough sets of these films to strip them onto master flats for all the common press sheet sizes. With digital imposition, you will be able to incorporate digital color bars, such as those available from GATF, into your marks set. The position of these bars can be easily moved as required. Positioning these color bars is very important, because in sheetwise, work-and-turn, and work-and-roll impositions, the color bars are typically located within the very last 0.375 in. (10 mm) of the back edge of the sheet. This allows the greatest amount of space on the rest of the sheet for the job itself.

Perfecting imposition is the exception to this rule. As you may recall from chapter 6, the perfecting press prints both sides of the sheet in the same pass, switching gripper edges on the sheet at some point within the press. If the color bars for the first side of a perfecting job are located at the very edge of the sheet, these color bars will still be wet when the second set of grippers clamp down on this area. This gets ink all over the grippers of the remaining press units, which can create severe maintenance problems. The final 0.375 in. (10 mm) of perfecting press sheets should therefore be left blank. Locate your color bars closer to the work for perfecting impositions such as our five text forms.

9. Note any special considerations for this imposition style or binding method. Our layout sheet has an area available for writing comments, which will be read by the person who actually performs the imposition, whether on a light table or a computer. Here are a few examples of the kind of issues about which you should alert them:

- *Perfect-bound covers.* The spine area between the inside front cover (IFC) and inside back cover (IBC) pages is where the glue will be applied just before the cover is fed into place. In this situation, a standard rule of conventional image assembly applies: never apply ink and glue in the same spot. This means that any image that prints to the binding edge of the IFC or IBC pages must be knocked out (eliminated) from the spine area, to avoid applying glue on top of an area that has already been printed. In fact, this glue area is larger than just the spine area. In order for the cover to firmly adhere to the text pages, some glue must wrap around the text pages—both the cover and the text must remain unprinted in this area, as well.

    How wide must this unprinted area be? The measure of this glue area is half the ***hinge,*** an area created by the nipping station (part of the cover application process). The nipping station uses great pressure to bring the backbone of the book block together with the spine of the cover. The

Providing an unprinted area on the inside of a cover for a perfect-bound book. This allows for some glue to wrap around the text pages.

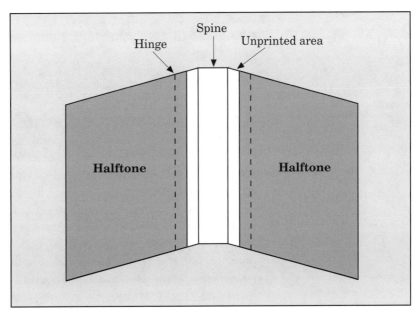

point where the hinge area ends is also called the score line. Since paperback books typically have a hinge of 0.25 in. (6 mm), leave 0.125 in. (3 mm) of unprinted paper near the binding edge of the IFC, IBC, and the first and last pages of the text. In our example, the customer would like to have a full-bleed halftone image on both inside covers, meaning that the image will bleed off the page at the top, face, and bottom, but stop 0.125 in. (3 mm) short of the spine along the binding edge.

- *Perfect-bound text.* Similar cautions apply to the text of a perfect-bound book. Extra space must be left unprinted where the last page of a signature meets the first page of the next signature, so that glue can penetrate and increase the strength of the book. Although this procedure applies to all types of perfect-bound books, it is especially important for notch-fold and burst-bound books whose text does not receive a cleanup trim from a backbone cutter. The unprinted space should extend into the text 0.125 in. (3 mm) from the binding edge.

- *Crossover images in perfect-bound text.* Bleed graphics and images that cross over (appear on both pages of a printer's spread, with the intent that both sides should line up to form the illusion of a single, unbroken image) should extend beyond the binding edge into the grind-off area, also called the binding gutter. In this way, inadequate grind-off will not result in the presence of unprinted paper near the spine.

  For crossover images, the trick is in positioning both sides of the image correctly, so that a believable illusion of continuity is achieved. It is easy to see why some people get confused when creating crossovers in a perfect-bound book. To illustrate both the correct method and the common mistake, two views of the center spread from a perfect-bound signature (pages 16 and 17, the center spread from the example's Form B) are shown. The first illustration (the wrong method) shows a single image spanning both pages, while the second illustration (the correct method) shows the importance of aligning image positions at the crossover point. For images that cross over within the same signature, this point is the same as the intended binding edge.

An incorrect method of creating a crossover for a perfect-bound book. The same image spans both pages of the reader's spread.

The correct method of creating a crossover for a perfect-bound book. The designer has aligned image positions at the crossover point, as shown in the enlargement at the bottom.

Crossover point

Fold

- *Compensating for bottling.* When a signature is folded, the natural resistance that occurs at the fold results in an effect called ***bottling;*** this condition forces the inner pages of the folded signature to rotate slightly away from the binding edge. Of course, saddle-stitched books do not suffer from bottling because the staples force the inner pages back into contact with the binding edge; however, bottling can be a major problem for perfect-bound books. In a perfect-bound signature, there is no method to force the inner pages into tight contact with the outer pages prior to spine grinding; the result can be pages in the final product that appear printed at an angle (even though the stripped films were perfectly square to the layout).

  Because of this problem, some of the most advanced imposition programs allow compensation for this bottling effect—in essence, entire pages are rotated toward the binding edge by a predetermined amount (the greater the paper thickness, the larger the rotation required).

- *High-page lips.* The special considerations described so far in step 9 pertain to perfect binding, which is appropriate, since the example is a perfect-bound book. There are still, however, two more important issues that pertain only to saddle-stitch binding methods.

  As discussed earlier in this chapter, figuring the location of each two-page spread across the width of a perfect-bound layout is a simple matter; merely equalize the margins between all spreads. When the signature is folded, the amount of paper at the face trim of every page is the same. Saddle-stitching, however, makes different demands. During the process of gathering signatures to be saddle-stitched, the signature must be opened to its center so that it can straddle the saddle on the conveyor chain. Whether this is done by hand or by a mechanical system involving vacuum suckers, a ***lip*** is necessary to allow these pages to unfold dependably.

  The lip is an amount of paper that extends beyond the rest of the signature. The customary amount of extra paper needed to form a lip is 0.25 in. (6 mm), although as little as 0.125 in. (3 mm) of extra paper is still useful. Lips beyond 0.375 in. (10 mm) are too large and may interfere with the reliability of automatic feeders. Folded signatures with lips greater than 0.75 in. (19 mm) are often pretrimmed before being gathered on the saddle-stitcher. This issue is relevant only for the saddle-stitch binding method. Since the signatures for perfect binding are merely stacked in the hopper to form a book block, it is not necessary to have a lip to assist in the gathering process. As you saw in the previous chapter, a folded signature emerges with the first page face down and the last page on top. In the language of the printer, this final page is known as the ***high page***, since it is the highest page number within that signature. In most instances, gathering pages for saddle-stitching will require a ***high-page lip;*** which is to say that the half of the signature with the larger face margin will be the top of the signature as it exits the folder.

Examining the pagination of the sixteen-page folding dummies quickly shows that the low page (the first page of the signature) is at the outside back corner, with its face trim opposite the guide side of the sheet. The high page is directly next to it, forming the other half of this printer's spread. Since the face trim of this page is located in the center of the sheet, a high-page lip can be achieved on saddle-stitched signatures by making these center face margins greater than the face margins at the edge of the sheet. The following illustration shows the correct margins for two nearly identical sixteen-page signatures. Aside from the difference in margin widths, these two layouts are virtually identical. One signature is imposed for burst binding, so it has equal face margins throughout (and since the binding method is burst binding, no grind-off is required); the other signature is imposed for saddle-stitching with a high-page lip.

In the case of eight-page signatures, the creation of a high-page lip is even easier—extra paper at the tail of the sheet will create the lip on the second half of the signature. Of course, this extra paper will be hard to come by if you are trying to squeeze a job onto the smallest possible sheet. Once again, the economics of ordering a smaller (and less expensive) sheet must be weighed against the compromises that such a purchase could create, including a lack of color bars and the inability to form a high-page lip.

- *Compensating for creep.* The most "notorious" special consideration has been saved for last. So much interest has been expressed in addressing this concern that automatic compensation for creep is now built into all of the major imposition software programs.

The top signature is imposed for saddle-stitching and has a high-page lip. The bottom illustration is imposed for burst binding and has equal face margins throughout.

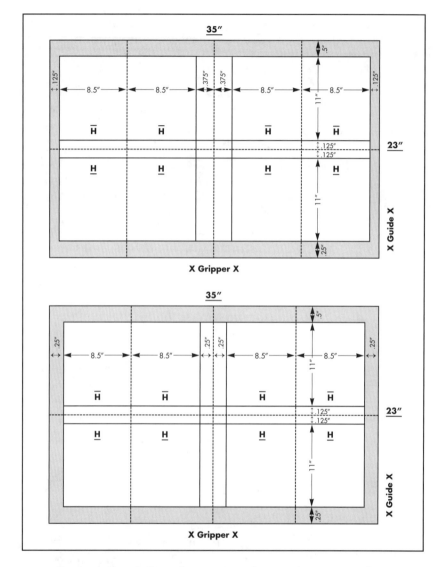

Creep, also referred to as ***push-out,*** is a natural consequence of the saddle-stitch binding method. The cause of creep is easy to understand. As shown in the accompanying illustration, nesting each folded signature inside the next causes the intended face trim of every new signature to extend slightly beyond that of the previous form. When the stitched booklets reach the cutter, the operator will probably trim the entire batch of booklets to exactly the trim size written on the job ticket. The result will be that the first and last page will indeed be the exact size specified, but every page thereafter will be incrementally smaller in the direction perpendicular to the binding. At the center

Creep, or push-out.

spread, the effect of creep will be the greatest, resulting in pages that are significantly narrower than those near the beginning of the book. For many projects, this is actually of little consequence. If the book has only a few pages, or the paper is of a light basis weight, the effect of creep on the internal margins of each page will not be readily apparent, and no compensation will be necessary. As the weight of the stock and/or the number of pages in the

Effect that creep has on trim size of interior pages of a saddle-stitched booklet.

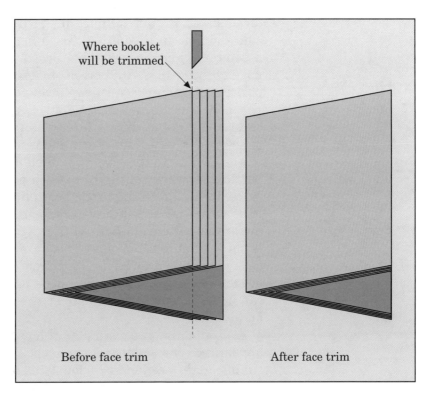

Where booklet will be trimmed

Before face trim

After face trim

booklet increases, however, a significant amount of push-out can occur, greatly affecting the relative position of elements on the page and on the face trim.

When designers create a document with a repeating design element (such as a header or footer) that comes close to the face trim, the human eye can easily memorize the relationship between this graphic and the edge of the page. Any change in the position of this content in relation to the page trim will be noticed by even the most casual observer, often making it necessary to move all the elements on a page toward the fold—a procedure referred to simply as ***adjusting for creep.*** The affected pages must be moved towards the binding edge in increments that are roughly equal to the amount of push-out created by the thickness of previous signatures. Generally, every page in a signature is adjusted by the same amount, beginning with the second signature. Making an additional adjustment for each subsequent signature produces a consistent face margin for these pages. The necessary adjustment is equal to the thickness of four sheets of stock (the same measure used earlier in this chapter to determine the thickness of a book's spine).

With most methods of digital imposition, compensating for push-out is quite simple, in sharp contrast to the difficult and inaccurate methods used in conventional image assembly. Typically, a stripper draws a thin line on every page of the orange vinyl layout to designate the correct position of the repeating graphic element. Next, the stripper measures in towards the fold of each page, drawing additional lines at intervals that match the calculated push-out for each form. Each line is identified with a letter corresponding to the form that should be stripped to that particular position. Finally, as each page of film is taped in place, the stripper aligns the horizontal marks to the trim lines on the layout, sliding each page over until the repeating graphic element aligns with the correct creep line. This is not as simple as it sounds, because the distance between each creep line may be not much more than the thickness of the line created by the stripper's ball-point pen! As you can imagine, such a technique is also prone to confusion and misregister.

Following are two examples of how creep can ruin the appearance of a saddle-stitched job. The first example is similar to the scenario previously mentioned: this booklet has five saddle-stitched signatures, and totals seventy-two pages. Each page has a header featuring three-point-wide horizontal rules that end only 0.125 in. (3 mm) away from each page's face trim. Taking a micrometer reading of four sheets of this paper yields a measurement of 0.02 in. (0.5 mm). Subtracting this number from the page width of each signature (beginning with the second form) tells us the effect of push-out on the page size. In other words, the pages on the final four-page signature will be 0.08 in. narrower than those on the first form.

If this job was imposed, printed, and saddle-stitched without making adjustment for creep, the distance from the header rules to the face trim on the eight pages in the center of the book would be only one-third of what it had been on the first eight pages! This was a rather obvious situation, in which the close proximity of the repeating design element to the face trim made an adjustment for creep clearly necessary. Keep in mind, however, that digital imposition programs automatically factor in creep based on the position of the first and last pages in the document. In a job such as this, it is more likely that you will want to manually enter a fixed amount of additional creep compensation on every signature, based on the width of the interior printer's spread. In this way, the distance from the repeating header rules to the face trim will never be less than what the designer had intended; unfortunately, the side effect will be that all pages will have less space at the binding edge gutter than in the original design.

The second example is more subtle, and just the sort of project you are likely to be unpleasantly surprised by someday. A customer brings in a project advertising houses in a new suburban subdivision. The 48-page booklet is an "image piece," meaning that the customer will spend freely for the most beautiful design, additional inks and varnishes, diecutting and foil-stamping, and a heavy coated stock. Looking over the document, you see no sign of elements that are likely to need adjusting for creep. In fact, the brochure has no repeating header or footer, and the folio is centered on each page. You decide, therefore, that no compensation is necessary and proceed to impose the booklet without adjusting for creep. Days later, you are stunned when the angry customer confronts you with the finished booklet. As it turns out, the center spread of this brochure features a map of homes available in the subdivision, and the 80-lb. coated cover stock used throughout has resulted in 0.06-in. (1.5-mm) creep—enough to trim off three houses at various spots near the face trim.

The lesson from this example is twofold: research every graphic on every page before you decide to impose without adjusting for creep, and always communicate to customers the dangers inherent in placing important information too close to the face trim. Folding, binding and trimming are, after all, inexact disciplines. To the designer obsessed with aligning page layout graphics within a thousandth of an inch, it may come as a surprise that the processes taking place after the job has left the pressroom are an order of magnitude less exact!

We have just covered the major stages of planning imposition for print production. These nine steps will help you to organize every job on the way to a successful resolution. Once you have planned your job, you will be ready to proceed—either in the conventional image assembly process described in the first part of our book, or in the new world of digital imposition. What is so different about *digital* imposition? What advantages can you expect to realize from using software and microprocessors instead of steel T-squares and X-Acto knives? Those very issues are addressed in the next chapter.

9 PostScript: Prelude to Digital Imposition

Chapter 1 covered the reasons why imposition was the last part of the printing process to be fully computerized. This chapter takes a look at where the digital imposition process fits into the larger prepress workflow. The illustration on the next page is a flowchart depicting the path work might take from the design studio to the pressroom of a printshop with an all-digital CTP workflow. As you can see, three opportunities are provided for digital imposition:

- As the final step within the page layout application, replacing the typical "print" command.
- After a PostScript file has been created, using PostScript imposition software.
- Following interpretation of the PostScript file by the RIP, through the use of RIP-based imposition software. This process may utilize templates created by a desktop imposition software program.

Each of these possibilities has its own advantages and disadvantages. The next chapter considers these categories and examines the variety of imposition software available today. Before we begin to compare the capabilities of these digital imposition methods, however, the rules and procedures under which these software programs operate must be defined. Without some knowledge of the process by which **PostScript** code is generated, you will not be able to grasp the methods these programs use to impose documents. Therefore it is necessary to take a quick look at PostScript, as well as its effect on document creation and output.

Overview of PostScript

The software giant Adobe was only a two-year-old start-up firm when it introduced the PostScript **page description language** in 1985. PostScript was a vast improvement over

Digital Workflow: Customer

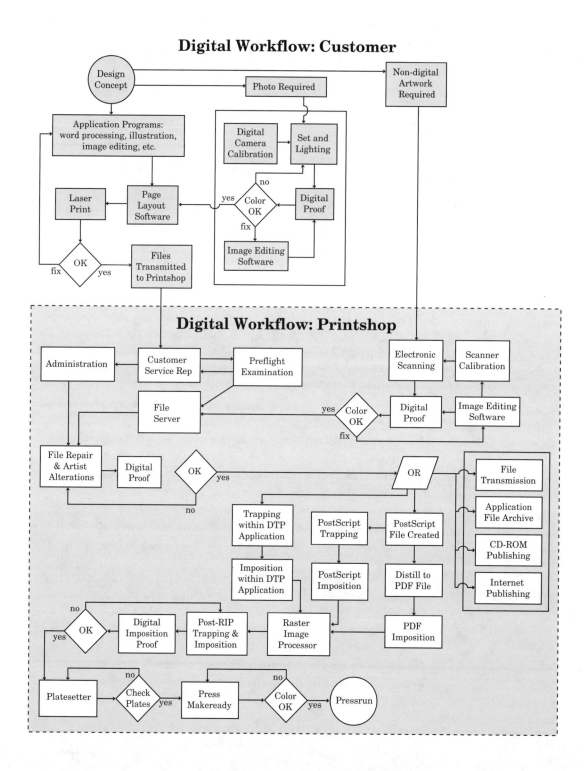

the many other printer languages available at the time, mainly because of its ***device-independent*** nature. This means, in short, that the PostScript language can convert any document created with a compatible application into an instruction set that can be understood by any compatible output device. Another major distinction between Adobe's offering and most other printer languages available at that time is that PostScript maintains fonts and most other graphics (with the notable exception of scanned images) as mathematical ***vector*** equations until the final rendering of the device-specific raster data. This allows fonts and other vector graphics to achieve output at the highest quality available on the device being used. For large, complex items (such as logos, illustrations, and digital images), PostScript allows external documents to be referenced from within the PostScript code. These files, therefore, do not have to be included within the PostScript code itself.

PostScript is a computer programming language, and PostScript files created during the output process are actually computer programs; the actual text that makes up any software program is called program code, or simply ***code***. But what is ***PostScript code,*** and how is it created? Typically two things must be present for desktop publishing documents to be converted into code—a PostScript-compatible document-creation application and a software program called a PostScript print driver.

Most documents that will be digitally imposed are created by specialized programs known as page layout software; popular examples include Adobe (formerly Aldus) PageMaker and QuarkXPress. These programs are designed for the purpose of allowing users to design documents and then convert them into PostScript code for output to compatible hardware. The tools available to the user in this type of software correspond directly to the features and functions allowed within the PostScript language. No "illegal" operations are possible in these programs because page layout applications are really graphical representations of the capabilities of PostScript.

Once a designer has completed work on a document in a page layout program and would like to see that page output from a compatible device (such as a laser printer, color proofer, imagesetter, or platesetter), he or she invokes the ***print command*** in the application. This begins a collaborative process between the page layout application and the PostScript print driver (more often referred to simply as the

PostScript driver). The page layout program begins by generating a list of all the parameters applicable to the entire document (such as software version, document name, page size), followed by a description of every item on the page, including references to external files whose data is not contained in the page layout document itself. This information is received and understood by the PostScript driver, which then begins the process of converting the description into PostScript code. When the process of generating this code is complete, the PostScript driver carries out a second function—it ***downloads*** (sends) this data through the network cable connecting the personal computer to the output device.

Components of PostScript Code

As do many other computer programs, the PostScript code has two components: the ***prolog*** and the ***script.*** The prolog is where the PostScript driver has recorded the information

Structure of a PostScript file. *Adapted from* Understanding Digital Color, *by Phil Green* (GATF*Press,* 1998).

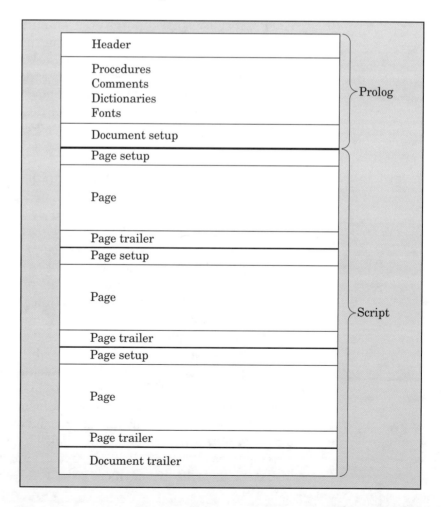

The PostScript code *(top)* that produced the 60-pt. Helvetica Bold letters "GATF" and the 10-pt. rule *(middle).*
Adapted from Understanding Digital Color, *by Phil Green* (GATF*Press*, 1998).

```
%!PS-Adobe-3.0
%%Title: GATF.PS
%%Creator: Phil Green
%%Pages: 1
%%BoundingBox: 18 23 577 819
/Helvetica-Bold findfont 60 scalefont setfont
%%EndProlog

10 setlinewidth
200 550 moveto
440 550 lineto
stroke

240 585 moveto
(GATF) show
showpage
%%Trailer
end
```

GATF

PostScript code is not difficult to understand. In this simple example, the prolog identifies the bounding box of the page (the area inside the page margins) and defines the font that will be used.

The *moveto* operator moves the current drawing position to the coordinates 200, 550, and then the *lineto* operator creates a horizontal line to the coordinates 440, 500. The *setlinewidth* and *stroke* operators define the line width and paint it on the page.

The font name and size have been defined in the prolog, so the letters "GATF" are simply identified (in parentheses) with the *show* operator. Finally, the *showpage* operator is the instruction to print the page.

that is global to the document as a whole. The prolog sketches out the parameters for constructing the output. The script is where the real action occurs. This portion of the file is divided into separate segments for each page, ending with a set of instructions called the document trailer. Since each page is a discrete component of the script, the order of these pages can be rearranged without negatively impacting the results. Moreover, multiple pages can be imaged simultaneously— for example, when an imagesetter exposes a row of dots across the width of a sheet of film, crossing two pages in a single pass.

To conform to the ***document structuring conventions*** established by Adobe, the document prolog can contain only description information, while the document script should contain only executable information. These executable commands within the PostScript language are called ***operators.*** If an operator must be accompanied by data (typically coordinates) in order to be executed, this data is known as an ***operand.*** These operators are used to recreate the graphics and text from the page layout document, as well as controlling the rotation and scaling of referenced graphics. For our purposes, the most important operator is the command ***showpage.*** This tells the output device that the entire page is now complete, and that the task of constructing a new page can begin. In essence, the PostScript code is saying "Show me a new page, so I can begin describing more graphics." The graphic file format known as EPS (encapsulated PostScript) is not allowed to contain the showpage operator; this is why EPS files (such as logos created in Adobe Illustrator or Macromedia FreeHand) can be only one page in length.

PostScript-Compatible Output Devices

This PostScript code is downloaded to a PostScript-compatible output device. Every PostScript-compatible device consists of two components: the ***raster image processor*** (or ***RIP)*** and a ***marking engine.*** Sometimes both components are housed within the same box, but quite often the RIP and marking engine are totally separate components from different manufacturers, working together to produce proofs, films, or plates. The RIP acts as a "virtual machine" for running the software program we have come to know as the PostScript file. Several different software programs can be used for this purpose, but many graphic arts RIP vendors utilize the ***Adobe CPSI*** (configurable PostScript interpreter) software program. These manufacturers can then proclaim that their devices feature "true Adobe PostScript." If this software is hosted by a specialized computer that serves no other purpose (such as the components inside a laser printer), the combination is described as a *hardware RIP.* If the software is running on a personal computer capable of being used for other tasks, we say the output device has a *software RIP.*

The marking engine is the system of motors, lasers, and consumables responsible for the physical creation of tiny marks on the desired material (or substrate). For an example, consider the Imation Rainbow 2730 dye sublimation proofer shown on the right in the following illustration. The RIP for this digital color proofer is a software program (supplied on CD–ROM) that runs on any PowerMac; the entire device pictured on the right is the marking engine.

The Imation 2730 dye sublimation proofer, which uses a software RIP supplied on a CD–ROM.

That still does not provide an adequate picture of how these components interact in the PostScript workflow. In the most simplified definition, the raster image processor converts the PostScript code into a series of on/off commands; the marking engine then carries out these commands, marking the output substrate as directed. The file containing these on/off commands is known as a *bi-level bitmap;* it consists of rows and rows of tiny black or white squares called *machine pixels.* These machine pixels correspond directly to the smallest marks (or *spots)* that can be consistently produced by the marking engine—for every machine pixel which is "on," a single spot is imaged by the marking engine. The spots are so small dozens (even hundreds) of them are clustered together to build a single halftone dot.

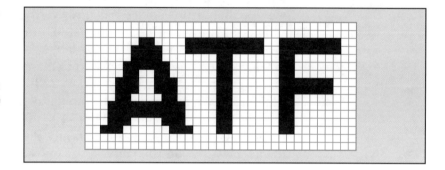

An enlarged example of a bi-level bitmap, consisting of rows of machine pixels. The resolution of the bi-level bitmap matches the capabilities of the marking engine.

This simplistic definition of the PostScript RIPing process serves to explain the basic flow of documents from creation to output; however, in order to achieve a clear understanding of what distinguishes certain imposition methods from each other, a deeper examination of the PostScript output function is required. Raster image processors do not perform just one function, but instead they are responsible for three processes: interpretation, rasterization, and screening.

The task of interpretation (also known as rendering) can occur very rapidly, because the RIP software is simply carrying out the commands contained within the PostScript code. As mentioned earlier, the RIP serves as a "virtual machine" for performing the tasks contained in the software program we know as a PostScript file. These files contain a series of commands (operators) that instruct the RIP to render (draw) the vector graphics contained within the page layout document; the vector graphics include text, rules, boxes, and anything else not made of pixels. Within the PostScript language, any vector object can be described as long as it can be built from three primitive shapes: straight lines, arcs, and curves.

The result of rendering (interpreting) the PostScript file is that the vector graphics that had been described in the Post-Script file have now been drawn as a series of **objects.** These rendered graphics exist in the RAM (random-access memory) of the RIP; it is possible to save this data (called the **object list)** to a hard drive for further manipulation or processing. Linotype-Hell (now known as Heidelberg Prepress) pioneered this object-list processing with its Delta RIP technology;

The result of rendering (interpreting) the Post-Script file is that the vector graphics that had been described in the PostScript file have now been drawn as a series of objects. At the right are three objects: two squares and one circle. The arrows show how the objects have been drawn.

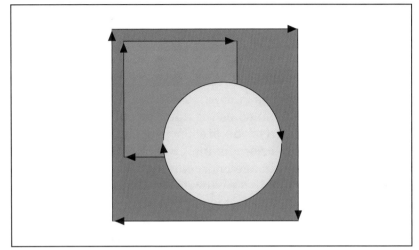

another commonly seen use for object list data is the PDF file (documents typically created with Adobe Acrobat).

Following the creation of the object list, the RIP continues to work on the PostScript file by ***rasterizing*** these objects. The process of rasterization converts the resolution-independent objects into tiny squares of variable density data, known as pixels. The file containing all of a rasterized file's pixels is known as the ***raster image.*** Another important aspect of the rasterization process is color separation. Although the pixels of the raster image can have variable density (shading from dark to light), each pixel must be contained within a certain color channel. Typically the channels of a raster image will be cyan, magenta, yellow, and black; however, additional channels for spot colors (requiring inks other than CMYK) are also common.

The process of rasteri-zation converts the resolution-independent objects (shown at the left) into tiny squares of variable density data, known as pixels (shown at the right).

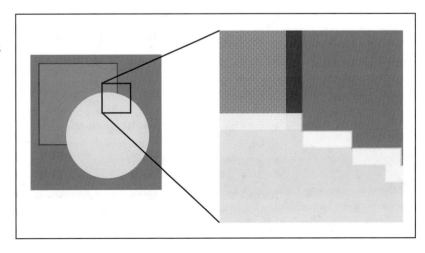

Some marking engines are capable of working directly with these raster images. A typical example of this sort of device would be a dye sublimation proofer. These devices produce varying densities of color by applying heat to a dye-coated ribbon with a variable-temperature head. In this case (as in most other cases), the resolution of the raster image matches the addressability of the marking engine; since the dye sub proofer is designed to deliver 300 spots of color (per color channel) within one linear inch of space, the raster image is prepared at 300 dpi. It is possible, however, to utilize a raster image that has fewer pixels per inch than the resolution of the output device. This seeming disparity can be overcome because the additional resolution is interpolated during the RIP's final process, called screening.

Screening refers to the conversion of the raster image's continuous-tone pixels into the on-off commands of the bi-level bitmap. These on-off commands (known as "machine pixels") are used to control the marking engine of all sorts of devices, from laser printers to imagesetters. The size of these tiny machine pixels is directly determined by the repeatability of the marking engine; for example, if the imagesetter is designed to deliver 2,400 blasts of laser light per inch, the bi-level bitmap will consist of a grid containing 2,400 on-off commands per linear inch.

Most PostScript-compatible output devices share one attribute in common: rather than being able to deliver a spot of variable density, they all must image spots that are of one consistent density. This restriction also applies to the printing press. To overcome this limitation methods have been developed to simulate the variable densities found in raster images and scanned photographs—the most common of these methods are halftone screening and stochastic screening. Halftone dots simulate highlights and shadows by using small or large clusters of spots, which are evenly spaced across the entire image. Stochastic screening uses very small clusters (typically three) of spots to create stochastic dots (the term "stochastic spot" is also commonly used), which are placed at random intervals. In a highlight area there are very few stochastic dots; as the image changes to a darker tone, the number of stochastic dots increases.

In both cases multiple "on" pixels are clustered together to form the halftone or stochastic dots we see on the proof or printing plate. Just as often, however (as in the case of image-setters and many on-demand printers), these dots are created

Enlargements of "digital" halftone dots.

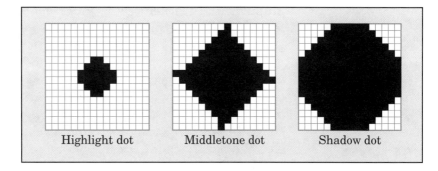

Highlight dot   Middletone dot   Shadow dot

Enlargements of stochastic dots.

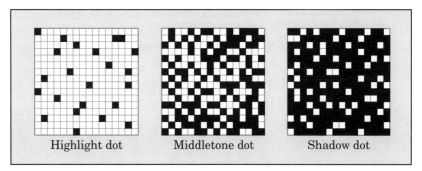

Highlight dot   Middletone dot   Shadow dot

when the nonimage area is exposed. When the nonimage area is defined through the use of "on" pixels, we refer to the device as having a "write-white" engine.

It is during the process of screening the raster images that externally referenced image data is incorporated. Scanned images, digital photographs, and other graphics consisting of pixel data bypass the rendering and rasterization stages of the RIP. During screening, the pixel data of these images are converted to halftone or stochastic dots at a predetermined number of lines per inch.

Encapsulated PostScript Files

We have just examined the procedure for creating and outputting PostScript code. However, there is another way to prepare documents for output without creating a traditional PostScript file. Most PostScript imposition software programs can create imposed signatures by using a digital file format called an encapsulated PostScript file (EPS). Although the subject of EPS files is very complex, enough to consume an entire chapter, this discussion will be limited to understanding the relation of the EPS file to digital imposition. There are three distinct kinds of EPS files commonly used in desktop publishing, and each one can be made in a variety of different ways. There are EPS files that can be saved from a bitmap editing program, such as Adobe Photoshop, ***EPSF*** graphics that feature vector data from programs such as Macromedia FreeHand, and the EPS we are interested in—a file that contains a single page worth of PostScript code, as well as two other components called the ***preview*** and the ***header***. Enormous confusion has been created within our industry by having these three similar, but slightly different, files referred to with a single name. The following illustration shows the components involved in each file. The print-to-disk EPS file has a header, a preview, and a data component. The preview is a low-resolution image (consisting of pixels, not vector data) that is not used by the RIP or the marking engine. It exists, instead, to provide a visual representation of the EPS file's contents. For example, to use this EPS file as a graphic in a QuarkXPress document, the preview allows one to position and scale the EPS file according to one's liking. The header is very similar to the document prolog of the PostScript file discussed previously. Likewise the data component of the EPS file bears a great similarity to the document

The vector graphic content of an encapsulated PostScript (EPS) file.

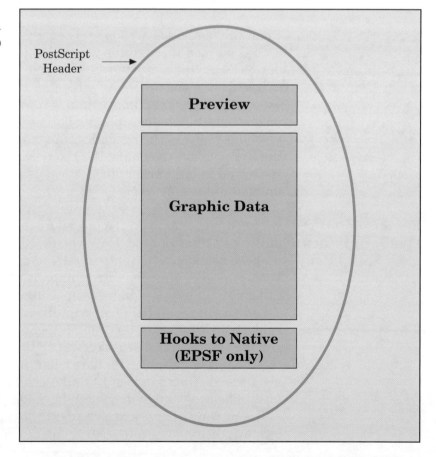

script of regular PostScript files, with one important exception: certain PostScript operators cannot be used within the EPS file format, including the operator showpage (this is true of all three varieties of EPS files). As mentioned earlier in this chapter, this restriction limits the EPS file format to a single page. In terms of its utilization, however, the EPS file is remarkably similar to a regular PostScript file. Once special downloading software is used to download the EPS file to the RIP, processing occurs in the same manner as with any other PostScript file.

These issues will relate directly to the information in the next chapter, which discusses the differences between the creation of imposed PostScript, software that imposes previously created PostScript files, and the imposition of multiple EPS files for interpretation to raster data. In addition the chapter discusses imposition at the RIP, including the newest approach: post-RIP imposition.

10   Digital Imposition Methods

Few issues are as closely linked as imposition methods and workflow. Today there is considerable discussion about creating the ultimate all-digital workflow. Vendors of raster image processors (RIPs), platesetters, and digital proofing devices all tout the unique advantages of their products in enhancing productivity by creating an optimal workflow. Yet, upon further discussion, these same vendors are quick to point out that every workflow is unique, and that the hardware and software involved should be flexible enough to accommodate multiple workflow scenarios.

Development of All-Digital Workflow

Is this just marketing hype, or is there something to be learned here? How is it possible that the printing industry has used computers to produce printed documents for over a decade, yet only recently has decided that nothing is more important than our workflow? The answer is that by defining an appropriate yet flexible digital workflow, we can be certain of achieving the greatest results with the least expenditure of time and effort. Only recently have computer systems become complex and flexible enough to assist in mapping the sequence in which production processes will occur. With these tools the newer generation of software and hardware becomes part of the work force as well as the workflow.

There has always been a variety of workflows involved in the print production process. After the advent of desktop publishing, the number of possibilities for moving a document from disk to paper dramatically increased. For many years, however, most printers used the following method of production when digital files were involved: First, the document was opened in the same software program used by the customer; second, a printer's employee who was relatively knowledgeable about desktop publishing would inspect the file and make any needed corrections; in the third step, the document would be printed out in single-page format to an imagesetter; finally, the fourth step was to pass the resulting film off to a stripper for inspection and image assembly.

Although this basic workflow is still used in many of the world's printing plants, the situation is rapidly changing. An ever-increasing number of options allow prepress technicians to perform the imposition process electronically, and with a great deal of flexibility relative to scheduling imposition within the workflow. The large number of digital imposition options available today can be divided into two categories: (1) PostScript imposition software and (2) RIP-based imposition.

The first category includes the following:

- Imposition software designed to operate within popular desktop publishing software programs, allowing the creation of paginated PostScript during the output process.
- Stand-alone imposition software designed to accept previously created (unpaginated) PostScript and EPS files (and in some cases, PDF and TIFF files), in order to rearrange these multiple files into a single, imposed PostScript document.
- A new crop of programs (running on desktop workstations) that specialize in directly imposing PDF files, without the requirement to first convert these PDF documents into PostScript.

The second category is comprised of the following:

- RIP-based solutions that process incoming PostScript, EPS, TIFF, or PDF documents into some sort of intermediate file format, which is then imposed into a single document before screening and output (this category is sometimes referred to as a "tiling" workflow).
- RIPs (or workstations attached to RIPs) that process PostScript, EPS, TIFF, PDF, or CEPS documents into a series of independent raster (or CT/LW) format files, then gather, impose, and finally screen the combined raster image during the output process, based on previously created imposition templates. Also known as an "element independent" workflow, this scenario allows for last-minute changes in imposition style (such as conversion from saddle-stitched to perfect-bound) without requiring that the pages be RIPed again.
- RIPs (or workstations attached to RIPs) that process PostScript, EPS, TIFF, PDF, or other documents into indepen-

dent, screened single pages. The RIP or another workstation is then used to combine and position these screened, bi-level bitmaps for imposed output (another form of "element independent" workflow). Although this provides the same flexibility to change imposition styles as in the previously mentioned option, any change in the output's LPI or dot gain compensation would require reprocessing of all pages.

PostScript Imposition Software

In the majority of today's prepress departments, most work is performed on desktop publishing workstations—small, relatively inexpensive computers that utilize the same applications used by designers to create digital documents. In commercial printing companies, these workstations are typically Apple Macintosh computers, although nearly all prepress departments also possess at least a few IBM-compatible workstations running the Windows operating system. These computers are the workstations on which documents are opened and checked, where corrections are made, and where the all-important "print" function is carried out. The term "desktop" software is a reference to software programs that can run on personal computers utilizing the Apple Macintosh or Microsoft Windows operating system.

Any worthwhile desktop imposition program must be capable of saving configuration information on page layout, page order, and binding methods as custom templates. Just as important is the ability to save custom marks files (including trims, folds, form IDs, and process control devices such as color bars) for later reuse. In fact every aspect of a job's imposition should be capable of being saved with the job, so that a later reprint of the same job will not require the imposition process to be done over again. Fortunately this functionality is ubiquitous throughout the sort of full-featured imposition programs that will be profiled in this chapter. (Contact information for all vendors mentioned in this chapter is presented in Appendix B.)

Not all of these programs, however, fit into the workflow in exactly the same way. Most offerings for digital imposition are designed to arrange the position of page layout documents after they have been converted into PostScript files. (These PostScript files are also called ***print-to-disk*** files.) Alternatives to creating PostScript prior to imposition do exist, however, and this is where our examination of PostScript imposition software will begin.

Creating
Imposed
PostScript
Documents

Programs from DK&A PrePress Inc. DK&A
manufactures a pair of software programs for
imposing digital documents: INposition and
INposition Lite. Both programs have the unusual
distinction of functioning as Quark XTensions—
software modules that work within the popular page
layout program QuarkXPress. Both programs take advantage of the output functions contained within Quark, so that
the interface to using DK&A's imposition offerings is quite
simple for experienced Quark users. This means, of course,
that companies purchasing INposition must have a working
version of QuarkXPress on every workstation where imposition is to take place.

DK&A INposition, in
the printer's spread
mode.
*Courtesy DK&A
PrePress Inc.*

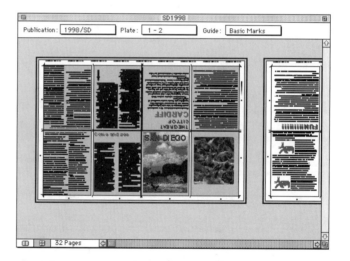

DK&A's products, however, can be used to impose more
than just Quark documents. Once the INposition XTension is
launched, users have the option of imposing PostScript and/or
EPS files from practically any application, as well as individual pages from multiple Quark documents. The latest version
of INposition adds the ability to impose native PageMaker
documents, as well as TIFF, PICT, and EPS files. If Acrobat
Exchange is loaded on the same workstation, the process of
converting PDF into PostScript for input to DK&A can be
automated. Once these documents are made a part of the
imposition, icon-sized previews are used to represent the
actual document pages. These previews provide visual feedback on the correctness of page sequence and orientation.

"Full-featured" is not a term likely to be associated with
DK&A's other PostScript imposition software offering, INpo-

sition Lite. Geared toward small printing establishments on smaller budgets, INposition Lite is a less-expensive program that functions in a similar fashion—with a few important exceptions. Only a single QuarkXPress document can be imposed (PostScript, EPS, and PageMaker files are not accepted); layout configurations are limited to a few preset varieties; there is no ability to introduce process control elements (other than the built-in color bar and form ID options); and custom marks files cannot be saved.

INposition Lite differs from the full version of INposition (and virtually every other PostScript imposition software program) in that information about the way in which the file was imposed and output cannot be saved with the document. INposition Lite, however, is sold for significantly less than the full version of INposition, and the lack of features makes it very simple to understand and operate. For prepress departments taking that first step into digital imposition (such as creating two-up or four-up output from an image-setter), this tool can be quite effective.

DK&A INposition, showing reader's spreads.
Courtesy DK&A PrePress Inc.

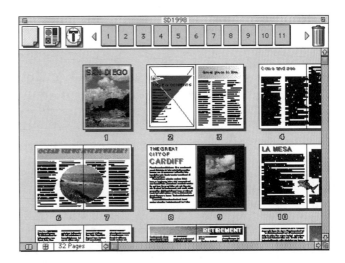

One drawback to using DK&A's PostScript imposition software programs is their inability to mix page sizes within a single publication. As one can infer from the interface, these programs have been designed for the publishing market—in which all pages of a single book or magazine will be of exactly the same size. Other users of imposition software (such as the packaging and label printing markets) would find restriction to a single page size to be a major limitation. Also absent from the INposition programs are other packaging-style functions (such as nesting and variable page rotation). To be fair very few PostScript imposition software programs actually include these functions. (A more in-depth discussion of what attributes are required for packaging imposition can be found in the next chapter.) The success of DK&A's products comes in large part from their ability to enhance the productivity of most desktop prepress departments without modifying the workflow of having a single operator open, correct, and output a document. They also operate within the framework of the industry's leading page layout program.

Specialized prepress functions. For many printing companies (especially smaller operations), this "all-in-one" workflow is ideal. If your concept of the ideal digital production environment is more akin to Henry Ford's production line, however, you will likely want to separate the tasks of inspecting, correcting, and outputting files. In the prepress courses at GATF's Center for Imaging Excellence, these functions are referred to as *preflighting, file repair,* and *output.* During GATF's "Preflighting" workshop, mid-sized and large printers are encouraged to train prepress workers for one of these specific functions, so that the effectiveness of each employee can be maximized. This can be a successful approach because it allows strippers, platemakers, and other conventional prepress workers to specialize in performing output tasks such as trapping and imposition. Performing these functions on previously-created PostScript files allows the retrained worker to focus on learning only two software programs—one for trapping, another for imposition. This is certainly easier than expecting the worker to quickly become competent at Quark, PageMaker, Illustrator, FreeHand, Photoshop, and the myriad other desktop publishing software programs.

If one is interested in separating these output functions from the rest of the process, one option is to use software designed to impose existing PostScript files. The majority of PostScript imposition software is of this variety, and it includes such familiar products as ScenicSoft Preps and Ultimate Impostrip; there are other players in this field, however, such as Imposition Publisher from Farrukh Systems and DynaStrip from Dynagram Software. These products all have a similar workflow; they manipulate the position of pages within any PostScript document that conforms to Adobe's Document Structuring Convention for PostScript data. In addition multiple documents can be combined into a single imposed file, and individual EPS pages can be added. After all pages have been arranged as desired, the resulting data is printed to the output device.

Ultimate Technographics. Ultimate Technographics touched off a revolution in digital workflow with the software program Impostrip, first released in 1989. The advent of Impostrip was clearly a historical landmark, as it was the first commercially available program for imposing PostScript documents. Today Ultimate continues to be at the forefront of digital imposition, by developing cutting-edge workflows such as server-based signature assembly and raster file imposition. Recent versions of Impostrip are available for both Macintosh and PC platforms, while Ultimate's Signature Server software can run on Mac, UNIX, or Windows NT (including Alpha) servers. After documents have been combined to create an imposed file via Impostrip, the companion program Ultimate Signature Server is used to perform the actual print operation. This is transparent to the user, however, since the print command is still issued from within Impostrip. If a separate computer is used to run the Signature Server software, workflow is enhanced by having control of the imposition workstation returned to the

Impostrip, a digital imposition program. *Courtesy Ultimate Technographics.*

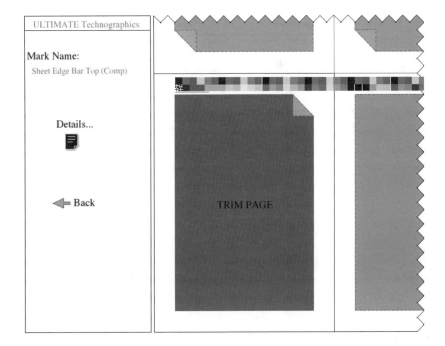

operator almost immediately after the print command is issued.

Ultimate's software can impose a wide variety of data formats, including separated or composite PostScript, EPS, and PDF files from Macintosh, PC, or UNIX workstations. Version 6.0 (just announced) promises support for PDF job tickets and increased CIP3 integration. Impostrip does not preview the contents of imposed pages during the imposition process; however, a high-quality preview of the entire signature can be generated by using Ultimate's Plate Preview application. Plate Preview is an actual Adobe CPSI Level 2 PostScript RIP that converts the signature into a TIFF file; the resulting TIFF image can be viewed from within Adobe Photoshop.

A professional-level tool for accomplishing a variety of different imposition tasks, Impostrip Second Generation comes with extensive tutorial-based documentation. Other interesting features of Impostrip include its ability to shift individual pages, the ability to save punch formats for imagesetters with internal register punch capabilities, and extensive functions for multi-web offset pagination. Impostrip also has excellent controls for color bar functions, allowing users to create their own basic color bars or use one of four GATF color bars, as well as adding Heidelberg CPC 4 registration marks. In addition complex folding patterns can be created visually using Ultimate's Origami animated folding utility. (Origami includes the Stahl library of folding styles.)

Ultimate's Origami animated folding utility.
Courtesy Ultimate Technographics.

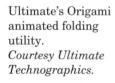

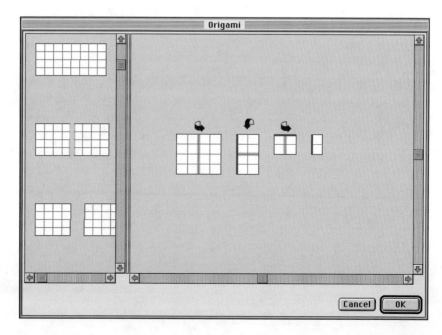

Ultimate's Trapeze trapping software. *Courtesy Ultimate Technographics.*

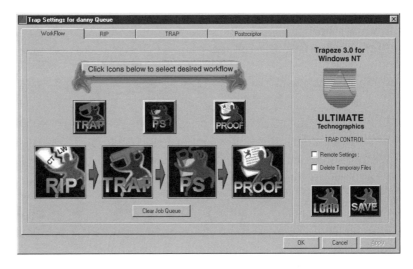

In addition to Impostrip, Ultimate also offers a specialized imposition software program called IMPress to address the specific needs of digital printing and on-demand publishing in a corporate environment.

As do many other desktop imposition software programs, Impostrip lacks packaging-specific imposition functions. Unlike any other desktop solution, however, Ultimate offers all the tools necessary to perform raster file imposition. This workflow utilizes the Adobe CPSI RIP built into Ultimate's Trapeze trapping software to RIP PostScript files into individual SIGI (Standard Interface for Generic Imposition) pages. An imposition template created with Impostrip can be sent to Trapeze, where rasterized SIGI pages can be merged with the imposition template for output. Similar approaches to raster imposition available from RIP vendors are profiled later in this chapter.

ScenicSoft Preps. One program that includes a range of functions needed for packaging imposition is Preps from ScenicSoft. (Chapter 11 discusses the special needs of the packaging industry at greater length.) Preps is used by a wide variety of companies in the printing industry because of its tremendous flexibility. Examples of this versatility include imposition of combination jobs, page nesting, and the ability to apply page rotation as compensation for bottling. Once PostScript or EPS (pre-separated or composite), and/or TIFF files are located, a wide variety of imposition controls are accessible. The latest version of Preps

Templates in Preps.
Courtesy ScenicSoft.

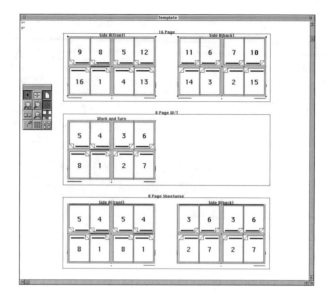

allows the direct use of PDF files and adds support for True-Type and multiple master fonts. Copious documentation is included (both in hard copy and on-line), to educate Preps users on the flexibility of the many options.

The integrated preview function in Preps provides on-screen viewing of imposed pages and flats directly within the application. Other useful features include the availability of built-in open prepress interface (OPI) functionality and a built-in color separation engine that allows flexibility in dealing with spot colors, including conversion of selected spot colors to

A preview image in
Preps.
Courtesy ScenicSoft.

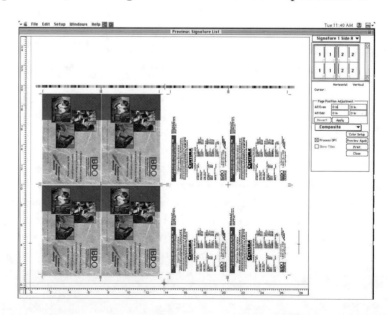

Color separation dialog box in Preps. *Courtesy ScenicSoft.*

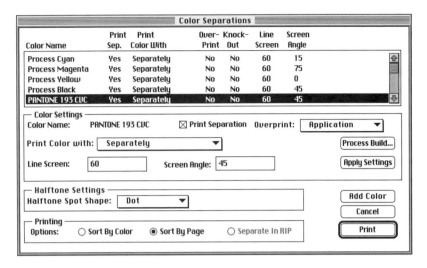

CMYK screen builds. Images that are linked via OPI but are in RGB mode are automatically separated as CMYK during output. ScenicSoft has also made this software available for both the Macintosh and Windows (95 or NT) platforms—which is not the case with many other desktop imposition programs. The templates and jobs created with Preps are cross-platform compatible, a significant benefit to any prepress department utilizing both Windows PCs and Macs.

Preps is sometimes supplied as a bundled application with an imagesetter, platesetter, or on-demand press; vendors supplying customized versions of Preps with their products include Scitex, Creo, Contex, and AGFA. Preps is currently available in three packages: the full-featured Preps Pro, the less-expensive Preps Plus (which has no built-in OPI functions), or the least-expensive version Preps XL (for the on-demand press market).

Farrukh Systems Limited. Imposition Publisher from the British firm Farrukh Systems is an imposition software program designed for use on Macintosh and PC workstations. Most notable for the implementation of a client/server architecture, Farrukh's desktop workstations communicate with a central UNIX, Windows NT, or Macintosh file server. This server stores all the files to be imposed, as well as Farrukh's Imposition Publisher Client Server software. By working directly from the same server as the stored data, imposed documents can be created and printed much faster than if documents were copied through the network.

Various dialog boxes in
Imposition Publisher.
*Courtesy Farrukh
Systems Limited.*

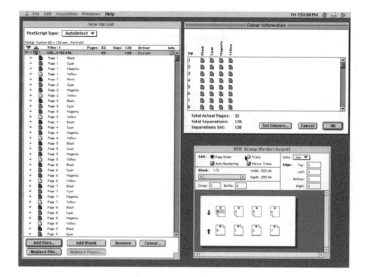

Imposition Publisher Client Server has many of the features
you would expect in any professional imposition software
package designed for the publishing industry. One of its most
interesting functions is the facility for designing and positioning color bars, including CPC 4 marks for Heidelberg presses.
Imposition Publisher lacks some of the functions necessary
for packaging and label printing, but a Flatwork feature is
available for imposing dissimilar-sized pages on a single film
or plate.

In addition to Imposition Client Server, there are three
other Farrukh products for digital imposition: Imposition
Publisher Personal Professional for a single Macintosh or PC

Output preview in
Imposition Publisher.
*Courtesy Farrukh
Systems Limited.*

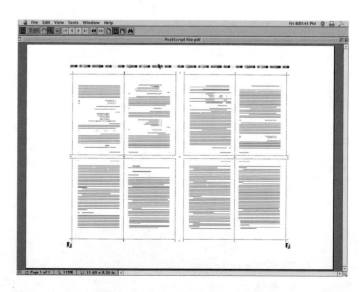

workstation, Imposition Publisher Studio Professional for single Macintosh or PC workstations (compatible with QuarkXPress, PageMaker and 60+ other DTP applications), and Imposition Publisher Page Pairer 2.0 on Windows NT and Sun servers for newspaper publishers for two- or four-up pairing of broadsheet and tabloid pages. Farrukh's offerings have already gained a significant number of followers in the European printing community—this is not surprising, as Imposition Publisher is the only imposition program of its kind available in French, German, Italian, and Spanish, as well as English.

Dynagram Software. A relative newcomer to the imposition market, Dynagram Software's product DynaStrip 2.0 is a PostScript imposition software program designed for use on a Windows 95 or Windows NT workstation. Based on a program first developed in 1994, DynaStrip 2.0 is a full-featured solution for imposing PostScript files (only) from a large variety of applications and computer platforms. Reportedly, the Canadian software developers of this program came from a printing industry background—and from the numerous features included in DynaStrip, that seems beyond question. Challenging impositions are no problem for this program, as functions to control nesting, compensate for bot-

The front and back forms for five signatures being imposed in DynaStrip 2.0. *Courtesy Dynagram Software.*

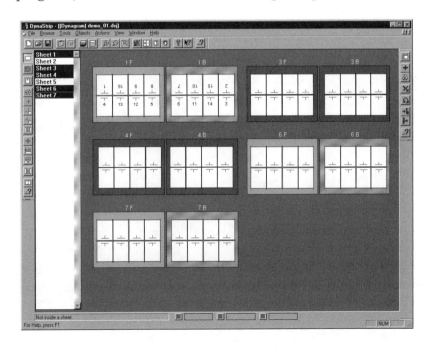

Imposing a form with two different sizes of pages in DynaStrip 2.0. *Courtesy Dynagram Software.*

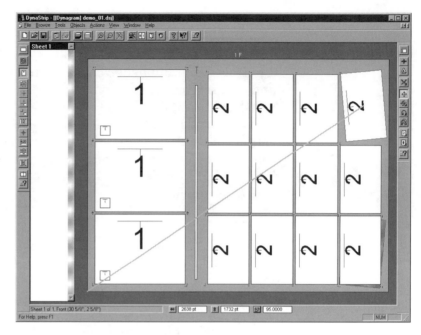

tling, and combine differing page sizes are standard. A more unusual feature of DynaStrip is its ability to scale, rotate, and offset any individual object, as well as individual pages. In order to see a preview of your imposition, however, you'll have to purchase the optional preview plug-in.

Similar to another Canadian software developer, Dynagram Software is proud of its visual interface for creating folding patterns. DynaStrip is capable of other unusual functions, including color merging (which allows colors bearing different

DynaFold in Dyna-Strip 2.0. *Courtesy Dynagram Software.*

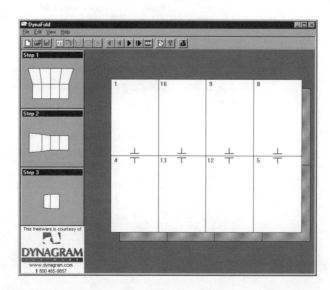

names to be combined onto a single plate) and selective printing of particular pages, marks, or other items. Other unusual features include the Color Layers function, which allows for full control (offset, scaling, rotation) over any object of any specific color (for compensation of press discrepancies or fine-tuning adjustments), and the Sheet Layers function, providing for multiple layers of objects and data (for last-minute corrections, placement of advertisements, superposing of small pages from different applications, etc.).

Dynagram Software also makes clear its interest in computer-integrated manufacturing, as the company has publicly released the specifications for DynaStrip Imposition Language (DSIL). This spec facilitates the integration of imposition with other computer-based functions such as estimating and postpress operations. All of these features are included in a program that sells below the list price of other major solutions; competitive upgrades are also available.

Imation Publishing Software Corp.
Last, but certainly not least, of the stand-alone PostScript imposition programs to be profiled is Imation Press-Wise. Formerly known as Luminous Technology Corporation, Imation Publishing Software Corp. now develops, supports, and markets PressWise. Despite the fact that other popular Imation products, such as TrapWise and Color Central (a GATF InterTech award winner) have been released for both Mac and Windows platforms, PressWise is currently available only for the Macintosh.

Imation PressWise is an application that offers the ability to impose multiple PostScript (both composite and pre-separated) files and standard EPS files. The latest release, PressWise 3.0, also allows the direct imposition of PDF files. Controls are available for a wide variety of publication-style impositions, although all pages within an imposition must be of the same dimension. This restriction reduces the appeal of PressWise for a packaging audience — however, Presswise 3.0 can impose nested or overlapping objects and supports unlimited form size for oversized flats of small repeated objects. High-quality page previews are available by actually RIPing the job to screen (utilizing another Imation application, PrePrint Pro).

Publication printers should be extremely happy with the productivity and flexibility of PressWise. Notable features

The page list dialog
box in Imation
PressWise.
*Courtesy Imation
Publishing Software
Corp.*

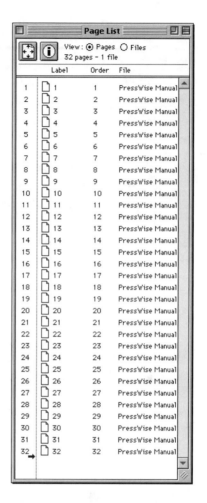

A 16-page head-to-head
sheetwise imposition
in Imation PressWise.
*Courtesy Imation
Publishing Software
Corp.*

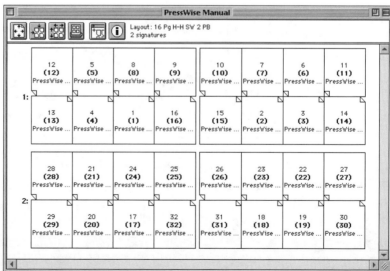

One side of a sixteen-page signature being imposed in Imation PressWise.
Courtesy Imation Publishing Software Corp.

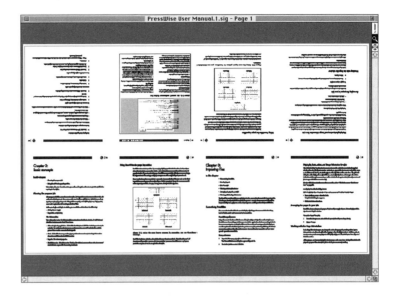

include a supplied library of commonly-used imposition styles, and an additional library of common imagesetter punch styles. Another benefit is that marks styles defined within PressWise can be applied to any imposition template, and can feature any EPS graphic (such as GATF's digital color bars, for instance) as part of the printer's marks.

Perhaps the greatest benefit in choosing Imation Press-Wise is its integration within the Imation OPEN automated environment through predefined pipeline packs. OPEN is a method of linking a variety of software (such as PressWise, TrapWise, and Color Central), so that jobs can travel through a predefined series of operations without human intervention. Although other prepress software companies also offer trapping applications that integrate with their imposition products, few other desktop vendors have automated the variety of capabilities that Imation offers within its OPEN workflow.

Quite Software Ltd. Would you buy an imposition software program that couldn't accept Post-  Script files? Perhaps the answer would be "yes" if that program specialized in imposing PDF files from within Acrobat Exchange. New to the pagination marketplace, the Acrobat plug-in Quite Imposing from England's Quite Software is the first Acrobat Exchange plug-in for PDF imposition. This plug-in is available for both PowerMac and Windows 95 or

The control panel in
Quite Imposing.

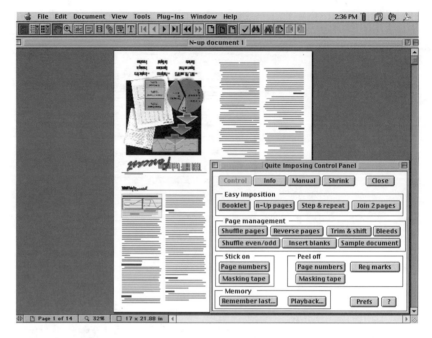

NT, allowing PDF files to be imposed without mandating the
creation of PostScript data.

Quite Software offers two different plug-ins (Quite Imposing
and Quite Imposing Plus), which offer a very inexpensive solution for PDF pagination. Although the operating procedures
for these plug-ins are unlike any other imposition software

One form of an eight-
page signature after
imposition with Quite
Imposing.

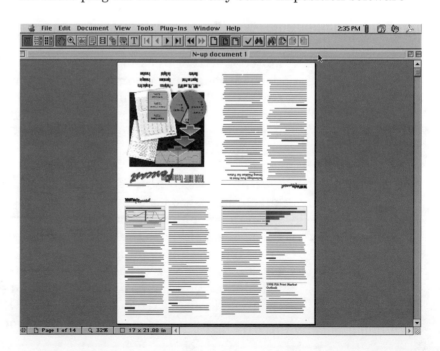

The plug-in menu for
Quite Imposing.

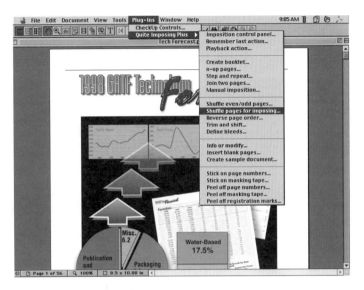

programs (as an example, you must use the Shuffle Pages
function to reorder and selectively rotate pages, as part of
creating a head-to-head layout), the tools are present to
accomplish a wide variety of output styles. Creep compensation and manual positioning for nested impositions are both
possible within the more advanced program, Quite Imposing
Plus. Furthermore, since all the imposition occurs directly to
PDF files, an imposed preview is always available.

Considering that this is the very first product available for
imposing documents from within Acrobat Exchange, this is a
software program that should become an essential tool for
prepress departments everywhere. Download a free demo
version by visiting Quite's website, *http://www.quite.com,*
and try it for yourself.

OneVision. Although the previous software is the first imposition plug-in for
Acrobat Exchange, it is not the first pro-
gram available for direct imposition of PDF files—that honor
belongs to OneVision's DigiScript. This German company's
software has become very popular in Europe for repairing
and modifying PostScript, EPS, and PDF files. DigiScript is
one of the few commercial programs available for Steve Job's
NeXT operating system, and it can run under OPENSTEP
on either Windows NT or the Macintosh platform. OneVision
plans to release a version of DigiScript for Mac OS X in the
near future.

The folding scheme
dialog box in Digi-
Script.
Courtesy OneVision.

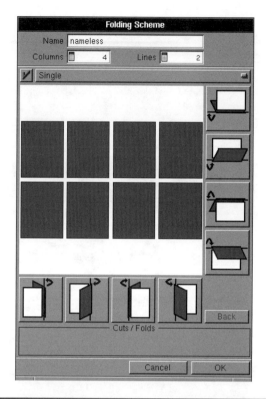

A preview of a form
being imposed in
DigiScript.
Courtesy OneVision.

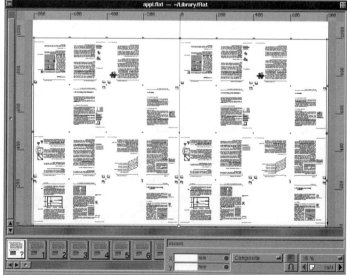

For users who have purchased DigiScript to repair and
edit PostScript or PDF files, the additional purchase of
OneVision Imposition software adds pagination functions to
the workstation. This program accepts both separated and
unseparated PostScript files, as well as data in EPS, TIFF,

The edit job dialog box
in DigiScript.
Courtesy OneVision.

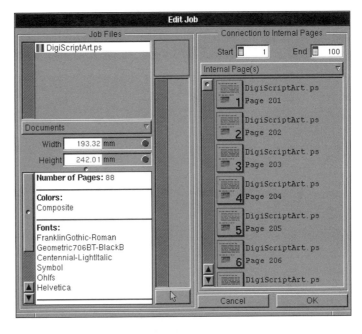

Adobe Illustrator, or PDF format. After imposition has been
defined, flats can be output as PostScript or converted into
EPS, TIFF, or PDF through DigiScript. All the functions of a
high-end imposition system are included, such as automatic
page arrangement, support of OPI print serving, and an integrated flat library of predefined sheet and film formats.

OneVision Imposition also includes a number of packaging-
style attributes, such as combination of different page sizes,
step-and-repeat imposition, and manual page placement. Perhaps the most interesting feature of OneVision Imposition,

Inspector dialog box in
DigiScript.
Courtesy OneVision.

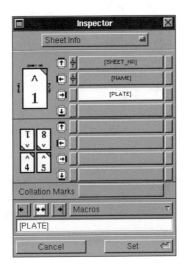

however, is its use of Display PostScript for on-screen representation of imposed data. This allows for a true "what you see is what you get" preview that can be zoomed up to 80,000% enlargement. Users of the complete OneVision package will have to make an investment of both capital and training time, but the benefits of editing and imposing such a wide variety of file formats are easy to see.

RIP-Based Imposition

Several leading products for creating digital impositions on desktop workstations have just been examined, but there is more to the picture. Many prepress departments take on the challenge of arranging graphics on a sheet by investing in raster image processors (RIPs) that include software for performing imposition. As mentioned on the second page of this chapter, some of these RIPs perform imposition after the creation of raster images, then screen these fully imposed raster flats during the output process. Alternatively, some RIP vendors process every individual page all the way to screened data before imposing these bi-level bitmaps. Of course, the electronic prepress industry also has a long history of support for vendors who "do their own thing," rasterizing PostScript into their own proprietary format for imposition and screening. (For the purpose of this book, a proprietary data format is one that can only be understood and interpreted by a single vendor's brand of RIP. Some readers will no doubt consider the CT/LW format popularized by Scitex to fit into this category; however, other vendors [such as Contex] also utilize CT/LW files.)

Whichever way the post-RIP imposition is performed, there are certain benefits offered by this workflow. Most of the promotional literature from purveyors of post-RIP imposition tout the benefits of a "late-binding" process. This refers to the ease with which page content may be changed late in the output process. With a late-binding imposition method, any individual page that requires a correction can be printed, RIPed, and inserted into the imposed flat as a single page. This is in contrast to a PostScript imposition software program, which would require the recreation and re-RIPing of an entire multipage imposed PostScript file. This introduces the possibility that pages which were not supposed to be changed might actually process differently when RIPed a second time, usually due to human error, such as failing to include all required fonts during the second printing.

Dozens of companies are currently in the business of manufacturing RIPs for various segments of the graphic arts industry, and the features available from these manufacturers change with every major trade show. Therefore, this book will not attempt to provide a comprehensive list of all RIPs that offer imposition. Instead we will look at a small sampling of the options available for the high-end prepress market.

Cortron. In its euRIPides workflow system, Cortron offers one of today's most advanced methods of controlling digital data. While some vendors are scrambling to allow PDF files to be used as input, Cortron has made the

generation of PDF files an integral part of the euRIPides methodology for processing and imposing files. Similar to Adobe's Extreme print architecture, Cortron's euRIPides immediately distills incoming data (in the form of PostScript, EPS, or PDF) into single-page PDF files; these PDF pages are then used to generate clean and verified "prime PostScript." Any errors found during the distilling process (such as missing fonts or RGB images) are reported to the screen for user interaction. These single-page files are stored on a file server for imposition in one of three styles: manual layout (allowing differing page sizes and nesting), automatic

Cortron's euRIPides Impose in page layout mode.
Courtesy Cortron.

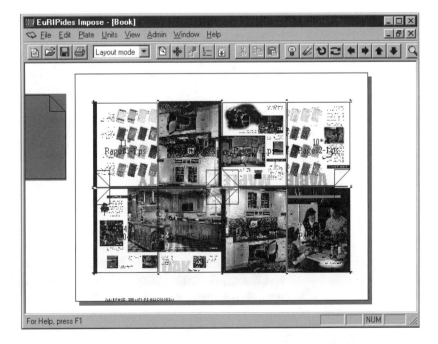

pagination for publication work, and template imposition for working from predefined job planning sheets or imported IT8.6 (DDES2) data.

This variety of imposition methods assures that most customers (including packaging printers) will find the imposition tool that suits their workflow. Cortron's use of single-page files also means that replacement of individual pages can be accomplished with relative ease. Integration of Imation's TrapWise trapping solution allows users to trap all files input to the system, including PDF files. For digital proofing, euRIPides includes the SoftProof station, with which images can be previewed on-screen prior to output on a hard proof device. Proofing the files either individually or post-imposition is easily done, since euRIPides can redirect output to a variety of devices (including large-format inkjet plotters, page proofers, CTP devices, and imagesetters).

Heidelberg Prepress. Heidelberg Prepress (formerly Linotype-Hell) is a recipient of the GATF InterTech award for its Delta RIP technology. Delta RIPs run on Windows NT hardware and allow for the creation of DeltaList files as an intermediate step in the processing of PostScript, EPS, or TIFF-IT data. Conceptually similar to the Cortron method of using PDF files to enhance the stability of the processed data, DeltaList files are used as an archival format that can be repurposed for any resolution or output format, which maintains the integrity and consistency of pages throughout the workflow. These DeltaList files can then be imposed at another workstation called the Signastation. Since the imposition created at the Signastation is composed of interpreted but unscreened data, the completed imposition can be output to a variety of proofing devices, imagesetters, or platesetters by varying only the screening, as needed. Imposing post-interpreted data especially increases productivity in the step-and-repeat mode, since data does not need to be RIPed again for each repeated image.

Heidelberg's Signastation can impose PostScript data or DeltaLists; the ability to directly impose PDF data is promised for the next release. When interpreted data is stored on a compatible file server, Signastation optimizes network throughput by sending only "skeleton files" back to the server for output.

Signastation currently uses the NeXTStep operating system; this configuration enables Signastation to use Adobe's Display PostScript Interpreter, for true WYSIWYG monitor soft proofing of all text, graphics, and images. LinoPreview is a subset of the Signastation software that is used as a basic preflight tool to check for common errors, such as missing fonts or images. Signastation will soon be available on Windows NT via OPENSTEP, or as a software package for the Macintosh once Apple's Mac OS X becomes available.

BARCO Graphics. The vendors mentioned so far facilitate the process of imposition at the RIP by converting the incoming  PostScript, EPS, PDF and TIFF-IT into a single, controllable format. Cortron and Gerber use open-platform PDF files, while Heidelberg Prepress favors the flat-file format of DeltaList. For our next vendor, the conversion of incoming data into a new format is nothing new. For years, BARCO Graphics has proudly touted the advantages of turning desktop and even CEPS system files into an object list file that they call the GRO format. BARCO's FastLane client/server hardware and applications have earned high praises for facilitating prepress functions in the packaging and label printing industry, but FastLane is now spreading to the commercial print market as well.

Various imposition layouts in Impose!, the imposition software used on BARCO workstations.
Courtesy BARCO Graphics.

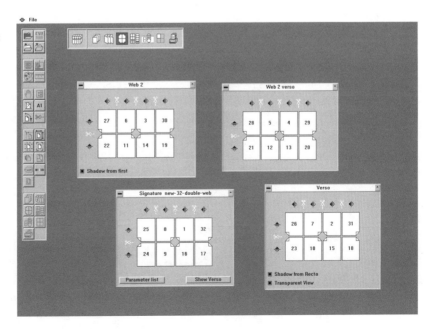

A preview of an impo-
sition for a book.
*Courtesy BARCO
Graphics.*

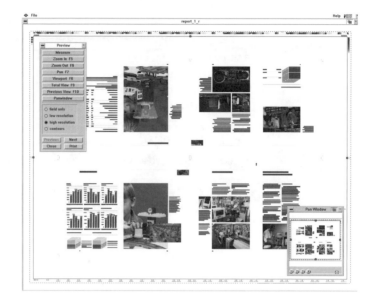

Impose!, the imposition software used on BARCO workstations, defines paginations by positioning individual GRO
elements. BARCO's late-binding workflow and object referenced script file allows these GRO files to be replaced, modified, or edited right up to the moment before RIPing. Similar
to post-RIP late-binding workflows, these changes can be

An imposition layout
in Impose! This layout
is for a 32-page signa-
ture to be printed
using double webs.
*Courtesy BARCO
Graphics.*

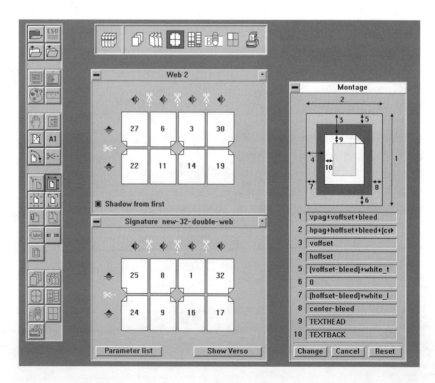

made without the need to re-execute the imposition scheme. After print preparation and imposition has been completed at a FastLane workstation, data follows an automated workflow track to a FastRip; this RIP uses a BARCO-written output driver for the intended imaging device.

In addition to a successful line of imagesetters and platesetters, BARCO's recent acquisition of Gerber Systems has brought large-format inkjet proofing capability to the FastRip family. BARCO's capability to drive the InterTech award-winning Gerber IMPRESS plotter as well as a variety of smaller-format laser printers goes under the moniker ImposeProof!

The three RIP manufacturers previously mentioned (Cortron, Heidelberg Prepress, and BARCO) have made imposition a function that occurs *before* final rendering at the RIP. They all point to the flexibility of using a stable, controlled data format that can be RIPed numerous times for a variety of different devices for proofing, imagesetting, or platesetting. The next three vendors have taken another route to that same destination—they impose individual pages *after* rasterization.

Krause America. Computer-to-plate vendor Krause America calls its work-flow PRI, short for Post-RIP Imposi-  tion. Page layout documents are printed from normal desktop publishing workstations and then RIPed by nearly any of today's popular high-end RIPs. (Krause allows the use of a wide variety of RIPs as part of its Extremely Open Architecture integration policy.) After the incoming PostScript files have been interpreted into screened bi-level bitmaps, these bitmap pages can be imposed and/or archived for later use. This imposition process occurs on Krause's imposition workstation (running on a Sun UltraSPARC MP computer) called the IPU. After the imposition is defined at the IPU, bitmap pages are pulled into press forms on-the-fly during plate exposure.

The advantages of this system include the same sort of flexibility and ease of page replacement that is part of the previous systems, but with an extra measure of security: since Krause's PRI workflow utilizes post-RIP screened data, there is no chance that PostScript errors will interrupt the platemaking process. Of course this concept cuts both ways—these screened pages have no flexibility to allow changes in line screen frequency, dot gain, or trapping before output. Krause also offers post-RIP proofing, so that these imposed raster files can be resampled and sent to a variety of proofing devices.

Scitex. Scitex also provides a workflow in which incoming files are RIPed before imposition, but the interpreted files are stored as independent pages in the CT/LW format. (CT/LW stands for Continuous Tone/LineWork and is a raster-based format popularized by Scitex, consisting of two files: a high-resolution LW file for rules, text, and other graphical elements, and a normal-resolution CT file for images and gradients.) Unlike Krause's screened bitmap data, however, CT/LW raster data is device-independent information; this means pages imposed on the Scitex Brisque DFE (Digital Front End) can be output to a variety of different devices without redundant RIPing. Alternately, the same imposed flat may be output at a variety of different screen rulings.

Electronic documents can be submitted to the Brisque as PostScript, EPS, TIFF-IT, or Scitex CT/LW. In a typical implementation of the Brisque Impose workflow, an imposition template (called an ICF, or imposition control file) is defined at a Macintosh workstation, using ScenicSoft Preps imposition software. Scitex's Brisque DFE workstation then RIPs submitted documents into individual pages of CT/LW

Layout assembly in the Brisque workflow. *Courtesy Scitex America Corp.*

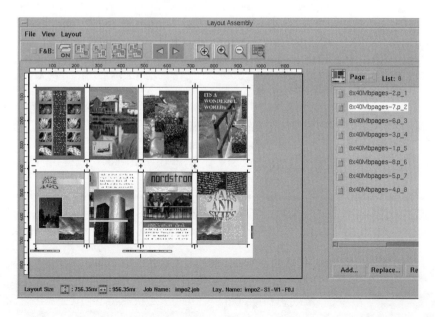

Dialog box for Improof
750C.
*Courtesy Scitex
America Corp.*

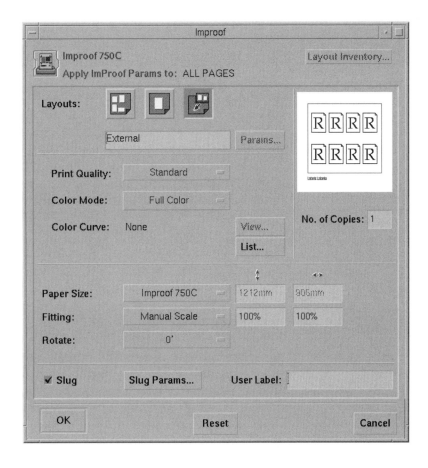

data, which are merged with marker file data, plate control
file data, and the ICF imposition template during output.
Both the imposition layout files and the CT/LW pages remain
fully editable right up until exposure is initiated.

PDF RIP parameters
dialog box.
*Courtesy Scitex
America Corp.*

Scitex has also added new features to the Brisque's flat preview function; fronts and backs can now be viewed simultaneously. The Brisque can also output related data in CIP3 format, using imposition information to preset downstream functions such as printing press ink fountain keys and paper cutter automation. The recently announced Brisque4 Impose platform incorporates elements of Adobe's Extreme RIP architecture, including normalization of PostScript to PDF and parallel RIPing. This is accomplished via four independent, multitasking CPUs, allowing simultaneous RIPing, trapping, and output to multiple Scitex proofing, plating, and imagesetting devices.

Contex. Preps is also a major component of the imposition method employed by RIP vendor Contex (a division of Xyvision, Inc.).  Documents can be submitted as PostScript, EPS, TIFF, or CEPS files to the Contex RIP (running on a Silicon Graphics UNIX server), where they are RIPed and held in the Contex CT1/LW1 format. From any Macintosh running Preps, the user can then define the imposition style and specify which RIPed pages are to be imposed, by using the Preps run list. With this small signature definition file and the ImposeMan software option loaded on the Contex workstation or server, entire jobs can be automatically paginated for output. The

The step-and-repeat dialog box in the ImposeMan imposition program.
Courtesy Contex Prepress Systems.

Step & Repeat Page

Page:

contex/job/LongJohn.job/LongJo_tr.lw

Basename of New Page:

stepped_4x3

Step Gap:

Across: 0.1000   ◈ mm
                 ◇ in
Down: 0.0000

Repeat:

Across: 4

Down: 3

Process Server: ms1

Start   Cancel

The ImposeMan impo-
sition software loaded
on a Contex work-
station or server.
*Courtesy Contex
Prepress Systems.*

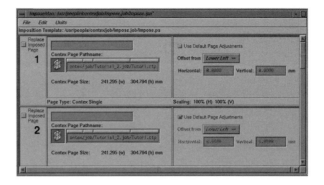

ImposeMan interface also provides for last minute insertion
or substitution of individual pages. Just as with the Scitex
implementation of post-RIP imposition, Contex ImposeMan
combines the flexibility of Preps running on desktop workstations with the advantages of a device-independent data
format for proofing, imagesetting, platemaking, or archiving.

Contex also offers step-and-repeat automation directly
from the Contex desktop to support label printing and flexographic applications. This straightforward interface allows
the user to define the number of repetitions across and down,
as well as the margin between rows and columns.

Summary

This sampling of digital imposition options has described
only a few of the many ways in which graphics can be
arranged on a press sheet electronically. The next chapter
discusses the special considerations that should be taken
into account when considering the purchase of one of these
digital imposition systems, along with factors that influence
whether or not a given imposition product is suitable for a
specific print market or prepress environment.

11 Special Considerations for Imposition

In preceding chapters the basic principles of image assembly as they relate to imposition and the important aspects of paper and press have been discussed; the effects of folding, binding, and finishing on the process of planning for imposition were also covered; and in the previous chapter, today's digital imposition methods were reviewed. At this point one might think that there is little left to say. Before putting this information to use in the real world, however, consider the advice this chapter offers about choosing a digital imposition system, or for those just starting to impose documents.

CTP and Imposition

Computer-to-plate (CTP) is an exciting field for today's printer. Whether the market is publications, packaging, or in-plant, printing companies around the world are rushing to adopt a new workflow that allows digital data to be imaged directly to printing plates without the use of film. While the absence of film from the process makes the use of digital imposition an absolute necessity, the tremendous number of choices available for creating imposed signatures makes it difficult to decide which products are best suited for CTP. As any vendor will tell you, it depends on your workflow. With the large investment that CTP users make in their systems, however, speed and flexibility will also be important factors.

Look for an imposition product that will fit into your current workflow, rather than causing you to change your production methods while you learn new software and hardware. Ideally choose a method that allows you to learn imposition before the CTP equipment arrives—because once it does, it is unlikely that you will have adequate freedom to experiment without undue time constraints and financial pressure. This scenario will be less likely, of course, if you are using RIP-based imposition, since you will probably take delivery of a new RIP as part of your CTP system. In some cases, however, prepress departments will already be using a RIP similar to that which will drive their platesetter, including identical imposition functions. An example might be a printing company that already uses a BARCO FastRIP and imagesetter for film output, and will simply be adding a platesetter to its stable of output devices. Another method of making the transition would be to learn a desktop imposition software program to drive your imagesetter, and then purchase a CTP system that utilizes that same software program to create imposition templates (such as ScenicSoft Preps paired with a Scitex Brisque DFE and a Lotem platesetter).

Perhaps you are not certain that your current workflow is worth keeping! In that case, look for new equipment that offers an integrated method of moving data from desktop workstations through imposition, trapping, RIPing, proofing, and final output. Although nearly every prepress vendor claims to have developed the ultimate in workflow productivity, some of these solutions are obviously easier to use than others. Of course, what their competitors ask you to give up in ease-of-use will often be repaid in high productivity (once you overcome the substantial learning curve). Also consider the availability of high-quality training on your chosen system. Do not believe the hardware vendors if they tell you that personalized training is unavailable for PostScript imposition software; several products (such as Ultimate's Impostrip) can be purchased with on-site training. As an alternative, some vendors of RIP-based imposition products offer training at one of their national technical centers. The key is to remember that personalized training is not always an option, so check before you buy.

Accurate image positioning. The challenges of imposition for CTP will become obvious the moment you think about making that first plate without film. For example, how much control will you have for assuring that the image hits the exact spot on the plate that you desire? To be truly useful for CTP, imposed signatures must be easily located in the center of the plate (or off-center, if desired), and set back the correct distance from the lead edge of the plate. Once a job has been imposed, individual signatures should be capable of moving from one plate size to another, or between presses, without requiring major changes in the imposition layout.

Incorporating marks and control elements. Providing the plethora of marks required by the pressroom and bindery is also a challenge. In a film-based workflow, you are probably accustomed to imaging and stripping several sets of film for the job, and then making additional exposures during platemaking from standing flats for side guides, collating marks, and color bars. Does the imposition system you are interested in purchasing make it easy to incorporate all of the various marks and process control elements you desire? Most programs will allow you to place one or more EPS files into the marks template, which you can use for everything from Form ID information to plate exposure control targets. GATF offers a wide variety of EPS files that are useful in CTP; especially helpful are the GATF Digital Plate Control Target and many varieties of color bars.

Be aware that most imposition programs simply flop the marks flat defined for the front of the sheet when imaging the back. While this guarantees that the marks will match when viewed through the sheet, it also means that EPS graphics used in the marks (such as digital color bars) will print as a mirror-image on the back side of the sheet. This renders the color bars useless for presses that require a consistent color sequence in order to be read by a scanning densitometer at the press console. You can get around these limitations (for instance, by manually replacing the normal EPS graphic with a "flopped" version before imaging the back of the sheet, or by imaging all forms in the job as "Fronts"), but this sort of workaround will impact your productivity.

Special Needs of the Packaging Industry

Accuracy of control marks. Probably no other part of the printing industry uses a greater variety of control marks on each press sheet than the packaging industry. In addition to simple marks such as color bars and sheet centers, packaging plants always add a number of other important targets. These include small color bars running next to each folding carton on the sheet, station ID marks, and register marks scattered throughout the sheet. If there is not enough space between packages for these targets, they are printed on the carton, typically in an area where they will go unnoticed, such as the bottom of a box or on a glue tab. Other marks are provided to indicate exactly where a carton should be diecut—when an entire sheet is cut apart with one massive cutting die, these marks (located along the edge of the trim) will be split in half. Bleeder marks are also common; these typically consist

A layout for printing nine cartons on one press sheet. In addition to the color bar at the back edge of the press sheet, small color bars run next to each folding carton (B). If there is not enough space between cartons, the color bar may be printed on a glue tab (A). The press sheet will also include station ID marks and register marks.

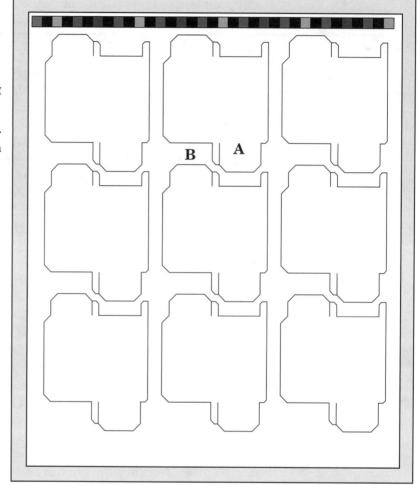

of a short, thick rule that bleeds off the edge of the package. Packages in the first position (closest to the press sheet's gripper) will be marked with a single line, packages in the second row will get two lines, etc. When a number of diecut boxes are stacked, any variance in the position of these marks will indicate a problem in registration. A sheet carrying multiple copies of the same carton might also carry station number marks, which identify each carton as a unique number. Using these marks a quality control inspector can determine if a particular carton was stripped out of position and is not being diecut correctly.

Acceptance of diecutting file formats. These cutting dies are the basis of an entire workflow system that is common to both packaging and label printing. In each case the printed piece will eventually be trimmed to a shape that is not rectangular and cannot be cut using a guillotine cutter, which is the basis of the publications industry's bindery process. Cutting dies are usually designed with some form of CAD/CAM (computer-aided drafting/computer-assisted manufacturing) equipment, not the typical desktop publishing programs that are used to design the packages and labels themselves. In the Americas, the most widely used format for storing the digital information produced by these CAD/CAM systems is called DDES2 (a similar file type named CFF2 is widely used in Europe). This format is also known as IT8.6 DDES-IADD, and was published as a standard by the International Organization for Standardization in 1991. More information on the IT8.6 standard can be obtained from NPES (the Association for Suppliers of Printing and Publishing Technologies) at their web site (www.npes.org).

However, the number of cutting die files being produced by illustration programs is on the rise. If one is going to use a desktop publishing program to create a die, be aware that the native Adobe Illustrator file format is the most widely supported among die manufacturers and packaging RIP vendors. Most packaging companies are proficient in using software that can translate files between these popular formats, such as CADMOVER from Kandu Software.

Any imposition system that is truly useful in a packaging environment will be able to accept a DDES2 file and use it as the basis for determining press sheet imposition. This may seem obvious, but in reality the acceptance of DDES2 data by imposition programs is uncommon (especially among desktop imposition programs). Anyone in the packaging business should insist on this feature.

Capability to execute special layouts. The predominance of diecutting in package printing results in special layout schemes used to maximize the number of pieces that can be printed on a sheet. Folding cartons, for example, are typically not rectangular, meaning that the printer can make more effective use of the press sheet by nesting packages. *Nesting* means that one portion of a printed piece will be located inside the negative space created by the irregular shape of another piece. This type of arrangement makes it impossible to cut the press sheet apart with a single, straight cut (such as that employed by a guillotine cutter). Nesting, therefore, is only done when a sheet is to be diecut. Since

Nesting eight #10 commercial envelopes on a 28×34-in. sheet of paper, as shown in the illustration, allows all envelopes to be cut straight grain. The envelopes marked A, however, are grain-parallel to the 9½-in. length of the envelope, and those marked B are grain-parallel to the 4⅛-in. length. *Courtesy William-house, a division of American Pad and Paper.*

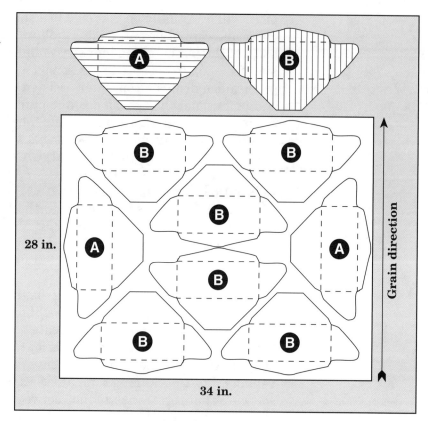

Nesting five #6¾ commercial envelopes on a 17×22-in. sheet of paper, as shown in the illustration, allows all envelopes to be cut diagonal to the grain. *Courtesy William-house, a division of American Pad and Paper.*

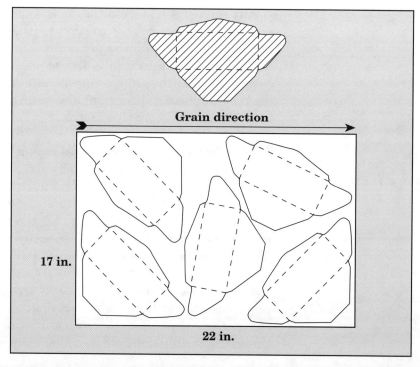

many imposition programs (both desktop and RIP-based) define each graphic element on the sheet as a rectangle, creating a nested imposition with these programs is nearly impossible. Although it is possible to accomplish nesting by deceiving the software (describing page sizes that are smaller than the actual cartons), such a process is extremely time-consuming and prone to human error.

Combination imposition. Imposition software applicable to the packaging and label printing industries will not only allow for nesting, but also for the use of combinations. A combination imposition combines multiple graphic elements of different sizes; this becomes a useful feature when several different labels must be printed on the same sheet, because it minimizes the number of different pressruns needed. Of course, it is highly likely that the most efficient use of a press sheet would be a combination run where all the elements are nested, but the amount of overlap between elements would change depending on which size elements are interacting. As you might expect, the resulting imposition can become very complex. Most digital imposition programs can only impose a single page size for each job, making them nearly useless for package and label printers. This should explain the dominance of a handful of companies (such as BARCO, Misomex, and Dalim) that sell imposition packages for these segments of the printing industry.

Trapping

Another special consideration when considering imposition systems is trapping—the creation of thin areas of overlap between adjacent colors, with the purpose of overcoming misregister that occurs during the printing process. While this is not an issue specific to packaging and label printing, these industries typically use the largest number of colors on some of the most unstable substrates. For this reason they must be assured of having complete control over creating traps during the imaging process. "But wait," one may say. "What does that have to do with imposition?" The answer is that digital prepress workflow is generally most efficient when trapping and imposition work together seamlessly; this means that one is likely to purchase and use the trapping option offered by the same manufacturer from which one has chosen an imposition method.

On the desktop, Imation pairs PressWise with TrapWise, Ultimate Impostrip interfaces directly with its Trapeze software, and DK&A recently acquired Trapper from Island Graphics to complement INposition. In the RIP-based imposition arena, integrated trapping solutions are offered by Harlequin, Contex, Scitex, BARCO, Heidelberg Prepress, and many other vendors. Using a trapping solution offered by your imposition vendor has the advantage of producing the highest degree of workflow automation. This means that the attributes of your trapping option may be just as important a part of your imposition method decision as the imposition program itself. An entire book could be filled with details on what differentiates one trapping system from another. Following are a few important considerations:

- If your pressroom has presses that are five-color or more, dealing with spot color inks will be a part of everyday life. Be certain that your trapping system makes it easy to deal with these spot colors, including traps between spot and process colors.

- Trapping page elements on the desktop is a function typically done in vector (object-oriented) mode, raster (pixel-based) mode, or a combination of both. Software that does not allow raster trapping will be unable to handle the tiny number of instances where you will need to trap two gradients or other continuous-tone areas. On the flip side, vector trapping is inherently faster and less processor-intensive than raster trapping, allowing the successful use of a relatively low-powered computer.

- Since raster trapping on the desktop is very processor-intensive, you will probably need to invest in a separate workstation dedicated to this function. Do not skimp— without a fast processor and lots of random-access memory (RAM), you will probably see long processing times, undependable results, and artifacts (small areas of strange and unexplainable colors and shapes, usually in the corners of trapped objects).

- Most trapping software (both desktop and RIP-based) handles images and other forms of continuous-tone (contone) data as a masked area, into which other colors will always be spread. In some rare instances, you may want to maintain the adjoining color and actually spread the contents of the contone area (such as gradient-filled type on a black background). Imation TrapWise and Ultimate Trapeze are the only desktop trapping solutions that let you choose whether to trap a contone area based on its mask, or on the value of its pixels relative to the adjoining pixels.

- Interestingly, many printers have survived a decade of digital workflow without investing in any special trapping software. When used to their fullest potential, the trapping functions within QuarkXPress, Adobe PageMaker, Adobe Illustrator, Macromedia FreeHand, and even Adobe Photoshop can be used to produce excellent results that satisfy most customers. Prepress workers sometimes forsake these tools and, as a result, end up inspecting and manipulating the same traps on the same logos and mastheads over and over. If adequate traps can be created in the original document and returned to the customer, it is highly probable that the correctly trapped file will be used in that designer's future jobs.

Networking

The next consideration for digital imposition relates to moving all that imposed data around the prepress department. As we slide deeper into this wired world, every prepress worker must become an expert in networking and moving data efficiently. One might think that the impact of imposition on your network will be no different from that of your current production methods—after all, if you are imaging thirty-two pages per hour on film, what does it matter whether they are printed individually or as eight-up signatures? There are two reasons: (1) imposition alters the workflow structure, and (2) equipment utilization creates demands.

Imposition alters the workflow structure. In prepress departments that are not utilizing imposition, the current imaging load is being spread out, a few pages at a time. This means that not only are you quicker to hit the print button for a couple of pages (especially since you need not worry about imposition), but also that the RIP processes these single pages quickly and begins imaging pages right away. Days are taken up by many trips back and forth from the desktop to the imagesetter, from the imagesetter to the processor, from the processor to the stripping department, and finally back to the desktop publishing workstation. With all that walking around, you really look busy! When imposition becomes a part of the process, it will take longer to click "print," and the ganged pages will take considerable time to process, resulting in fewer trips to the imagesetter and to the stripping department. As a result, a slow network does not mean more time waiting for PostScript to travel through the network; it simply means that the waiting will be lumped together into fewer, bigger segments, making you look and feel less productive! In reality, the throughput of your network will be unchanged. Imposition will simply make the network bottleneck more apparent.

Equipment utilization creates demands. The second reason for concern about the impact of imposition on the network is that an investment in imposition software has been made in order to make the best use of a large-format imagesetter or a new platesetter. In order to achieve a reasonable return on investment from this new device, you will have to do more work than you have ever done before. More pages in less time—undoubtedly, the management decision to purchase this equipment was based on just such a strategy. This makes the previous scenario even worse, because now every moment you spend watching the clock spin will be blamed for the lack of productivity from your new purchase.

Network advancements to solve potential problems. Given these issues, what sort of adjustments can be made? Inevitably, improving the network infrastructure will become a top priority. Fortunately recent advancements in 100BaseTX (Fast Ethernet) as well as alternative high-speed networking strategies such as FDDI (fiber distributed digital interface), HiPPI (high-performance parallel interface), and differential SCSI (small computer system interface) all offer increased throughput. Along the way it is also likely that many will give up AppleTalk as you have come to know it in favor of the faster, more cross-platform-compatible AppleShareIP. This new network operating system looks and feels like AppleTalk but uses the streaming TCP/IP (transmission control protocol/Internet protocol) common to UNIX computers and the Internet.

Another important component of reducing network transmission time from the desktop is the use of OPI (open prepress interface) image serving. The longest transmission times in a typical workflow involve copying image data through the network. Print time can be greatly reduced, however, if the high-resolution images are stored on a file server. Be certain that an overall imposition strategy includes some form of high-quality, dependable image serving, and be aware that, in many cases, integrating a second vendor that specializes in OPI will produce better results than buying a prepackaged solution from a single source. Using one computer to accomplish OPI image serving, RIPing, trapping, and imposition eliminates copying data through the network between these processes. Many manufacturers, however, establish a secondary, high-speed connection between servers and RIPs in order to keep this traffic off the Ethernet network. This can sometimes be a better solution than expecting a single computer to perform all those functions simultaneously.

Finally, do not underestimate the advantage of imposing at the RIP for packaging, label printing or any other digital version of step-and-repeat platemaking. If the same image appears on an imposed signature thirty-two times, some desktop imposition programs will require you to send the PostScript data for that page thirty-two times! (More sophisticated programs, such as ScenicSoft Preps, take advantage of the forms cache functionality within PostScript Level 2 to overcome this problem.) Imposing at the RIP means that the data can be copied and reused from only a single original, saving valuable print time from the desktop workstation. Of course the advantage of this strategy becomes less dramatic when nonrepeating publication work is involved.

Default vs. Alternate Settings

Be aware of the automatic or default choices that any imposition program wants to make for you! Whether the software runs on the desktop or at the RIP, certain functions may occur without your intervention and you will need to watch out for them. Typically these default settings are good, all-around choices for most imposition scenarios—but it is important to realize that they are only suggestions, and that it is okay to use alternative settings. Consider, for example, the amount of bleed on a page. Although the industry "standard" is 0.125 in. (3 mm), half-web printers typically use less, while packaging and label printers often use more. Another example would be the automatic creation of multiple imposed forms. Generally if you define an imposition and then add more pages than will fit on a single form, the software will create full forms until the number of pages is less than needed for a complete signature. It will then offer you the option of using a smaller sheet, or running a two-up or four-up form. Although this sounds like the ultimate in convenience, most saddle-stitch impositions should place these partial forms at the beginning of the document, not at the end. Automatic form creation will typically cause the small signatures to be in the middle of the booklet, but the bindery supervisor would probably prefer that the small signatures run as the first and last pages, so that the weight of the rest of the book does not prevent the partial form from jogging properly during the binding process.

Summary

Consider these points carefully when evaluating choices for an imposition method. Read all you can, peruse the vendor's websites, and be sure to spend time working with your final choices before you sign the contract. The correct choice will make your workflow more efficient and remove the bottleneck of manual stripping, while an incorrect choice may hobble you with an inefficient process that you cannot afford to get rid of. For those who already have an imposition system but are keeping your eyes open for a new method, or just planning to take some time before you make your choice, the final chapter will elaborate on the possible future of digital imposition.

12 The Future of Electronic Imposition

Given the rapid succession of changes that have challenged the printing industry recently, it would seem impossible to predict what the future will hold. As long as there are pundits, however, there will be predictions—so here are a few of mine.

Computer-Integrated Manufacturing

The use of centralized computing power to control manufacturing processes has a decades-long tradition—everywhere, that is, but in the graphic arts! For all our current high-tech trappings, we are really behind the times when it comes to integrating our many different computer systems. For decades other manufacturing industries have been using computer systems to bring together order entry, cost estimating, inventory control, and production automation. By integrating computer technology into the manufacturing process, it minimizes the number of times that data must be entered and allows projects to be tracked throughout the production cycle. This familiar concept is one of the printing industry's hot new topics, under the acronym *CIM* (computer-integrated manufacturing).

CIP3

A number of coalitions and vendor-supported groups are working towards a more uniform implementation of computing resources in the printing and publishing industry. To cite one example, a committee of leading graphic arts vendors and printers working to allow our current systems to talk to one another goes by the name CIP3 (International Cooperation for Integration of Prepress, Press, and Postpress). One of the earliest results of the CIP3 committee's efforts has been agreement on a digital file format called a Print Production Format file for press ink fountain key settings. Many of the vendors mentioned in earlier chapters have already

One of the first implementations of CIP3 was a digital file format for press ink fountain settings. The data, contained either on a floppy disk *(top)* or magnetic strip *(bottom)* allows the operator to preset the ink fountain keys.

released CIP3 ink key software or have announced their intention to do so. With this type of software an imposed signature is analyzed for the amount of ink coverage that will be required across the sheet. The resulting information is then saved in a file format that can be understood by the computer console of a modern, semi-automated printing press. This information presets the amount of ink that the press will release from its ink fountains, allowing the job to be run at the correct densities with less wasted time and paper at startup.

**Electronic
Job Tickets**

Ink fountain settings are just the tip of the iceberg. In the near future we are likely to see agreement on data file formats to drive automated paper cutters and preset binding equipment such as folders and perfect binders. Eventually CIP3 standards will streamline the passage of information from estimating and order-entry software into preflight, trapping, and imposition software.

A great innovation in the next generation of imposition software will be that information gathered by the sales force and the preliminary job planning work done by the estimator will not be wasted. Instead these numbers will automatically arrive with the job files and preset most of the relevant settings in your imposition program. For this to work, printers will all need to agree on exactly what constitutes a digital work order. While electronic job tickets are not a new idea, the concept that all will use some sort of relatively standardized docket is a very ambitious goal. The early lead in this field seems to be going to Adobe, which has quietly been supporting the efforts of the DNPS (Digital Networked Production Systems) committee. Look for digital job jackets to become an integral part of the next version of the portable document format (PDF), where it will add to the growing acceptance of PDF as a new standard for digital publishing.

**PDF as an
Intermediate
File Format**

Beyond the issue of an electronic job jacket, look forward to more imposition vendors embracing PDF as an intermediate file format. Just as Cortron's euRIPides workflow currently translates every incoming page into a PDF file, we are likely to see many imposition vendors adopting the flexible yet reliable PDF as a middle ground for digital data. Why PDF? Because this manageable, predictable subset of the PostScript language allows data to be edited and then output at a variety of different resolutions, making imposition proofing more practical. Additionally PDF files have true page independence, which allows individual pages to be processed on multiple RIPs simultaneously. Vendors whose current workflows already offer some of these advantages (such as the CT/LW imposition of Scitex and Contex, or the object list workflow of BARCO's GRO format) are unlikely, however, to change directions. Instead, they will simply offer robust support for PDF as an incoming data file format. Indeed the ability to impose customer-supplied PDF files will be an absolute necessity for the next generation of imposition software.

Single-Program Workflow

Just as PDF will have an enormous impact on all aspects of publishing, so will the role of PDF and PostScript editors such as OneVision's DigiScript. Companies such as OneVision foresee a future when most prepress department personnel will not use QuarkXPress, PageMaker, or Illustrator, but instead will use a single program to manipulate and correct PDF and/or PostScript files created by designers. In Europe this workflow method is already in place. Since DigiScript already offers some imposition functions as part of its broad range of services, it is easy to see that many companies may prefer this Swiss Army Knife approach to electronic publishing.

Display PostScript

The next operating system from Apple Computer (called OS X) will also have an enormous impact on imposition. Currently most methods of doing imposition on the desktop (and even a few RIP-based methods) require the use of a Macintosh computer. Once OS X is a part of the picture, every imposition software program will benefit, because OS X uses a technology known as Display PostScript, which replaces the Macintosh's current display method known as QuickDraw. (The just-mentioned DigiScript from OneVision runs on Steve Job's NeXT computer platform, which already utilizes this method of drawing information onto a computer monitor.) Display PostScript will allow entire pages to be previewed in WYSIWYG (What You See Is What You Get) mode during the imposition process, leveling the playing field among desktop imposition programs.

Client/Server-Based Applications

Another "new" computer technology (actually, new only to those of us in the printing industry) that will undoubtedly become more predominant in the future is client/server-based applications. In today's printing plant large data files and relatively slow networking systems have kept us from enjoying the same distributed computing power that other industries have enjoyed for a decade. That situation, however, is changing. Faster workstations, robust servers, and high-speed networking have finally brought some client/server applications to the imposition field, such as Farrukh's Imposition Publisher and Ultimate Impostrip's Signature Server.

Client/server applications use a single, powerful software program on a central server to do the work requested by multiple users scattered around the network. Each user workstation has only a small "client" version of the program, and the data to be processed is ideally located on the same server as the main application. In this way the client simply reaches through the network to use the data and facilities of the main server.

Since today's servers are capable of much higher network transmission speeds than the typical workstation—and because high-speed connections such as fiber distributed digital interface (FDDI) are typically run only between servers and RIPs—client/server applications can speed job processing and increase network throughput while simultaneously lowering the "cost per seat" when a large number of users is required. On the negative side setting up a client/server application for only one or two users is likely to be more expensive than our current stand-alone scenarios.

Centralized Prepress Departments

From a scenario in which the power of imposition is concentrated in a central server, it takes only a small leap of faith to contemplate a future in which centralized prepress departments perform preflight, file correction, trapping, and imposition for a geographically widespread collection of printing plants. If this sounds improbable, think again. In a few locations around the United States, corporate printers with multiple locations have already established links between sites, using high-speed telecommunications lines. These digital connections, such as T3 or high-bit-rate digital subscriber lines (HDSL), are widely available in metropolitan areas, but what about the more rural areas in which corporate printers often locate? Look no further than computing giant Bill Gates for the answer. His private company Teledisic is committed to launching a fleet of satellites that will provide high-capacity, low-cost broadband access to cellular data transfer methods (LMDS). Initial plans call for a network of 288 satellites to be in place by the year 2002. With a combination of advanced data connections and computer-to-plate technology, a printer can staff a single prepress department for a virtually unlimited number of production sites. Using this same scenario today's service bureaus will be able to survive the demise of film by offering file preparation and imposition services to printing companies that invest in platesetters. Many of these service bureaus will likely become technology integrators, using their knowledge and ability to guide printers to appropriate equipment solutions.

Such a distributed production scheme will require prepress workers to be knowledgeable about an incredible array of imposition styles—everything from the simple sheetfed and web publication styles described in this book, to challenging multi-web and folding carton layouts. Success in producing this diversity of production styles will be enabled by the increasing ease of use that newer versions of today's imposition software are sure to possess. Visual tools such as Ultimate's Origami animated folding utility, coupled with CIP3 automation and Display PostScript, will ease the challenge of placing graphics on a sheet.

Primacy of Basic Print Production Knowledge

One component of this process will not change, however: knowledge of how the fundamental principles of print reproduction combine with layout and design. No matter how interactive or integrated the imposition software may be, the user will be unable to take full advantage of it without a basic knowledge of paper and a thorough grasp of the printing, folding, binding, and finishing operations. Spend all the time you need examining the available options for desktop or RIP-based imposition but, before you begin using your new equipment, make sure you have come to terms with the basics of printing functions. Whether the tools are servers and platesetters or triangles and T-squares, the underlying concepts are the same. No imposition strategy will be successful until these essential concepts are understood.

A GATF Master Layout Sheets

This appendix contains a number of master layouts sheets for four-, eight-, and sixteen-page signatures. You are encouraged to photocopy these forms to assist in planning your impositions. Each layout sheet consists of two pages. The first page shows general information about the layout (e.g., stock information, job information, and imposition information) as well as the front of the form. The second page shows the back of the form (with the exception of work-and-turn layouts, which are blank on the second side).

The name of each layout sheet is in a form of shorthand. The first layout sheet is called "12.5×19/8.5×11/mec/sht/nolip." The "12.5×19" indicates the paper size, and the "8.5×11" indicates the page size. The "mec" indicate that the binding method to be used will be "mechanical." The "sht" indicates that the imposition style will be "sheetwise," and the "nolip" indicates that there will be no lip on the folded signature. These layouts have been provided for the most common sheetfed impositions on five standard paper sizes.

Since the masters provided in this appendix cannot cover every possible imposition scenario, there are also two blank layouts (one in the saddle-stitch style, the other suitable for perfect-bound or mechanical binding) provided for each sheet size. These are for your use when creating custom layouts. Additionally, keep in mind that the relative size of gutters and margins has been intentionally exaggerated, to allow room for display of measurement information.

When using these layouts, bear this important considerations in mind: all page numbers shown are based upon the exclusive use of "up" folds. Check with your bindery before assuming that this folding sequence is correct for your purposes.

**Master Layout
Sheets in
Appendix**

12.5×19/8.5×11/mec/sht/nolip
12.5×19/8.5×11/ss/sht/nolip
12.5×19/8.5×11/pb/sht/nolip
12.5×19/8.5×11/cov/sht/nolip
12.5×19/blank/ss/blank/blank
12.5×19/blank/pb/blank/blank

17×22/8.5×11/mec/sht/nolip

17.5×23/8.5×11/mec/sht/nolip
17.5×23/8.5×11/ss/sht/hilip
17.5×23/8.5×11/ss/sht/lolip
17.5×23/8.5×11/ss/w&t/nolip
17.5×23/8.5×11/ss/per/nolip
17.5×23/8.5×11/pb/sht/nolip
17.5×23/8.5×11/pb/per/nolip
17.5×23/blank/ss/blank/blank
17.5×23/blank/pb/blank/blank

23×35/8.5×11/mec/sht/nolip
23×35/8.5×11/ss/sht/hilip
23×35/8.5×11/ss/sht/lolip
23×35/8.5×11/ss/w&t/nolip
23×35/8.5×11/ss/per/nolip
23×35/8.5×11/pb/sht/nolip
23×35/8.5×11/pb/per/nolip
23×35/blank/ss/blank/blank
23×35/blank/pb/blank/blank

25×38/8.5×11/mec/sht/nolip
25×38/8.5×11/ss/sht/hilip
25×38/8.5×11/ss/sht/lolip
25×38/8.5×11/ss/w&t/nolip
25×38/8.5×11/ss/per/hilip
25×38/8.5×11/pb/sht/nolip
25×38/8.5×11/pb/per/nolip
25×38/8.5×11/cov/sht/nolip
25×38/blank/ss/blank/blank
25×38/blank/pb/blank/blank
25×38/blank/cov/blank/blank

GATF Master Layout Sheets

12.5×19/8.5×11/mec/sht/nolip

Stock information

Press style: Sheetfed
Paper size: 12.5" × 19"
Grain direction:
Weight:
Type:
Color:

Job information

Customer name:
Job number:
Project description:
Signature:
Form shown: *Front*

Imposition information

Page size: 8.5" × 11"
Quantity up: 2 up
Quantity out: 1 out
Binding:
Grind-off/Spine width: n/a
Imposition style: Sheetwise

Comments: *No lip*

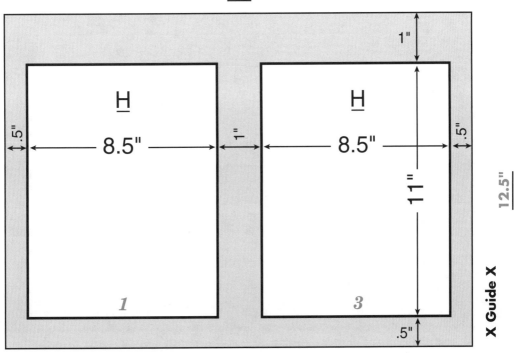

12.5×19/8.5×11/mec/sht/nolip

Signature:
Form shown: *Back*

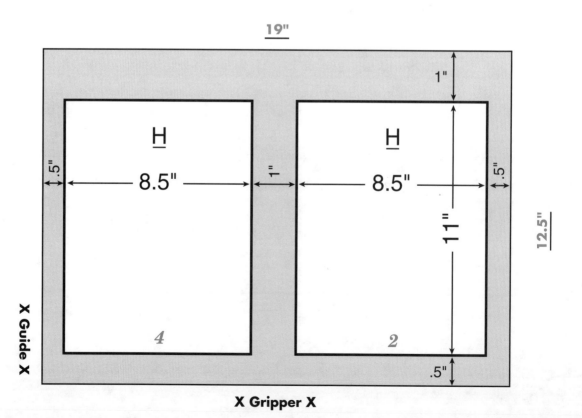

GATF Master Layout Sheets

12.5×19/8.5×11/ss/sht/nolip

Stock information

Press style: Sheetfed
Paper size: 12.5" × 19"
Grain direction: Grain-short
Weight:
Type:
Color:

Imposition information

Page size: 8.5" × 11"
Quantity up: 2 up
Quantity out: 1 out
Binding: Saddle-stitch
Grind-off/Spine width: n/a
Imposition style: Sheetwise

Job information

Customer name:
Job number:
Project description:
Signature:
Form shown: *Front*

Comments: *No lip*

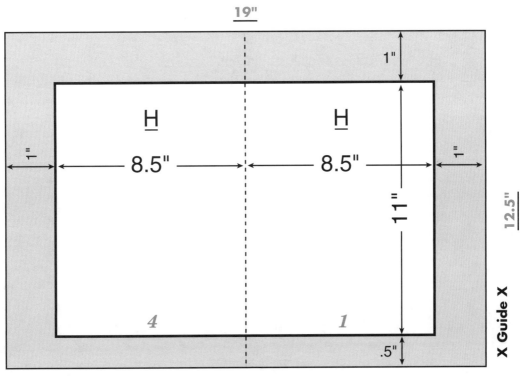

12.5×19/8.5×11/ss/sht/nolip

Signature:
Form shown: *Back*

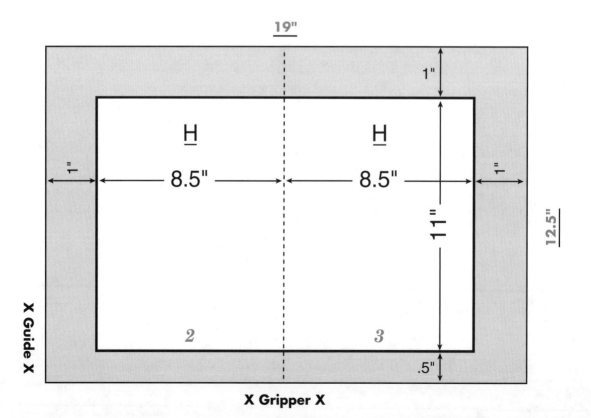

GATF Master Layout Sheets

Stock information

Press style: Sheetfed
Paper size: 12.5" × 19"
Grain direction: Grain-short
Weight:
Type:
Color:

Imposition information

Page size: 8.5" × 11"
Quantity up: 2 up
Quantity out: 1 out
Binding: Perfect-bound
Grind-off/Spine width: .125"
Imposition style: Sheetwise

Job information

Customer name:
Job number:
Project description:
Signature:
Form shown: *Front*

Comments: *No lip*

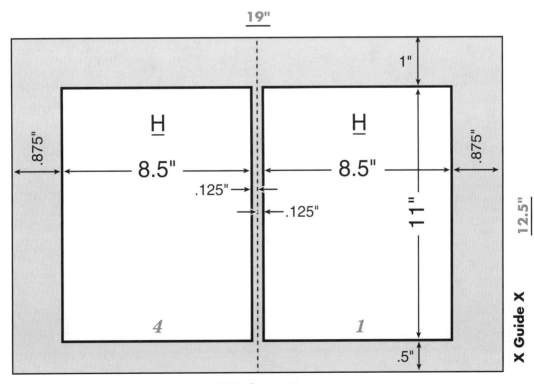

12.5×19/8.5×11/pb/sht/nolip

Signature:
Form shown: *Back*

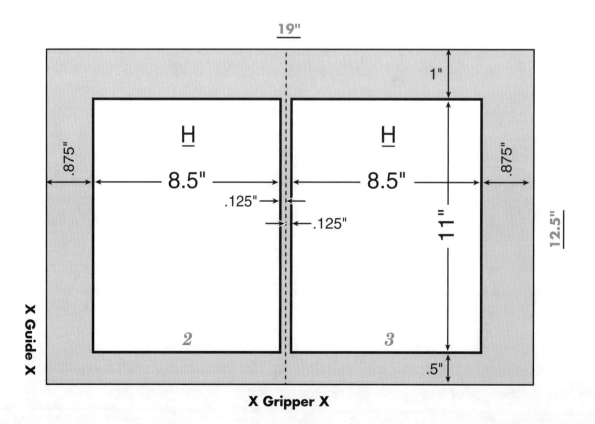

GATF Master Layout Sheets

Stock information

Press style: Sheetfed
Paper size: 12.5" × 19"
Grain direction: Grain-short
Weight:
Type:
Color:

Imposition information

Page size: 8.5" × 11"
Quantity up: 1 up
Quantity out: 1 out
Binding: Perfect-bound cover
Grind-off/Spine width: .25"
Imposition style: Sheetwise

Job information

Customer name:
Job number:
Project description:
Signature:
Form shown: *Front*

Comments: *No lip*

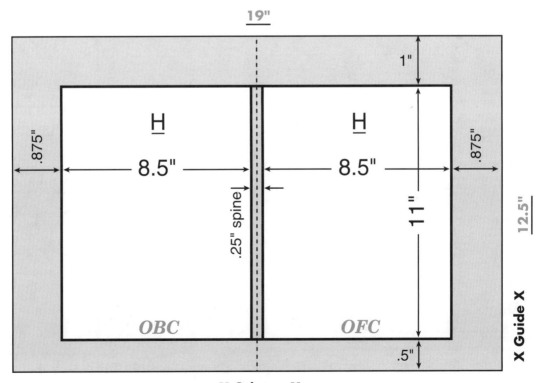

12.5×19/8.5×11/cov/sht/nolip

Signature:
Form shown: ***Back***

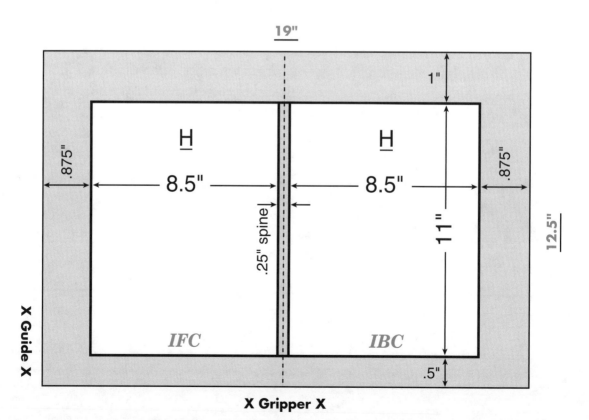

GATF Master Layout Sheets

12.5×19/blank/ss/blank/blank

Stock information

Press style: Sheetfed
Paper size: 12.5" × 19"
Grain direction: Grain-short
Weight:
Type:
Color:

Imposition information

Page size:
Quantity up:
Quantity out:
Binding: Saddle-stitch
Grind-off/Spine width: n/a
Imposition style:

Job information

Customer name:
Job number:
Project description:
Signature:
Form shown:

Comments:

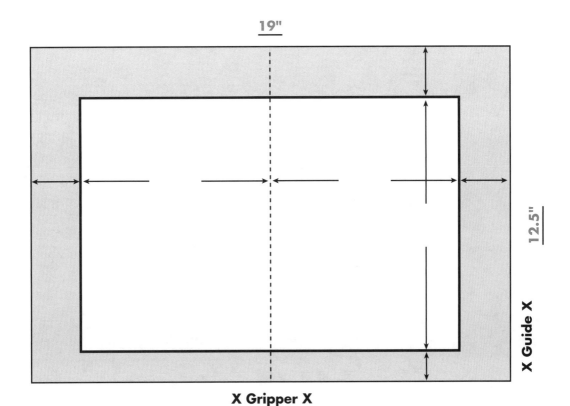

12.5×19/blank/ss/blank/blank

Signature:
Form shown: *Back*

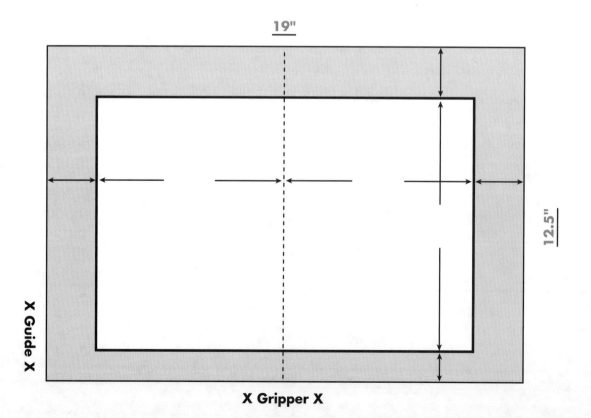

GATF Master Layout Sheets

12.5×19/blank/pb/blank/blank

Stock information

Press style: Sheetfed
Paper size: 12.5" × 19"
Grain direction: Grain-short
Weight:
Type:
Color:

Imposition information

Page size:
Quantity up:
Quantity out:
Binding: Perfect-bound
Grind-off/Spine width: n/a
Imposition style:

Job information

Customer name:
Job number:
Project description:
Signature:
Form shown:

Comments:

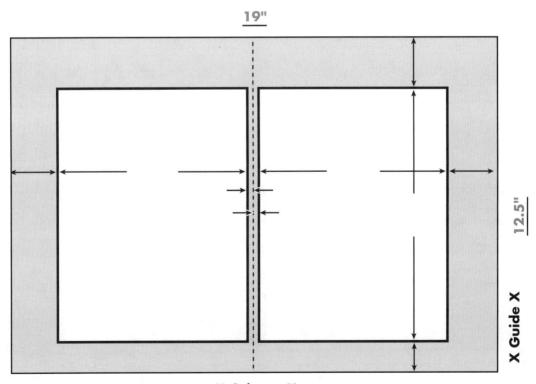

19"

12.5"

X Guide X

X Gripper X

12.5×19/blank/pb/blank/blank

Signature:
Form shown: *Back*

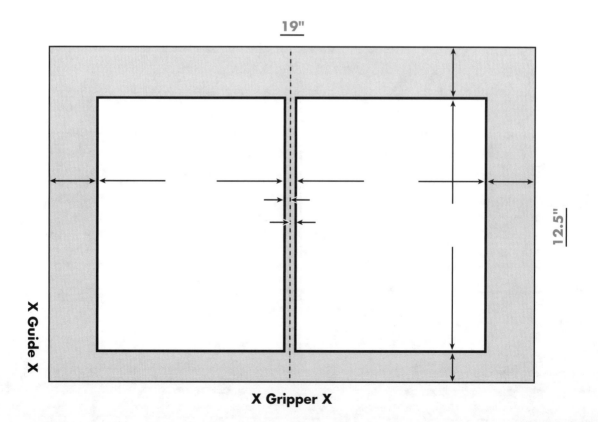

GATF Master Layout Sheets

Stock information

Press style: Sheetfed
Paper size: 17" × 22"
Grain direction:
Weight:
Type:
Color:

Imposition information

Page size: 8.5" × 11"
Quantity up: 1 up
Quantity out: 4 out
Binding:
Grind-off/Spine width: n/a
Imposition style: Sheetwise

Job information

Customer name:
Job number:
Project description:
Signature:
Form shown: *Front*

Comments: *No bleeds*

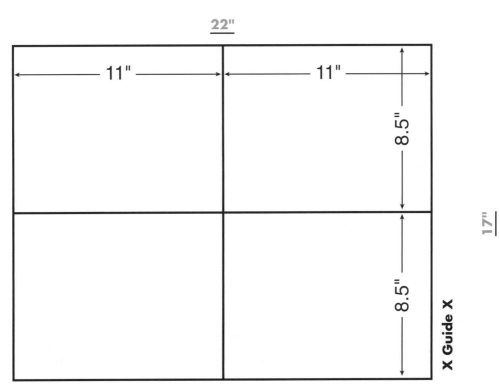

17×22/8.5×11/mec/sht/nolip

Signature:
Form shown: *Back*

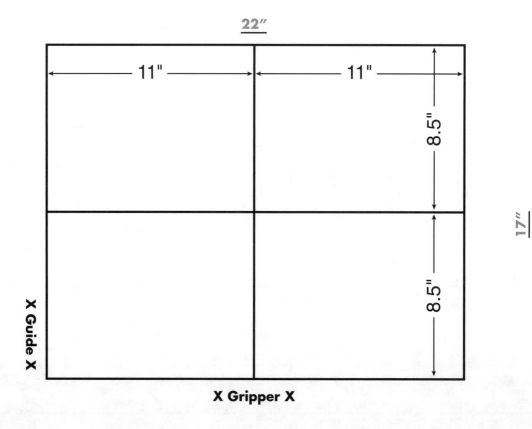

GATF Master Layout Sheets

17.5×23/8.5×11/mec/sht/nolip

Stock information

Press style: Sheetfed
Paper size: 17.5" × 23"
Grain direction: Grain-long
Weight:
Type:
Color:

Imposition information

Page size: 8.5" × 11"
Quantity up: 4 up
Quantity out: 1 out
Binding:
Grind-off/Spine width: n/a
Imposition style: Sheetwise

Job information

Customer name:
Job number:
Project description:
Signature:
Form shown: *Front*

Comments: *No lip*

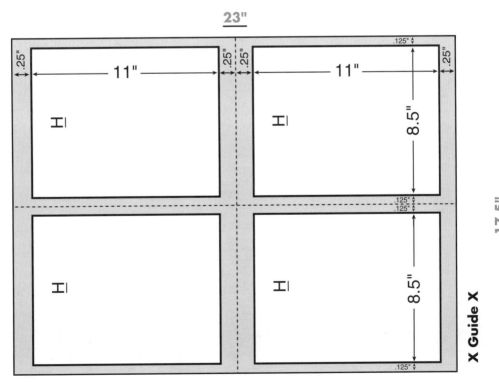

17.5×23/8.5×11/mec/sht/nolip

Signature:
Form shown: *Back*

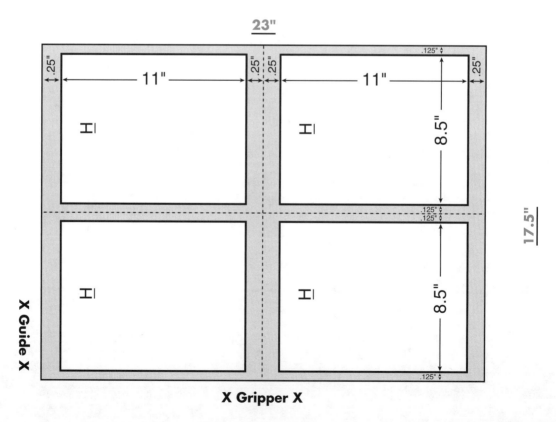

GATF Master Layout Sheets

17.5×23/8.5×11/ss/sht/hilip

Stock information

Press style: Sheetfed
Paper size: 17.5" × 23"
Grain direction: Grain-long
Weight:
Type:
Color:

Imposition information

Page size: 8.5" × 11"
Quantity up: 4 up
Quantity out: 1 out
Binding: Saddle-stitch
Grind-off/Spine width: n/a
Imposition style: Sheetwise

Job information

Customer name:
Job number:
Project description:
Signature:
Form shown: *Front*

Comments: ***High-page lip***

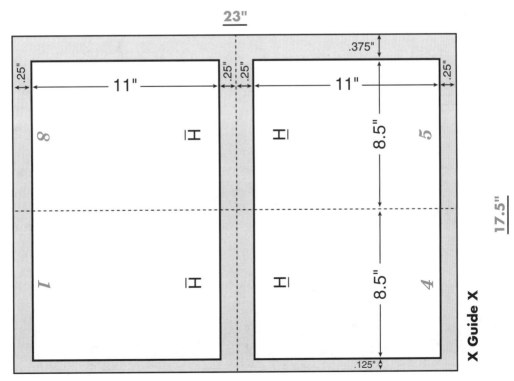

17.5×23/8.5×11/ss/sht/hilip

Signature:
Form shown: *Back*

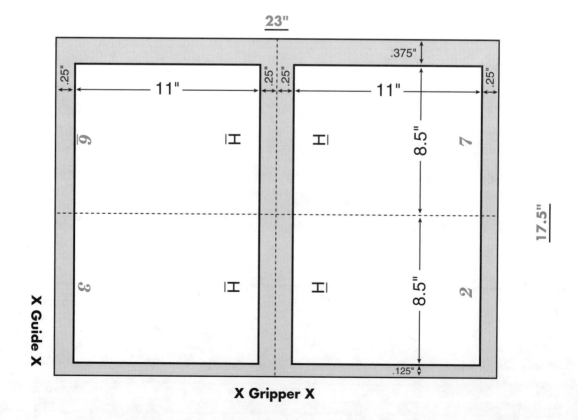

GATF Master Layout Sheets

17.5×23/8.5×11/ss/sht/lolip

Stock information

Press style: Sheetfed
Paper size: 17.5" × 23"
Grain direction: Grain-long
Weight:
Type:
Color:

Imposition information

Page size: 8.5" × 11"
Quantity up: 4 up
Quantity out: 1 out
Binding: Saddle-stitch
Grind-off/Spine width: n/a
Imposition style: Sheetwise

Job information

Customer name:
Job number:
Project description:
Signature:
Form shown: *Front*

Comments: *Low-page lip*

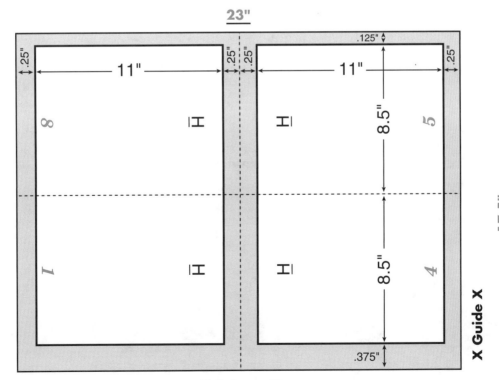

17.5×23/8.5×11/ss/sht/lolip

Signature:
Form shown: *Back*

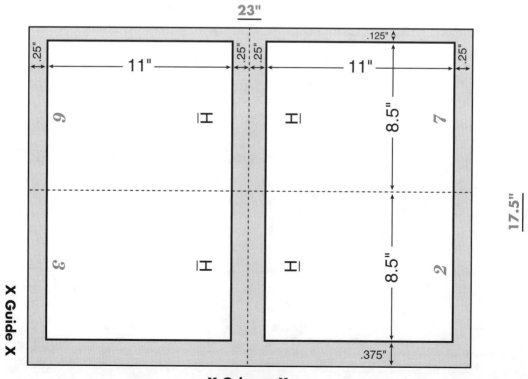

GATF Master Layout Sheets

17.5×23/8.5×11/ss/w&t/nolip

Stock information

Press style: Sheetfed
Paper size: 17.5" × 23"
Grain direction: Grain-long
Weight:
Type:
Color:

Imposition information

Page size: 8.5" × 11"
Quantity up: 2 up
Quantity out: 2 out
Binding: Saddle-stitch
Grind-off/Spine width: n/a
Imposition style: Work & turn

Job information

Customer name:
Job number:
Project description:
Signature:
Form shown: *Work & turn*

Comments: *No lip*

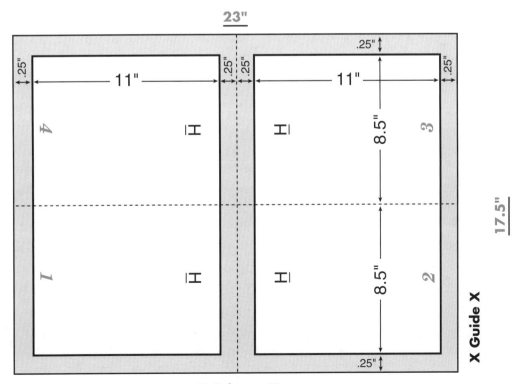

17.5×23/8.5×11/ss/per/nolip

Stock information

Press style: Sheetfed
Paper size: 17.5" × 23"
Grain direction: Grain-long
Weight:
Type:
Color:

Job information

Customer name:
Job number:
Project description:
Signature:
Form shown: *Front*

Imposition information

Page size: 8.5" × 11"
Quantity up: 4 up
Quantity out: 1 out
Binding: Saddle-stitch
Grind-off/Spine width: n/a
Imposition style: Perfecting

Comments: *No lip, perfecting*

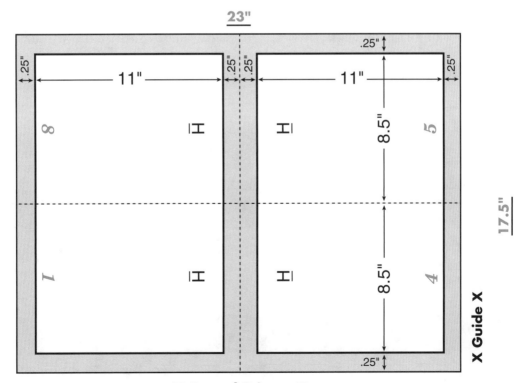

17.5×23/8.5×11/ss/per/nolip

Signature:
Form shown: *Back*

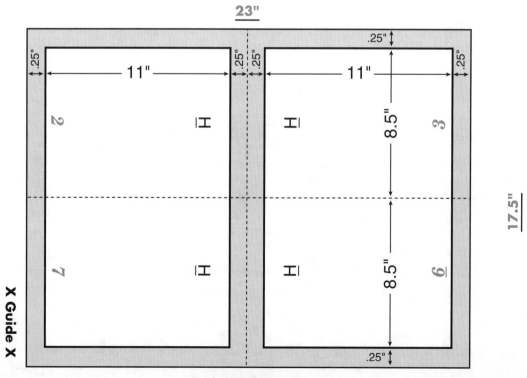

GATF Master Layout Sheets

17.5×23/8.5×11/pb/sht/nolip

Stock information

Press style: Sheetfed
Paper size: 17.5" × 23"
Grain direction: Grain-long
Weight:
Type:
Color:

Imposition information

Page size: 8.5" × 11"
Quantity up: 4 up
Quantity out: 1 out
Binding: Perfect-bound
Grind-off/Spine width: .125"
Imposition style: Sheetwise

Job information

Customer name:
Job number:
Project description:
Signature:
Form shown: *Front*

Comments: *No lip*

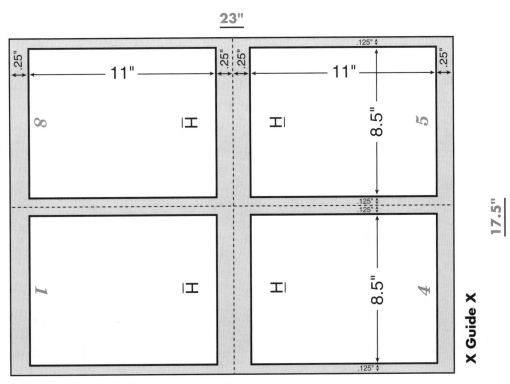

17.5×23/8.5×11/pb/sht/nolip

Signature:
Form shown: ***Back***

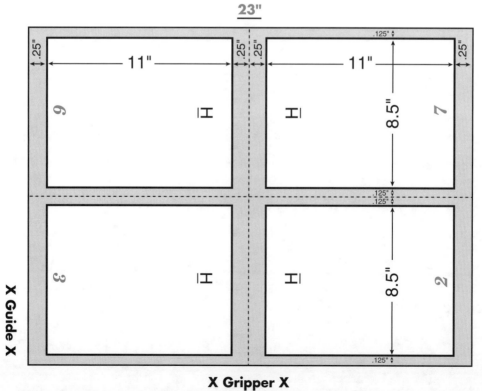

GATF Master Layout Sheets

17.5×23/8.5×11/pb/per/nolip

Stock information

Press style: Sheetfed
Paper size: 17.5" × 23"
Grain direction: Grain-long
Weight:
Type:
Color:

Imposition information

Page size: 8.5" × 11"
Quantity up: 4 up
Quantity out: 1 out
Binding: Perfect-bound
Grind-off/Spine width: .125"
Imposition style: Perfecting

Job information

Customer name:
Job number:
Project description:
Signature:
Form shown: *Front*

Comments: *No lip, perfecting*

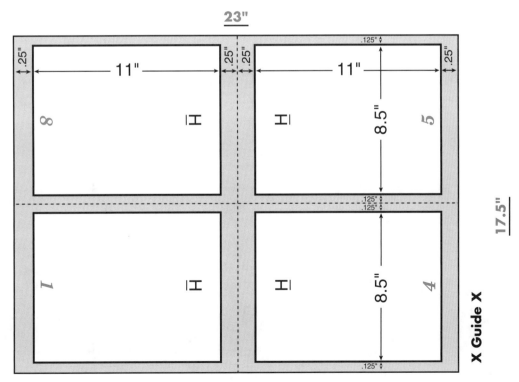

17.5×23/8.5×11/pb/per/nolip

Signature:
Form shown: *Back*

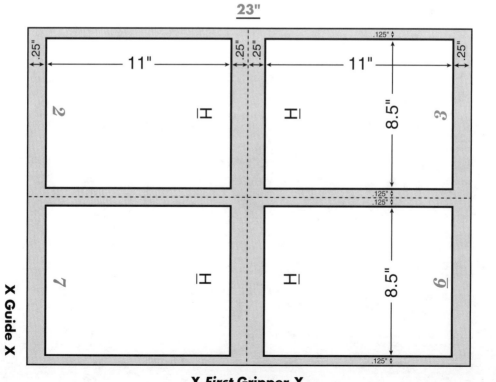

GATF Master Layout Sheets

17.5×23/blank/ss/blank/blank

Stock information

Press style: Sheetfed
Paper size: 17.5" × 23"
Grain direction: Grain-long
Weight:
Type:
Color:

Imposition information

Page size:
Quantity up:
Quantity out:
Binding: Saddle-stitch
Grind-off/Spine width: n/a
Imposition style:

Job information

Customer name:
Job number:
Project description:
Signature:
Form shown:

Comments: *No lip*

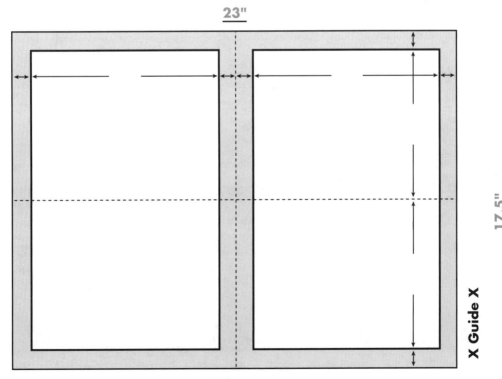

23"

17.5"

X Guide X

X Gripper X

17.5×23/blank/ss/blank/blank

Signature:
Form shown: *Back*

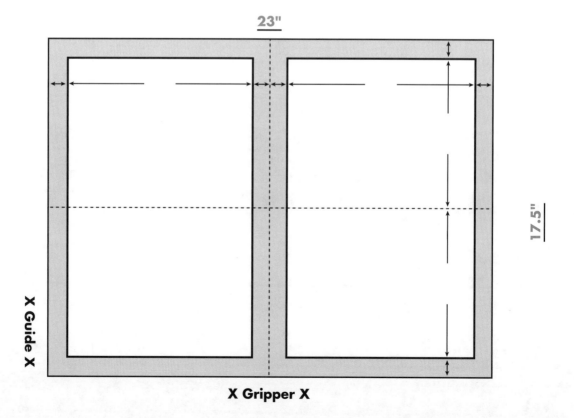

GATF Master Layout Sheets

17.5×23/blank/pb/blank/blank

Stock information

Press style: Sheetfed
Paper size: 17.5" × 23"
Grain direction: Grain-long
Weight:
Type:
Color:

Job information

Customer name:
Job number:
Project description:
Signature:
Form shown: *Front*

Imposition information

Page size:
Quantity up:
Quantity out:
Binding: Perfect-bound
Grind-off/Spine width: .125"
Imposition style:

Comments: *No lip*

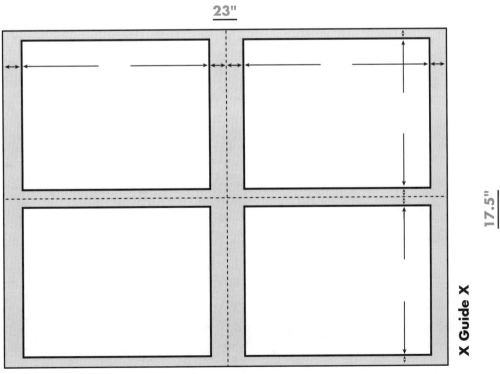

23"

17.5"

X Guide X

X Gripper X

17.5×23/blank/pb/blank/blank

Signature:
Form shown: *Back*

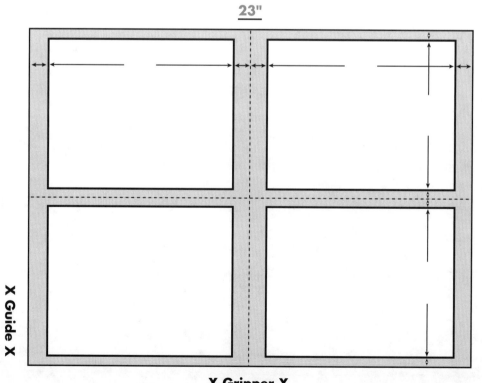

GATF Master Layout Sheets

Stock information

Press style: Sheetfed
Paper size: 23" × 35"
Grain direction: Grain-short
Weight:
Type:
Color:

Imposition information

Page size: 8.5" × 11"
Quantity up: 8 up
Quantity out: 1 out
Binding: Mechanical
Grind-off/Spine width: n/a
Imposition style: Sheetwise

Job information

Customer name:
Job number:
Project description:
Signature:
Form shown: *Front*

Comments: *No lip*

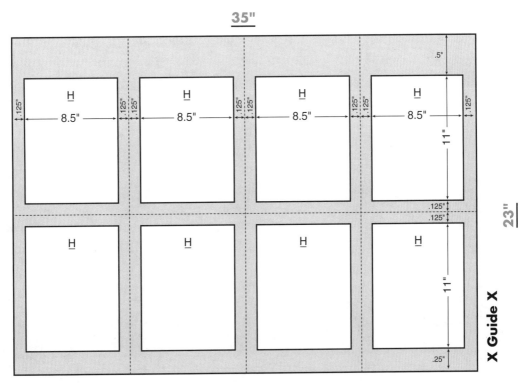

23×35/8.5×11/mec/sht/nolip

Signature:
Form shown: *Back*

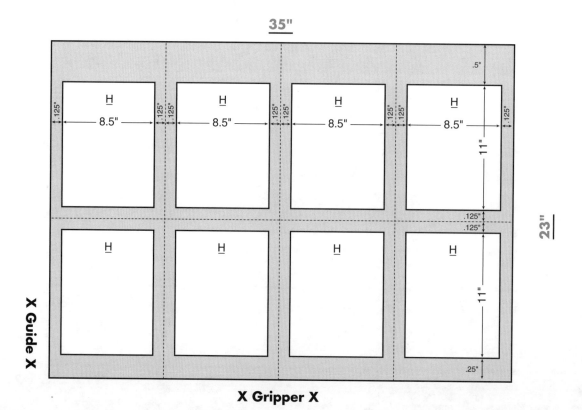

GATF Master Layout Sheets

23×35/8.5×11/ss/sht/hilip

Stock information

Press style: Sheetfed
Paper size: 23" × 35"
Grain direction: Grain-short
Weight:
Type:
Color:

Imposition information

Page size: 8.5" × 11"
Quantity up: 8 up
Quantity out: 1 out
Binding: Saddle-stitch
Grind-off/Spine width: n/a
Imposition style: Sheetwise

Job information

Customer name:
Job number:
Project description:
Signature:
Form shown: *Front*

Comments: ***High-page lip***

35"

1	*16*	*13*	*4*
8.5"	8.5"	8.5"	8.5"
H̄	H̄	H̄	H̄
H	H	H	H
8	9	12	5

.5"
.125"
.375" .375"
.125"
11"
.125"
.125"
11"
.25"

23"

X Guide X

X Gripper X

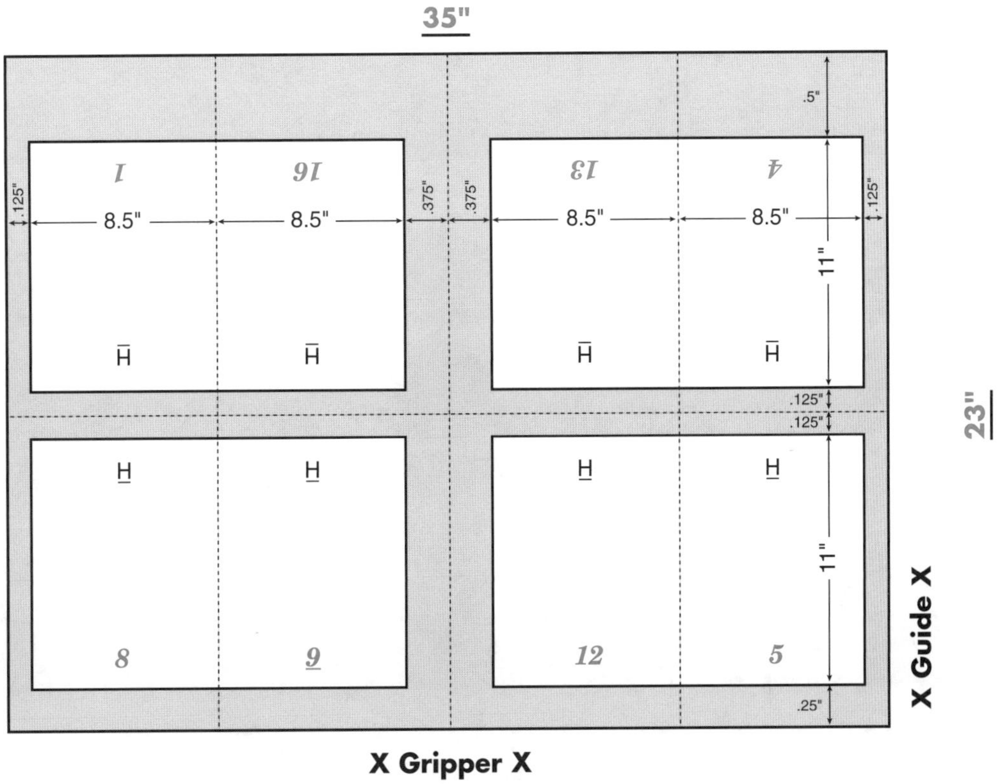

23×35/8.5×11/ss/sht/hilip

Signature:
Form shown: *Back*

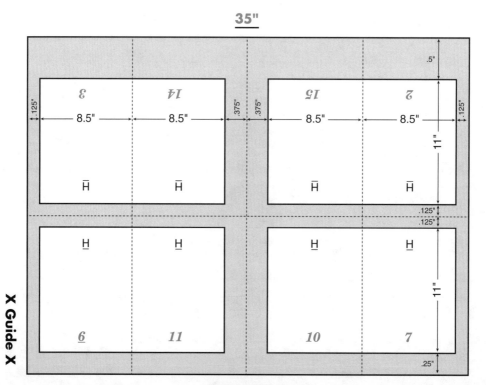

GATF Master Layout Sheets

23×35/8.5×11/ss/sht/lolip

Stock information

Press style: Sheetfed
Paper size: 23" × 35"
Grain direction: Grain-short
Weight:
Type:
Color:

Job information

Customer name:
Job number:
Project description:
Signature:
Form shown: *Front*

Imposition information

Page size: 8.5" × 11"
Quantity up: 8 up
Quantity out: 1 out
Binding: Saddle-stitch
Grind-off/Spine width: n/a
Imposition style: Sheetwise

Comments: *Low-page lip*

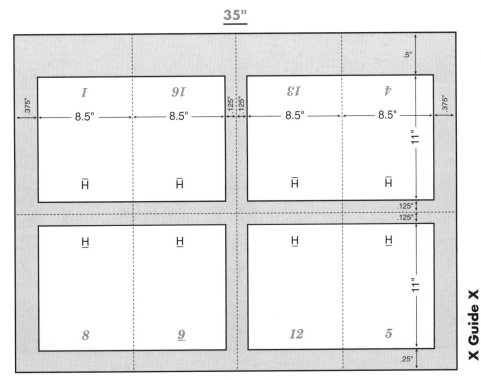

23×35/8.5×11/ss/sht/lolip

Signature:
Form shown: *Back*

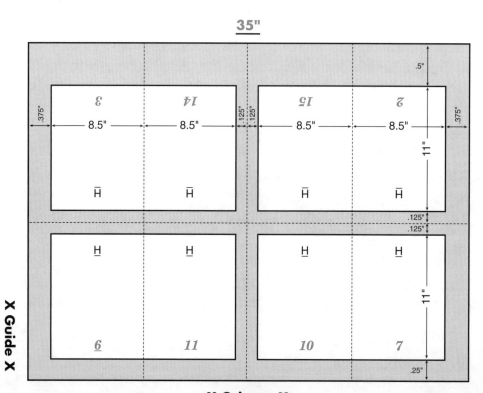

GATF Master Layout Sheets

23×35/8.5×11/ss/w&t/nolip

Stock information

Press style: Sheetfed
Paper size: 23" × 35"
Grain direction: Grain-short
Weight:
Type:
Color:

Job information

Customer name:
Job number:
Project description:
Signature:
Form shown: ***Work & turn***

Imposition information

Page size: 8.5" × 11"
Quantity up: 4 up
Quantity out: 2 out
Binding: Saddle-stitch
Grind-off/Spine width: n/a
Imposition style: Work & turn

Comments: ***No lip***

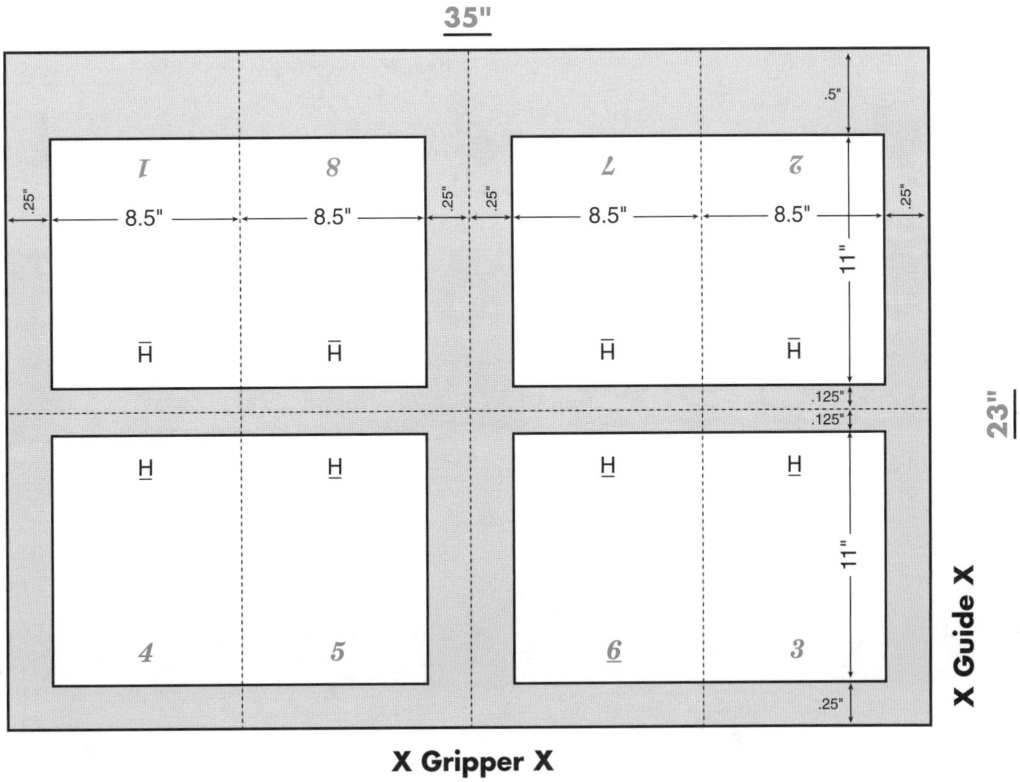

GATF Master Layout Sheets

Stock information

Press style: Sheetfed
Paper size: 23" × 35"
Grain direction: Grain-short
Weight:
Type:
Color:

Imposition information

Page size: 8.5" × 11"
Quantity up: 8 up
Quantity out: 1 out
Binding: Saddle-stitch
Grind-off/Spine width: n/a
Imposition style: Perfecting

Job information

Customer name:
Job number:
Project description:
Signature:
Form shown: *Front*

Comments: *No lip, perfecting*

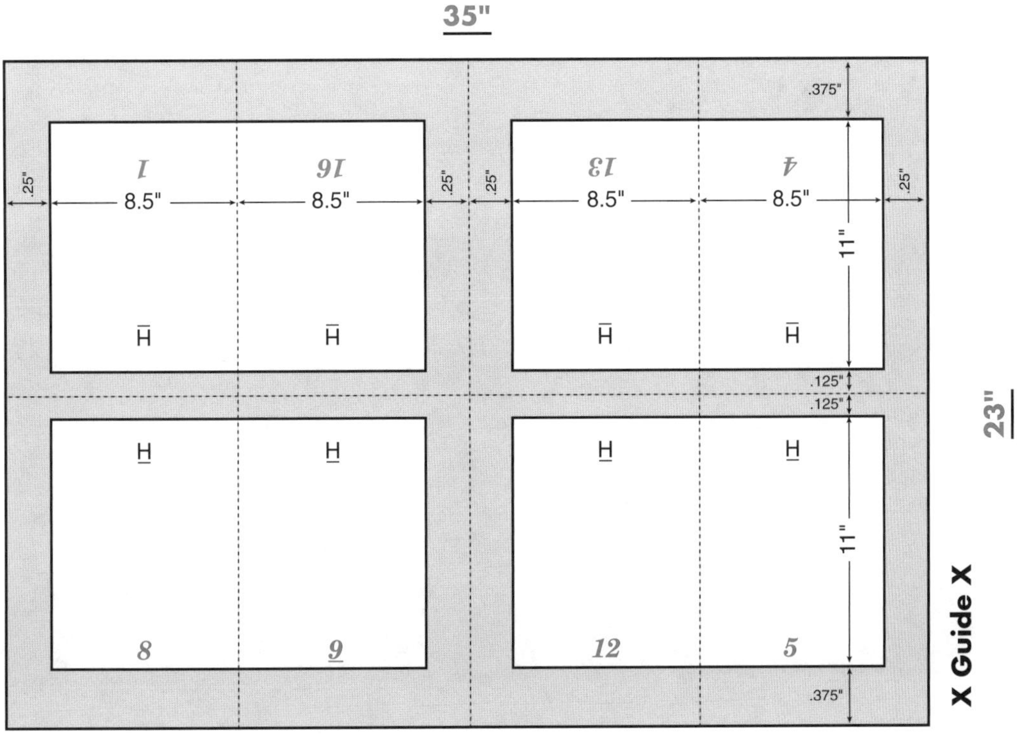

35"

X Guide X

X *Second* Gripper X

23×35/8.5×11/ss/per/nolip

Signature:
Form shown: ***Back***

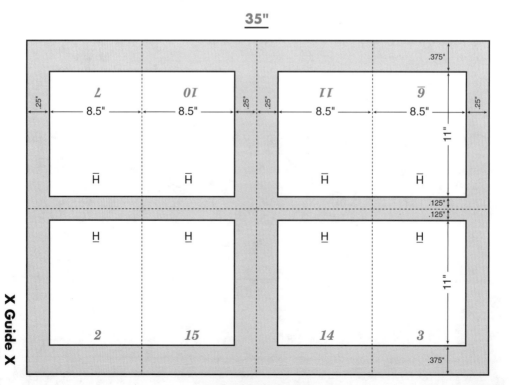

23×35/8.5×11/pb/sht/nolip

Stock information

Press style: Sheetfed
Paper size: 23" × 35"
Grain direction: Grain-short
Weight:
Type:
Color:

Imposition information

Page size: 8.5" × 11"
Quantity up: 8 up
Quantity out: 1 out
Binding: Perfect-bound
Grind-off/Spine width: .125"
Imposition style: Sheetwise

Job information

Customer name:
Job number:
Project description:
Signature:
Form shown: *Front*

Comments: *No lip*

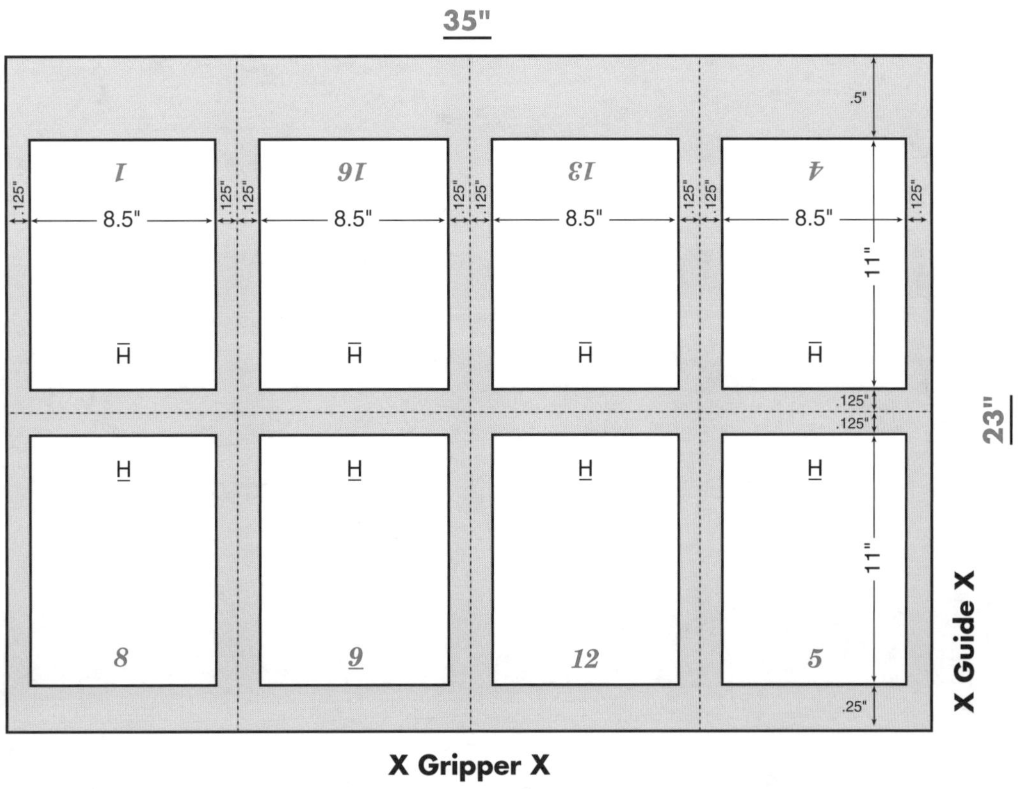

35"

.125"	I	16	13	4	.5"

8.5" 8.5" 8.5" 8.5"

.125" .125" .125" .125" .125" .125" .125" .125"

H̄ H̄ H̄ H̄

11"

.125"
.125"

H H H H

11"

8 9 12 5

.25"

23"

X Guide X

X Gripper X

23×35/8.5×11/pb/sht/nolip

Signature:
Form shown: *Back*

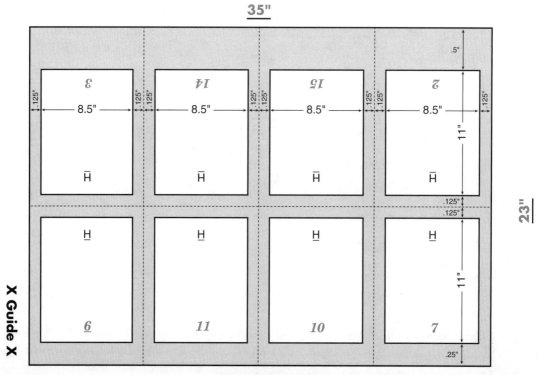

GATF Master Layout Sheets

23×35/8.5×11/pb/per/nolip

Stock information

Press style: Sheetfed
Paper size: 23" × 35"
Grain direction: Grain-short
Weight:
Type:
Color:

Imposition information

Page size: 8.5" × 11"
Quantity up: 8 up
Quantity out: 1 out
Binding: Perfect-bound
Grind-off/Spine width: .125"
Imposition style: Perfecting

Job information

Customer name:
Job number:
Project description:
Signature:
Form shown: *Front*

Comments: *No lip, perfecting*

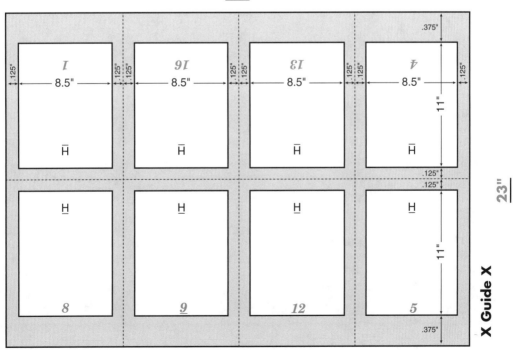

23×35/8.5×11/pb/per/nolip

Signature:
Form shown: ***Back***

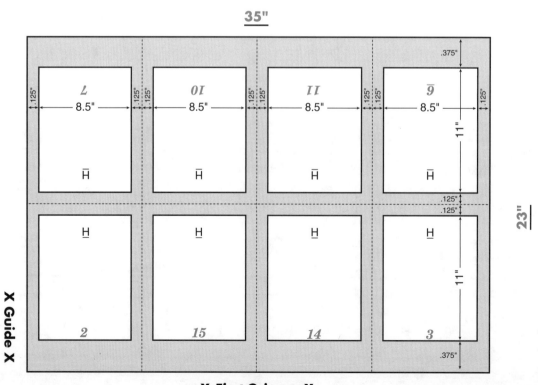

GATF Master Layout Sheets

23×35/blank/ss/blank/blank

Stock information

Press style: Sheetfed
Paper size: 23" × 35"
Grain direction: Grain-short
Weight:
Type:
Color:

Imposition information

Page size:
Quantity up:
Quantity out:
Binding: Saddle-stitch
Grind-off/Spine width: n/a
Imposition style:

Job information

Customer name:
Job number:
Project description:
Signature:
Form shown:

Comments:

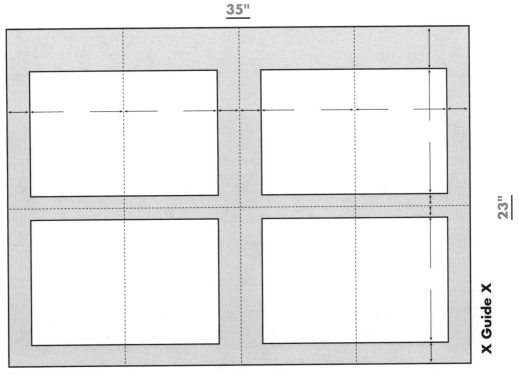

35"

23"

X Guide X

X Gripper X

23×35/blank/ss/blank/blank

Signature:
Form shown: *Back*

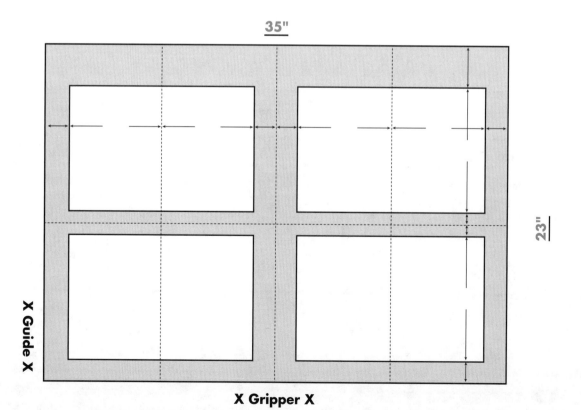

GATF Master Layout Sheets

23×35/blank/pb/blank/blank

Stock information

Press style: Sheetfed
Paper size: 23" × 35"
Grain direction: Grain-short
Weight:
Type:
Color:

Imposition information

Page size:
Quantity up:
Quantity out:
Binding: Perfect-bound
Grind-off/Spine width: n/a
Imposition style:

Job information

Customer name:
Job number:
Project description:
Signature:
Form shown:

Comments:

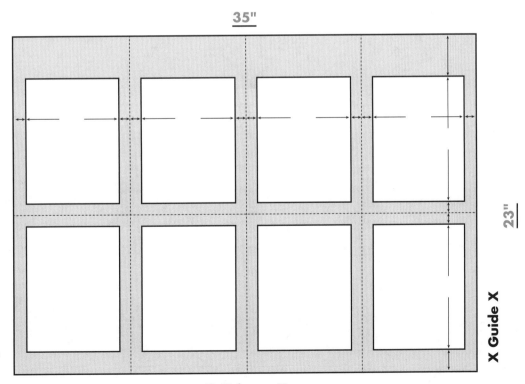

35"

23"

X Guide X

X Gripper X

23×35/blank/pb/blank/blank

Signature:
Form shown: *Back*

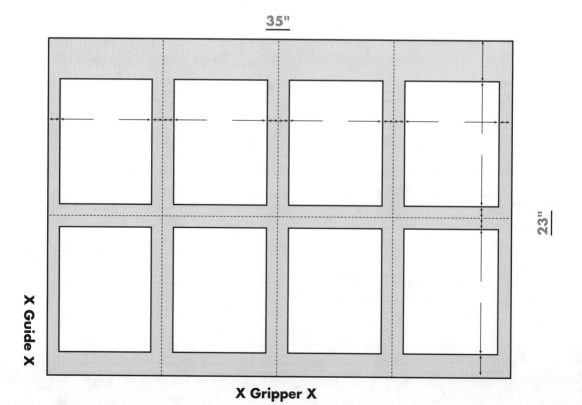

GATF Master Layout Sheets

25×38/8.5×11/mec/sht/nolip

Stock information

Press style: Sheetfed
Paper size: 25" × 38"
Grain direction: Grain-short
Weight:
Type:
Color:

Imposition information

Page size: 8.5" × 11"
Quantity up: 8 up
Quantity out: 1 out
Binding: Mechanical
Grind-off/Spine width: n/a
Imposition style: Sheetwise

Job information

Customer name:
Job number:
Project description:
Signature:
Form shown: ***Front***

Comments: ***No lip***

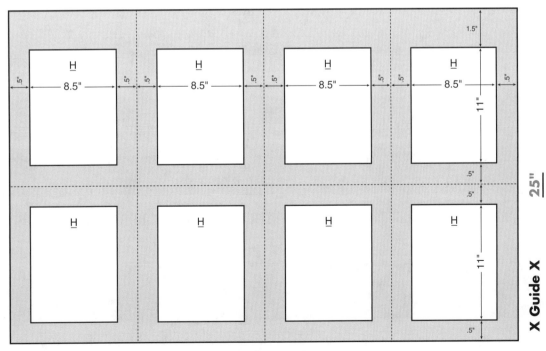

25×38/8.5×11/mec/sht/nolip

Signature:
Form shown: *Back*

GATF Master Layout Sheets

Stock information

Press style: Sheetfed
Paper size: 25" × 38"
Grain direction: Grain-short
Weight:
Type:
Color:

Imposition information

Page size: 8.5" × 11"
Quantity up: 8 up
Quantity out: 1 out
Binding: Saddle-stitch
Grind-off/Spine width: n/a
Imposition style: Sheetwise

Job information

Customer name:
Job number:
Project description:
Signature:
Form shown: *Front*

Comments: *High-page lip*

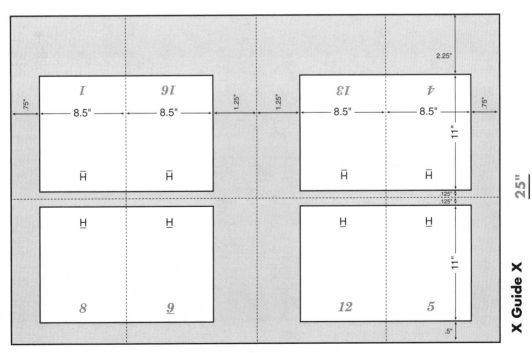

25×38/8.5×11/ss/sht/hilip

Signature:
Form shown: *Back*

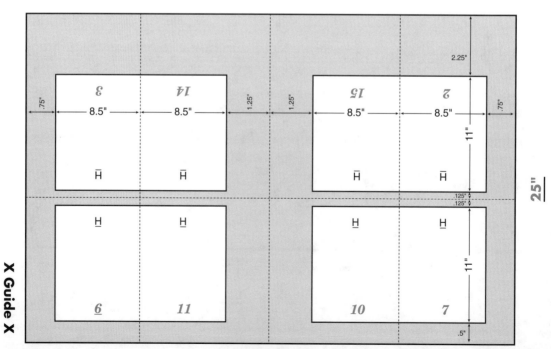

GATF Master Layout Sheets

25×38/8.5×11/ss/sht/lolip

Stock information

Press style: Sheetfed
Paper size: 25" × 38"
Grain direction: Grain-short
Weight:
Type:
Color:

Imposition information

Page size: 8.5" × 11"
Quantity up: 8 up
Quantity out: 1 out
Binding: Saddle-stitch
Grind-off/Spine width: n/a
Imposition style: Sheetwise

Job information

Customer name:
Job number:
Project description:
Signature:
Form shown: *Front*

Comments: ***Low-page lip***

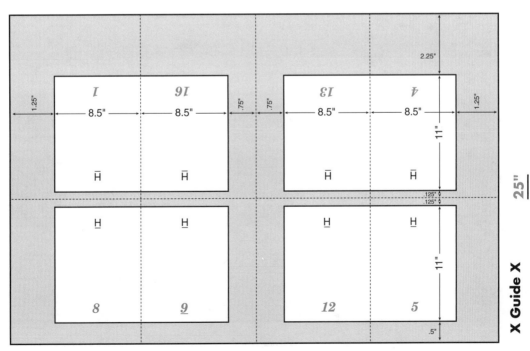

25×38/8.5×11/ss/sht/lolip

Signature:
Form shown: ***Back***

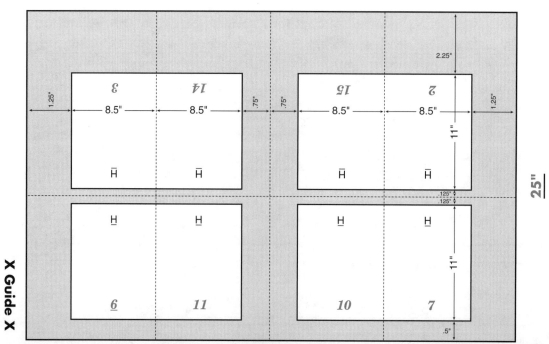

GATF Master Layout Sheets

25×38/8.5×11/ss/w&t/nolip

Stock information

Press style: Sheetfed
Paper size: 25" × 38"
Grain direction: Grain-short
Weight:
Type:
Color:

Imposition information

Page size: 8.5" × 11"
Quantity up: 8 up
Quantity out: 1 out
Binding: Saddle-stitch
Grind-off/Spine width: n/a
Imposition style: Work and turn

Job information

Customer name:
Job number:
Project description:
Signature:
Form shown: *Work and turn*

Comments: *No lip*

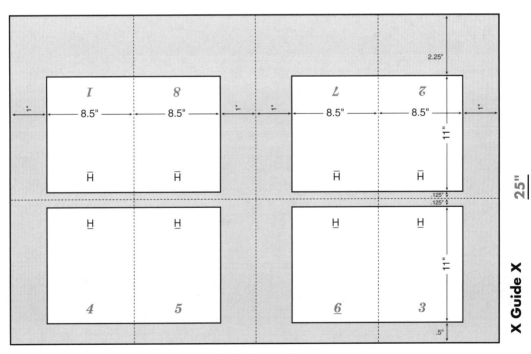

GATF Master Layout Sheets

25×38/8.5×11/ss/per/hilip

Stock information

Press style: Sheetfed
Paper size: 25" × 38"
Grain direction: Grain-short
Weight:
Type:
Color:

Imposition information

Page size: 8.5" × 11"
Quantity up: 8 up
Quantity out: 1 out
Binding: Saddle-stitch
Grind-off/Spine width: n/a
Imposition style: Perfecting

Job information

Customer name:
Job number:
Project description:
Signature:
Form shown: *Front*

Comments: ***High-page lip, perfecting***

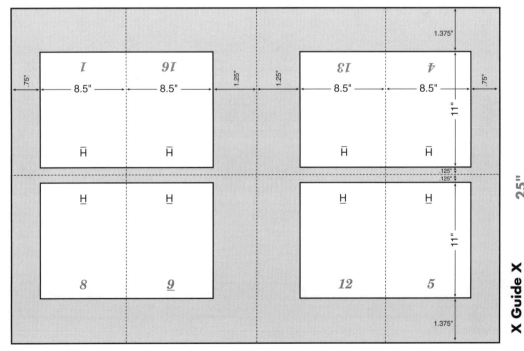

25×38/8.5×11/ss/per/hilip

Signature:
Form shown: *Back*

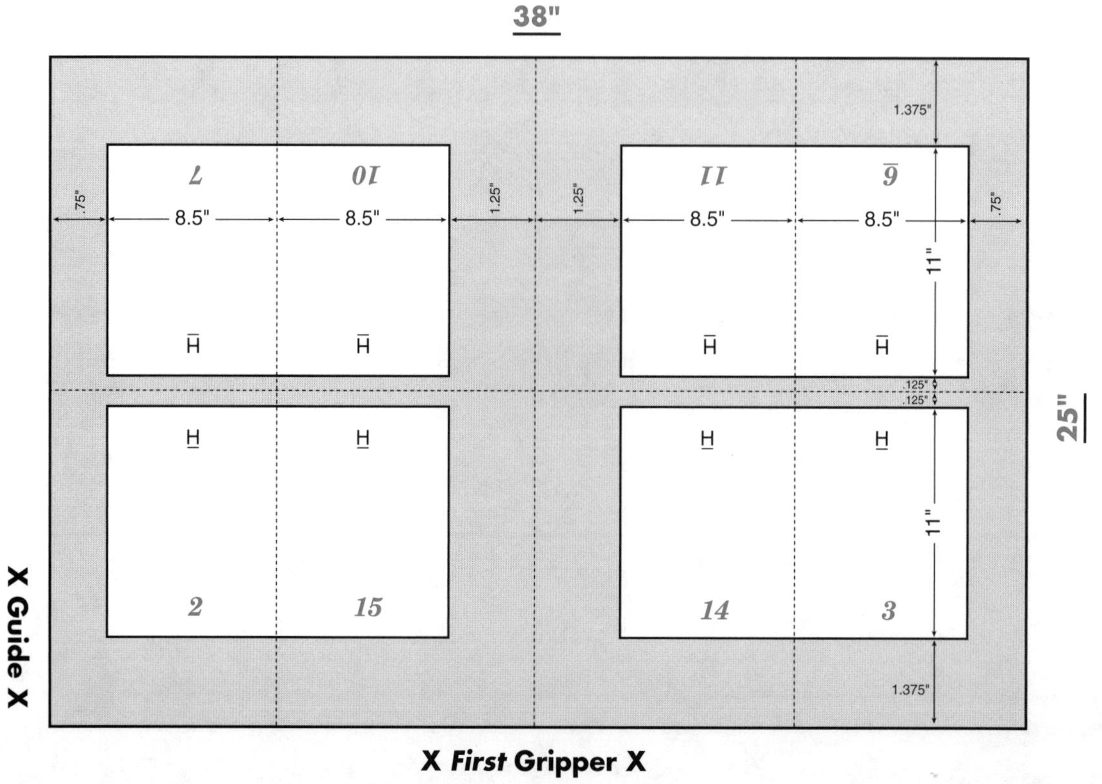

GATF Master Layout Sheets

25×38/8.5×11/pb/sht/nolip

Stock information

Press style: Sheetfed
Paper size: 25" × 38"
Grain direction: Grain-short
Weight:
Type:
Color:

Job information

Customer name:
Job number:
Project description:
Signature:
Form shown: *Front*

Imposition information

Page size: 8.5" × 11"
Quantity up: 8 up
Quantity out: 1 out
Binding: Perfect-bound
Grind-off/Spine width: n/a
Imposition style: Sheetwise

Comments: *No lip*

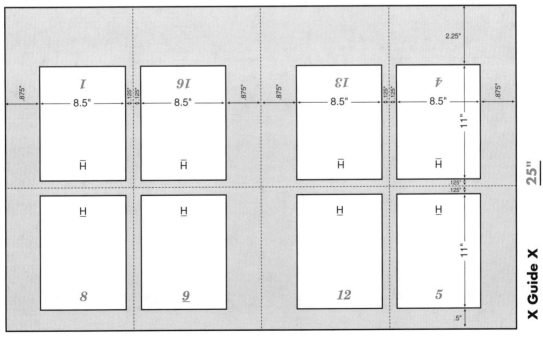

25×38/8.5×11/pb/sht/nolip

Signature:
Form shown: *Back*

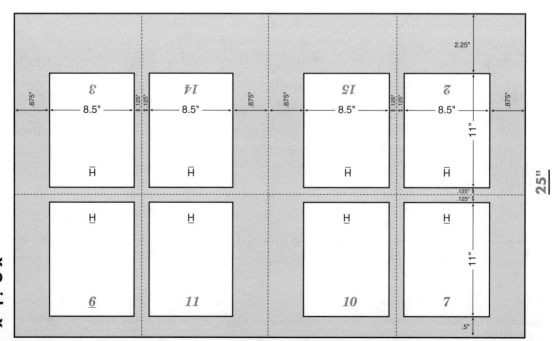

GATF Master Layout Sheets

25×38/8.5×11/pb/per/nolip

Stock information

Press style: Sheetfed
Paper size: 25" × 38"
Grain direction: Grain-short
Weight:
Type:
Color:

Job information

Customer name:
Job number:
Project description:
Signature:
Form shown: *Front*

Imposition information

Page size: 8.5" × 11"
Quantity up: 8 up
Quantity out: 1 out
Binding: Perfect-bound
Grind-off/Spine width: n/a
Imposition style: Perfecting

Comments: *No lip, perfecting*

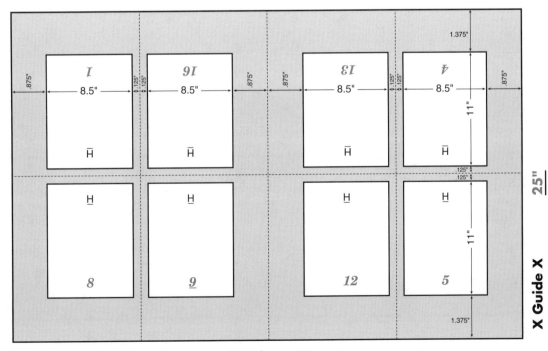

25×38/8.5×11/pb/per/nolip

Signature:
Form shown: ***Back***

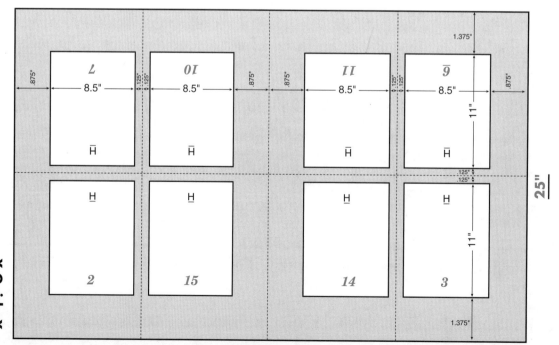

GATF Master Layout Sheets

25×38/8.5×11/cov/sht/nolip

Stock information

Press style: Sheetfed
Paper size: 25" × 38"
Grain direction: Grain-short
Weight:
Type:
Color:

Imposition information

Page size: 8.5" × 11"
Quantity up: 1 up
Quantity out: 4 out
Binding: Perfect-bound cover
Grind-off/Spine width: .25"
Imposition style: Sheetwise

Job information

Customer name:
Job number:
Project description:
Signature:
Form shown: *Front*

Comments: *No lip*

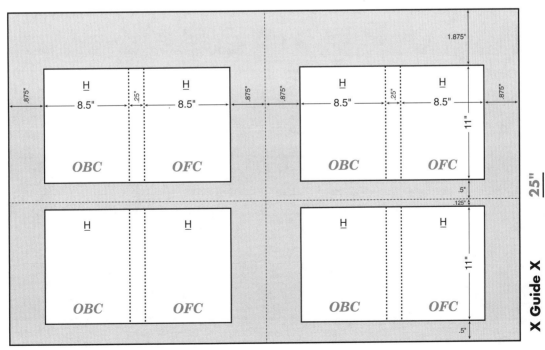

25×38/8.5×11/cov/sht/nolip

Signature:
Form shown: ***Back***

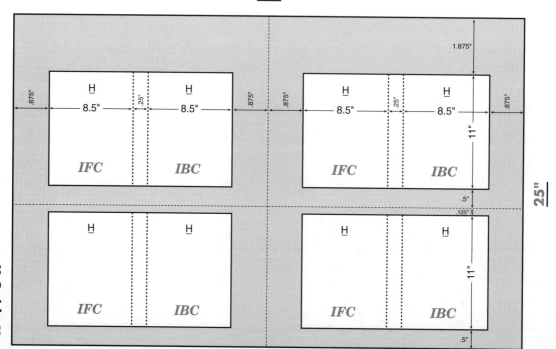

GATF Master Layout Sheets

25×38/blank/ss/blank/blank

Stock information

Press style: Sheetfed
Paper size: 25" × 38"
Grain direction: Grain-short
Weight:
Type:
Color:

Imposition information

Page size:
Quantity up:
Quantity out:
Binding: Saddle-stitch
Grind-off/Spine width: n/a
Imposition style:

Job information

Customer name:
Job number:
Project description:
Signature:
Form shown:

Comments:

38"

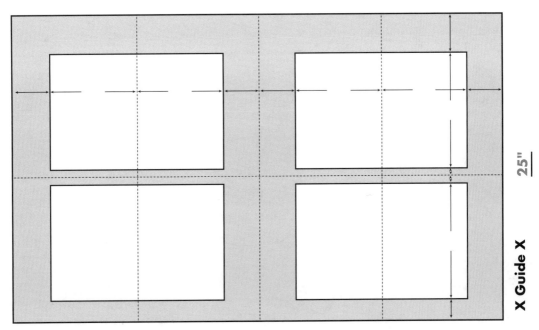

25"

X Guide X

X Gripper X

25×38/blank/ss/blank/blank

Signature:
Form shown: *Back*

38"

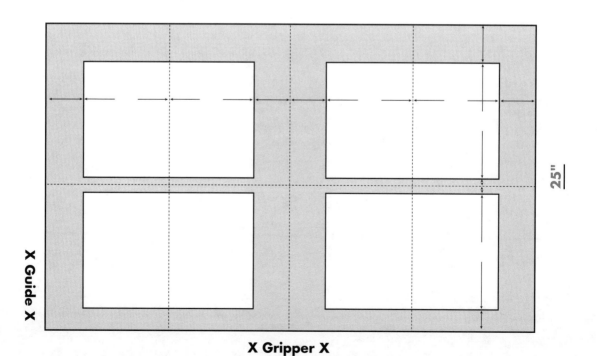

25"

X Guide X

X Gripper X

GATF Master Layout Sheets

25×38/blank/pb/blank/blank

Stock information

Press style: Sheetfed
Paper size: 25" × 38"
Grain direction: Grain-short
Weight:
Type:
Color:

Imposition information

Page size:
Quantity up:
Quantity out:
Binding: Perfect-bound
Grind-off/Spine width: .125"
Imposition style:

Job information

Customer name:
Job number:
Project description:
Signature:
Form shown:

Comments:

38"

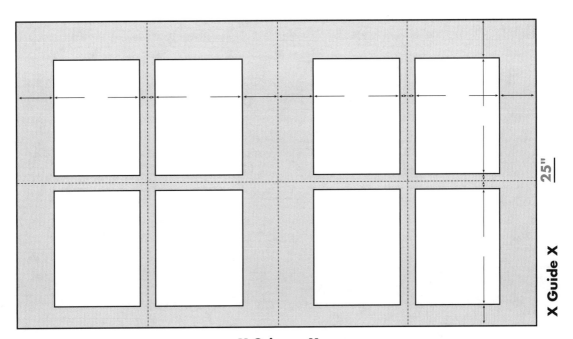

25"

X Guide X

X Gripper X

25×38/blank/pb/blank/blank

Signature:
Form shown: *Back*

38"

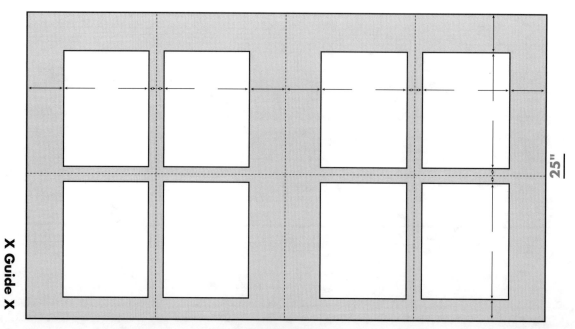

X Guide X

X Gripper X

25"

GATF Master Layout Sheets

Stock information

Press style: Sheetfed
Paper size: 25" × 38"
Grain direction: Grain-short
Weight:
Type:
Color:

Job information

Customer name:
Job number:
Project description:
Signature:
Form shown:

Imposition information

Page size:
Quantity up:
Quantity out:
Binding: Perfect-bound cover
Grind-off/Spine width:
Imposition style:

Comments:

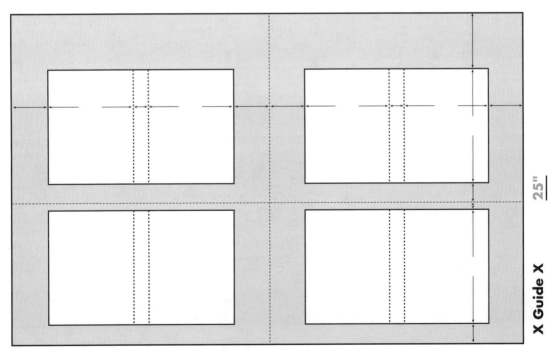

38"

25"

X Guide X

X Gripper X

25×38/blank/cov/blank/blank

Signature:
Form shown: *Back*

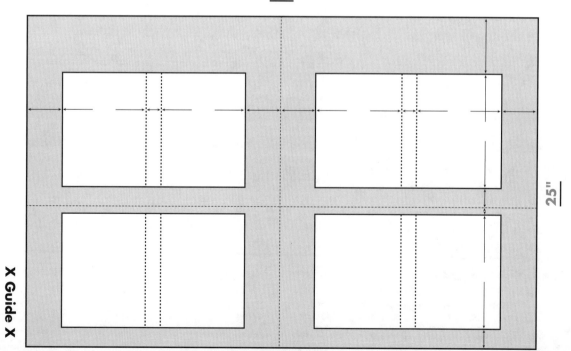

B   Vendor Addresses

BARCO Graphics
721 Crossroads Court
Vandalia, OH 45377
Phone: 937/454-1721
Fax: 937/454-1522
http://www.barco.com/graphics

Contex Prepress Systems
30 New Crossing Road
Reading, MA 01867-3254
Phone: 781/756-4400
Fax: 781/756-4310
http://www.contex.com

Cortron
7855 Ranchers Road
Minneapolis, MN 55432
Phone: 612/572-1555
Fax: 612/572-0364
http://www.cortron.com

DK&A PrePress Inc.
1010 Turquoise Street, Suite 300
San Diego, CA 92109
Phone: 800/598-8118
Fax: 619/488-9418
http://www.dka.com

Dynagram Software
881 De Saint-Vallier Est
Québec, QB G1K 3P9, Canada
Phone: 800/465-9857
Fax: 418/694-2048
http://www.dynagram.com

Farrukh Systems Limited
Clarendon House
125 Shenley Road
Borehamwood, Herts, UK
WD6 1AG
Phone: 011-44-181-207-4249
Toll-free from the U.S.:
    800-601-6907
Fax: 011-44-181-207-5992
http://www.farrukh.co.uk

Heidelberg Prepress
1000 Gutenberg Drive
Kennesaw, GA 30144
Phone: 516/821-7292
http://www.heidelbergusa.com/
    prepress

Imation Publishing Software
    Corp.
1011 Western Avenue, Suite 900
Seattle, WA 98104
Phone: 206/689-6700
Fax: 206/689-6702
http://ips.imation.com

Krause America
36 Park Drive East
Branford, CT 06405
Phone: 203/483-9883
Fax: 203/483-5486
http://www.krause-america.com

OneVision, Inc.
438 Division Street
Sewickley, PA 15143
Phone: 412/741-4811
http://www.one-vision.com

Quite Software Ltd.
105 Ridley Road
Forest Gate
London UK E7 0LX
Phone: 011-44-181-257-1044
Fax: 011-44-181-522-1726
http://www.quite.com

ScenicSoft
11400 Airport Road
Everett, WA 98204
Phone: 425/355-6655
Fax: 425/355-6898
http://www.scenicsoft.com

Scitex America Corp.
Eight Oak Park Drive
Bedford, MA 01730
Phone: 617/275-5150
Fax: 617/275-3430
http://www.scitex.com

Ultimate Technographics Inc.
One Westmount Square,
    Suite 1700
Montreal, QB H3Z 2P9, Canada
Phone: 514/938-9050
Fax: 514/938-5225
http://www.ultimate-tech.com

Glossary

accordion fold
Two or more folds parallel to each other with adjacent folds in opposite directions, resembling the bellows of an accordion. Alternative term: *fanfold*.

acetate
Clear plastic sheeting used to prepare overlays or used as a base for stripping films.

adhesive binding
Applying a glue or another, usually hot-melt, substance along the backbone edges of assembled, printed sheets. The book or magazine cover is applied directly on top of the tacky adhesive. Alternative term: *perfect binding*.

Adobe Acrobat
A popular software program for the conversion of documents into the portable document file (PDF) format. Through Acrobat or another PDF, users can read electronic versions of printed documents that maintain the attributes (bold and italic type and other formatting choices) assigned to a printed original.

album binding
To enclose and cover a document on the short side of a page instead of in the more common method of binding upright on the long side of the page. Alternative term: *oblong binding*.

alley
The spaces between tabular copy.

apron
A blank space at the edge of a foldout that permits the sheet to be folded and tipped in the finishing process without marring the copy.

argon-ion laser
A laser light source in which argon-ion gas is stimulated to produce a monochromatic blue-green beam of light that is used to expose images onto orthochromatic or blue-sensitive photographic film, paper, or electrostatic printing plates.

art knife
A tool with a small, sharp blade used for lightly cutting tracing paper, screen printing stencil films, and other materials. The most popular tool of this type is the X-Acto™ knife.

artwork
A general term for photographs, drawings, paintings, and other materials prepared to illustrate printed matter.

assembling
Collecting individual sheets or signatures into a complete set with pages in proper sequence and alignment. Assembling is followed by binding.

author's alterations (AA)
Changes requested by the author or author's representative after the original copy has been typeset. Alternative terms: *author's corrections; artist's alterations.*

automatic picture replacement
Computer technology that enables the operator to replace for-position-only artwork with the actual images that will be used during printing.

back margin
The distance between the fold edge and the edge of the body of the type (text matter) next to the fold. Alternative terms: *binding margin, gutter margin.*

back matter
Material printed at the end of a book, including the appendix, addenda, glossary, index, and bibliography. Alternative term: *end matter.*

backbone
The portion of a bound book that connects the front and back covers. Alternative term: *spine.*

backing up
Printing the reverse side of a sheet that has already been printed.

backup register
Correct relative position of the printing on one side of the sheet or web and the printing on the other side.

banding
An electronic prepress term referring to visible steps in shades of a gradient.

base density
The small-value nonimage-area optical density of a transparent base after the photographic material has been exposed and processed. It consists of the density of the base material plus any overall slight fogging of the base by the photographic process or other influence.

basis weight	The weight in pounds of a ream (500 sheets) of paper cut to its basic size in inches. Some basic sizes include 25×38 in. for book papers, 20×26 in. for cover papers, 22.5×28.5 in. or 22.5×35 in. for bristol, and 25.5×30.5 in. for index. For example, 500 sheets of 25×38-in., 80-lb. coated paper will weigh eighty pounds.
bindery	A facility where finishing operations such as folding, joining signatures, and covering are performed.
binding	Joining the assembled pages of a printed piece together. Binding takes many forms including saddle-stitching, adhesive binding, mechanical binding, loose-leaf binding, and Smyth sewing.
binding, mechanical	Clasping individual sheets together with plastic, small wire, or metal rings. Two examples are three-ring binding and spiral binding.
binding dummy	Blank pages of assembled signatures stitched and trimmed to show the amount of compensation needed for creep.
binding lap, low folio	Approximately ⅜ in. (10 mm) of extra paper on the low page number (folio) side of a folded signature, as required for mechanical feeding (saddle-stitching). Alternative term: *low-page lip*.
bit	The smallest unit of information used in a computer file. It has one of two possible values—zero or one—used to indicate "on" or "off" or "yes" or "no" in the storage and transfer of electronic information and images. A contraction of the term "binary digit."
bitmap	An image represented by an array of picture elements, each of which is encoded as one or more binary digits.
black printer	(1) The plate that prints black ink in four-color process printing. (2) The halftone film used to burn the plate that will print black ink or the printing screen used in process-color reproduction to print the color black and add detail to the print. The letter "K" is often used to designate this color. Alternative term: *key plate*.

blank	(1) A thick paperboard, coated or uncoated, produced on a cylinder machine and designed for printing. Thickness ranges from 15 to 48 points (0.380 to 1.220 millimeters). (2) An unprinted page or sheet side. (3) Unprinted cardboard, metal sheets, or other substrates used for making displays and signs.
bleed	Pictures, lines, or solid colors that extend beyond the edge or edges of a page so that when margins are trimmed, the image is trimmed even with the edge of the page.
bleed tab	A bleeding ink square at the edge of a page that functions as a guide for locating specific material.
blind folio	A page number counted but not actually expressed (printed).
blockout	To opaque, mask, or spot out an area on a negative or positive so that it will not transmit light.
blueline	A blue-on-white print made by exposing sensitized paper to a negative. It is used as a final proof before platemaking.
board	A heavy, thick sheet of paper or other fibrous substance, usually with a thickness greater than 6 mil (0.006 inch).
body	The printed text of a book not including endpapers or covers.
book	A set of written, printed, or blank sheets bound together as a volume.
book block	A book that has been folded, gathered, and stitched but not cased-in.
book paper	A term used to describe a group of papers of a higher grade than newsprint, which are used primarily for book and publication printing and a wide variety of commercial printing applications. Book papers, as a class, include coated and uncoated papers in a wide variety of basis weights, colors, and finishes.
booklet	Any pamphlet sewed, wired, or bound with adhesive. It contains very few pages and is not produced for permanence.

border
A printed line or design surrounding an illustration or other printed matter.

bristol
A heavyweight paper, usually six points or more in thickness, used for printing.

buckle folder
A bindery machine in which two rollers push the sheet between two metal plates, stopping it and causing it to buckle at the entrance to the folder. A third roller working with one of the original rollers uses the buckle to fold the paper. Buckle folders are best suited for parallel folding.

bulk
The thickness of a pile of an exact number of sheets under a specified pressure.

bulking dummy
Blank sheets of the actual stock, folded and gathered to show the thickness of the book.

burnout mask
An assembly of cutout image masks that are used to crop image size and to minimize the number of unwanted images (e.g., cut lines) that have to be corrected. Any printing form with a number of pages will have cut lines in the margins that must be eliminated. Used when stripping or creating film positives.

burst binding
A special perforating device on web presses that slits the spine edge so that glue can penetrate the pages during perfect binding. With this method, it is not necessary to mill the spine off the book at the perfect binder, thus allowing for an additional 0.125 in. (3 mm) of trim.

butt
To adjoin two pieces of film or two colors of ink without overlapping.

byte
A single group of bits (most often eight) that are processed as a unit. Also the smallest addressable unit of main storage in a computer system.

caliper
The thickness of a sheet of paper or other material measured under specific conditions. Caliper is usually expressed in mils (thousandths of an inch).

camera film

A high-contrast, silver-based orthochromatic graphic arts film designed specifically for exposure using a graphic arts camera. Alternative term: *lith film.*

camera-ready copy

All printing elements prepared to be photographed on the graphic arts camera: text type set in the correct point size and properly mounted to the page grid; headlines, copy blocks, and screened prints; keylines showing the exact size and position of halftones or four-color photographs to be stripped in; and spot color elements mounted to acetate overlays, properly registered over the black copy, and marked for screen percentage and colors. Manual pasteup techniques or computer-based pagination systems may be used to create the layout. Alternative term: *camera-ready art.*

cardboard

Layers of paper laminated into sheets that are at least 0.006 in. (0.15 mm) or more in thickness.

carrier

A gravure term for film flat. Alternative terms: *cab; backing sheet.*

case binding

The process that produces a hardcover book. Printed covering material is glued to rigid board material and then affixed to the book with endpapers. Alternative term: *edition binding.*

casebound book

A book bound with a stiff, hard cover. Alternative term: *hardbound book.*

casing-in

Applying adhesive and combining a sewn and trimmed text with a cover (case).

center spread

Facing pages in the center of a newspaper section or signature.

centerline

A line or mark added to copy, a page negative, or a film flat to denote the center of trim margins on a page or form. The centerline is also used as a registration mark.

choke

A camera or contacting process whereby various images are made thinner without changing shape or position. The image area remains essentially the same except for a narrow reduction around its perimeter. Chokes are used to provide a printing overlap between a color or tinted background and display matter, to outline letters, or to achieve other special effects when preparing negatives. Alternative term: *"skinny."*

circumferential register	The alignment of successive ink films on top of each other on the printed sheets, usually accomplished on a rotary printing press by moving the plate cylinder toward the gripper or tail.
collate	The process of sorting the pages of a publication in the proper order.
collating mark	A distinctive, numbered symbol printed on the folded edge of signatures to denote the correct gathering sequence.
collimator	An optical instrument that produces a beam of parallel light rays or forms an infinitely distant virtual image that can be viewed without parallax. In printing, a collimator is used to check register and alignment between two or more photographic images separated from each other, such as superimposed flats.
colophon	(1) Traditionally, the printer's signature and the date of completion written at the beginning or end of a book. (2) The publisher's trademark printed on the cover or title page. (3) A modern colophon at the back of a book often includes information about the paper, typeface, and typesetting method used, how the illustrations were produced, and what printing process was employed.
color bar	A device printed in a trim area of a press sheet to monitor printing variables such as trapping, ink density, dot gain, and print contrast. It usually consists of overprints of two- and three-color solids and tints; solid and tint blocks of cyan, magenta, yellow, and black; and additional aids such as resolution targets and dot gain scales. Alternative terms: *color control strip; color control bar.*
color break	Indicating on tissue overlays attached to the mechanical what image areas will print in what colors (usually line and screen tints). This is done so that a different plate can be prepared for each color in a multicolor job.
color overlay	Transparent film sheets, usually made of acetate, that are superimposed over each other to represent each color in a reproduction.

color sequence

The order in which colors are printed on a substrate as indicated by the order in which the inks are supplied to the printing units on the press. Color sequence determines how well the inks will trap on the substrate. Alternative term: *color rotation.*

Color-Key

Trademark for a color proofing system that generates a set of process-color transparent overlays from separation negatives so that registration and screen-tint combinations can be checked before printing.

comb, plastic binding

A curved or rake-shaped plastic strip inserted through slots punched along the binding edge of the sheet.

combination

A stripping layout containing a variety of different printing forms instead of a group of identical forms as in a step-and-repeat assembly.

combination layout

A layout that combines several different forms on the same plate. Alternative term: *gang-run layout.*

common-line mask

A cover used to ensure proper alignment when adjoining film flats have images that share a border line along one side. Alternative term: *common cropper.*

composite

A single film carrying two or more images (usually line, halftone, or screen tint) as a result of photocombining (contacting) two or more separate film images. Alternative term: *one-piece film.*

comprehensive dummy

Design produced primarily to give the customer an approximate idea of what the printed piece will look like. Alternative terms: *comprehensive; comp.*

contact film

Blue-sensitive, continuous-tone film with a relatively high maximum density, excellent resolution, and a special anti-halation backing that allows exposure through its base without loss in quality. This film has been designed specifically to reproduce a same-size reverse (positive) image from an original negative, or a negative image from a film positive as the films are held together in a vacuum frame. Darkroom (high-speed) contact films may be handled under red or yellow safelights while roomlight (slow-speed) films may be handled under yellow fluorescent or subdued white lighting.

continuous tone	An unscreened photographic image or art (such as a wash drawing) that has infinite tone gradations between the lightest highlights and the deepest shadows.
continuous-tone proof	An illustration without halftone dots, which is produced on a digital color proofing device.
control strips	(1) Continuous or step wedges (film) with graduated densities that are preexposed under exacting conditions and used to test development solution in automatic processors. (2) Any test image printed on the trim edge of a sheet and used to visually assess ink settings.
converting	Any manufacturing or finishing operation completed after printing to form the printed item into the final product. Envelope creation, bagmaking, coating, waxing, laminating, folding, slitting, gluing, box manufacture, and diecutting are some examples. Converting units may be attached to the end of the press, or the operation may be handled by a special outside facility.
corner marks	Lines indicating the final size of a job. Alternative term: *crop marks.*
creasing	(1) Pressing lines into a book cover during binding. (2) Crimping or indenting along the binding edge of sheets or pages so that they will lie flat and bend easily. (3) Indenting bristol or boxboard to guide subsequent folding or forming.
creep	The slight but cumulative extension of the edges of each inserted spread or signature beyond the edges of the signature that encloses it. This results in progressively smaller trim size on the inside pages. Alternative terms: *pushout; shingling; binder's creep.*
crop	To opaque, mask, mark, cut, or trim an illustration or other reproduction to fit a designated area.
crop marks	Small lines placed in the margin or on an overlay, denoting the image areas to be reproduced.
cropping	(1) Indicating what portion of the copy is to be included in the final reproduction. (2) Trimming unwanted areas of a photograph film or print.

cross-direction	The position across the grain, or at a right angle to the machine direction, on a sheet of paper. The stock is not as strong and is more susceptible to relative humidity in the cross-direction.
cross-grain	Folding at a right angle to the direction of the grain in the paper stock. Folding the stock against the grain.
crossover	A photo or other image that extends across the gutter onto both pages of the spread. Alternative terms: *breakacross; reader's spread.*
cutoff length	The distance between corresponding points of repeated images on a web: the circumference of the plate cylinder.
cut-size paper	Paper sized specifically for printing, copying, or duplicating, such as 8.5×11-in., 11×14-in., and 11×17-in. paper.
degradee	The French term for fade. In the graphic arts, a degradee is a halftone tint that varies from a given small dot size to a given large dot size.
diecutting	Using sharp steel rules to slice paper or board to a specific shape on a printing press or a specialized stamping press.
digital color proof	Proof printed directly from computer data to paper or another substrate without creating separation films first. Proof made with computer output device, such as laser or ink-jet printer.
dimensional stability	How well an object maintains its size. How well a sheet of paper resists dimensional change when changes occur in its moisture content.
D_{max}	The maximum density that can be achieved in a given photographic or photomechanical system.
D_{min}	The lowest density that can be achieved in a given photographic or photomechanical system.
dongle	A small piece of hardware that plugs into a computer port to allow access to restricted areas of a network or to copy-protected software. Alternative term: *hardware key.*

dot
: The individual element of a halftone. It may be square, elliptical, or a variety of other shapes.

dot area
: In photomechanical reproduction, a screen breaks the wide tonal range found in the original into discrete intervals (from 1% to 99%), creating a halftone dot pattern. The value of each increment, or interval, in the halftone is expressed as the percentage of dot area covered.

dot gain
: The optical increase in the size of a halftone dot during pre-press operations or the mechanical increase in halftone dot size that occurs as the image is transferred from plate to blanket to paper in lithography. Alternative terms: *dot spread; ink spread.*

double burn
: Photoprinting different line and halftone negatives in register and in succession, on the same photosensitive surface.

double spread
: A printing image that extends across and fills two pages of a brochure, book, or folder. If located in the center of a book or folder, it is called a center spread. Alternative terms: *spread; double-page spread; double truck.*

dowel
: A short plastic or metal pin used for plate and film position register, typically during step-and-repeat exposure.

drawdown
: The duration of time required to remove air from a vacuum frame to allow the original film and the contact film to achieve uniform contact before exposure.

dummy
: (1) A preliminary layout showing the position of illustrations, text, folds, and other design elements as they are to appear in the printed piece. (2) A set of blank pages prepared to show the size, shape, style, and general appearance of a book, pamphlet, or other printed piece.

Dylux®
: DuPont trademark name for photosensitive polymer proof papers that produce dry proofs and require no processing.

elliptical dot screen
: A halftone screen characterized by oval-shaped dots. Such screens are designed to avoid the sudden jump between midtone densities where the corners of square dots join. They also help to reduce image graininess.

emulsion   Photographic term for a gelatin or colloidal solution holding light-sensitive salts of silver in suspension. It is used as the light-sensitive coating on photographic film or plates in photo-mechanical printing processes.

encapsulated PostScript™   A file format used to transfer PostScript™ image information from one program to another.

end product   The final package or printed piece ready for customer use after all folding, gluing, and other binding, finishing, and/or converting operations are completed.

equivalent weight   The term used to denote the respective weights of the same paper in two different sheet sizes.

estimating   The process of determining approximate cost, specifying required quality and quantity, and projecting waste.

exposure   (1) The period of time during which a light-sensitive surface (photographic film, paper, or printing plate) is subjected to the action of light. (2) The product of the intensity and the duration of the light acting upon a photographic emulsion.

film   Sheets of flexible translucent or transparent acetate, vinyl, or other plastic base materials that are coated with a photographic emulsion.

film image assembly   Positioning, mounting, and securing various individual films to one carrier sheet in preparation for platemaking. Alternative term: *film assembly*.

film processor   A machine that treats and develops photographic films and papers with chemicals under controlled conditions to produce permanent visible images.

finishing   All forms of completing graphic arts production, including folding, trimming, and assembling sections; binding by sewing, wire stitching, or gluing; and diecutting or gold stamping.

flat   An assembly consisting of a sheet of film or goldenrod paper and the negatives or positives attached (stripped) to it for exposure as a unit onto a printing plate.

flexography | A method of rotary letterpress printing characterized by the use of flexible, rubber or plastic plates with raised image areas and fluid, rapid-drying inks. Alternative term: *aniline printing*.

flop | To place a photographic film positive or negative with the emulsion facing up instead of down.

fog | A photographic defect in which the image is either locally or entirely veiled by a deposit of silver. Fogging is caused by stray light or improperly compounded chemical solutions.

foil | (1) A thin metal or plastic membrane (less than 0.006 in. thick) that is often used as a substrate in the flexographic printing process. (2) A thin decorative metal used in foil stamping. (3) A European term for polyester materials.

fold marks | Guides on the pasteup that indicate where a printed piece will be creased.

folding dummy | A mockup that shows the placement of page heads, the binding edge, and the gripper and side-guide edges, as well as page sequence and signature arrangement.

folding to paper | Folding sheets without regard to alignment of headers, footers, and other images throughout the signatures.

folding to print | Folding sheets so that the headers, footers, and other image areas are aligned throughout the signatures.

foldout | An oversize leaf, often a map, an illustration, or a table, folded to fit within the trim size of a book and tipped (pasted) in.

folio | (1) In printing, a page number, often placed at the outside of the running head, at the top (head) of the page. (2) In descriptive bibliography, a leaf of a manuscript or early printed book, the two sides designated as "r" (recto, or front) and "v" (verso, or back). (3) Formerly, a book made from standard-size sheets folded once, each sheet forming two leaves, or four pages.

foot margin | The distance between the bottom edge of the body of type (text matter) on a page and the bottom edge of the trimmed page. Alternative term: *tail margin*.

footer	A book's title or a chapter title printed at the bottom of a page. A drop folio (page number) may or may not be included. Alternative term: *running foot.*
form	Either side of a signature. A form usually contains a multiple of eight pages, but may be more or less.
former	A smooth, triangular-shaped, metal plate over which a printed web passes prior to entering an in-line folder. The former folds the moving web in half lengthwise. Alternative term: *former board.*
forwarding	Backing, rounding, shaping, lining up, and head-banding, among other operations performed before a casebound book is covered.
four-color process printing	The photomechanical reproduction of multicolor images achieved by overprinting specified amounts and areas of yellow, magenta, cyan, and black inks.
fourdrinier	A paper machine that forms a continuous web of paper on a horizontal, forward-moving, endless wire belt.
French fold	A press sheet in which all of the pages are printed on one side and folded, first vertically and then horizontally, to produce a four-page signature. The blank side is folded inward before the other folds are made.
front matter	The pages preceding the text of a book, including the title and copyright pages, the preface, foreword, table of contents, list of illustrations, and dedication.
frontispiece	An illustration facing the title page of a book; frequently printed on enamel paper and tipped (glued) in.
full bleed	An image extending to all four edges of the press sheet leaving no visible margins.
gang	(1) A grouping of different or identical forms arranged to print together in one impression. Alternative terms: *gang up; gang run; gang printing.* (2) Multiple photographic images scanned as one unit.

gatefold

A four-page book insert that is larger than some dimension of the page and opens from each side of the center.

gathering

Assembling a set of signatures sequentially. Alternative terms: *assembling; collating; inserting.*

glue lap

The area of a printed package or container reserved for the adhesive material used to fasten the folded carton.

goldenrod

A sheet of paper used to prepare negative film flats. It serves as a base for drawing the layout and attaching the film negatives. When exposure openings are cut through it, the remainder serves as an exposure mask, since its yellowish-orange color does not transmit light.

grain direction

(1) In papermaking, the alignment of fibers in the direction of web travel. (2) In printing, paper is said to be "grain-long" if the grain direction parallels the long dimension of the sheet. The paper is referred to as "grain-short" if it parallels the short dimension of the sheet. (3) In book binding, the grain direction of all papers used must run parallel to the book backbone.

grammage

The weight in grams of a single sheet of paper with an area of one square meter.

gravure

An intaglio printing process in which minute depressions, sometimes called cells, that form the image area are engraved or etched below the nonimage area in the surface of the printing cylinder. The cylinder is immersed in ink, and the excess ink is scraped off by a blade. When paper or another substrate comes in contact with the printing cylinder, ink is transferred.

gripper bite

The amount of paper that extends beneath the press gripper.

gripper edge

The leading edge of a sheet when it is being moved, in the grip of mechanical fingers, to and through the image transfer, or impression, operation on press.

guide edge

The side of a sheet at right angles to the gripper edge that is used to control the lateral (side-to-side) position of the sheet as it travels through the press or folder.

guillotine cutter   A manual or electronic device with a long, heavy, sloping blade that descends to a table or bed and slices through a stack of paper.

gutter   The inside margin (white space) between facing pages or columns of type. In bookbinding, the margin at the binding edge. Alternative terms: *gutter margin; back margin.*

hairline register   A standard for accuracy in which the maximum deviation between printing colors is 0.003 in. (0.08 mm).

halftone   A printed reproduction of a continuous-tone image composed of dots that vary in frequency (number per square inch), size, or density, thereby producing tonal gradations. The term is also applied to the process and plates used to produce this image.

head   (1) A line of display type signifying the title of a work or conveying crucial information. A headline. (2) The top of a page, book, or printing form.

head margin   The distance between the top edge of the trimmed page and the top edge of the body of type (text matter) on a page.

head trim   The amount of paper that is cut off above the sheet above the head margin; usually about 0.125 in. (3 mm).

header   A book's title or a chapter title printed at the top of a page and often with a folio (page number). Alternative term: *running head.*

helium-neon laser   A red laser light source in which helium-neon gas is stimulated to produce a monochromatic red light. This light is used to expose red-sensitive photographic films or paper, plates, or cylinders. It is also used in some scanners for electronic dot generation.

highlight   The lightest or whitest area of an original or reproduction, represented by the densest portion of a continuous-tone negative and by the smallest dot formation on a halftone and printing plate.

humidity, relative   The amount of moisture present in the air, expressed as a percentage of the amount of moisture required to saturate the air at a given temperature.

image area	On a lithographic printing plate, the area that has been specially treated to receive ink and repel water.
image carrier	The device on a printing press that carries an inked image either to an intermediate rubber blanket or directly to the paper or other printing substrate. A direct-printing letterpress form, a lithographic plate, a gravure cylinder, and a screen used in screen printing are examples of image carriers.
image fit	The agreement in distance between the register marks on each color from the gripper to the tail edge of the press sheet.
imposition	The process of placing graphics into predetermined positions on a press-size sheet of paper. Page layout is the process of defining where repeating elements such as headlines, text, and folios (page numbers) will appear on multiple pages throughout a document, while imposition can be thought of as defining where these completed pages will appear on much larger sheets of paper.
imposition, head-to-head	Arranging pages on a form during stripping so that the top of one page is located near the top of the opposite page.
imposition layout	A guide that indicates how images should be assembled on the sheet to meet press, folding, and bindery requirements.
imposition systems	Step-and-repeat imaging cameras or computerized methods of assembling the units of pages into signatures for printing. The latter method is often referred to as digital imposition.
impression	(1) The printing pressure necessary for ink transfer. (2) A single print.
in-line converting	Converting done directly from the last printing station or drying unit into the converting machinery in one continuous operation.
in-line finishing	Manufacturing operations such as numbering, addressing, sorting, folding, diecutting, and converting that are performed as part of a continuous operation right after the printing section on a press or on a single piece of equipment as part of the binding process. In-line finishing is common in web printing operations.

insert
(1) In stripping, a section of film carrying printing detail that is spliced into a larger film. (2) In printing, a page that is printed separately and then bound into the main publication. (3) Assembling signatures one inside of another in sequence.

insert, free-converting
A four-page, eight-page, etc., self-contained signature typically added to a newspaper.

jacket
The wrapper placed around a finished casebound book.

job jacket
The work order on which the instructions for each phase of production are written. The job jacket may also contain the original copy, photos, and line art for the job.

joint
The flexible portion of a casebound book where the cover meets the spine. It functions as a hinge, permitting the cover to be opened and closed without damaging the spine. Alternative term: *hinge.*

key
(1) The master layout or flat that is used as a positioning guide for preparing color artwork and/or stripping other film flats. The key is often prepared from the black printer but may include detail from other colors where registration marks do not appear in the black. Alternative term: *key flat.* (2) In photography, the emphasis on lighter or darker tones in a negative or print. High key indicates the prevalence of light tones; low key the prevalence of darker tones.

key plate
In color printing, the standard plate to which the other color plates are registered. The key plate is normally the plate with the most detail, never the yellow plate.

knife
(1) In folding machines, the three or four blades at different levels and at right angles to each other that force the paper between the folding rollers. The sheet of paper is pushed from one knife folding mechanism to the other until the desired number of folds have been made. Alternative term: *tucker blade.* (2) A sharp steel blade that trims excess from sheets and/or cuts them to a specific size. Automatic trimmers and cutters have knifes that can be programmed to make precise cuts.

knockout
Type that appears as unprinted stock on a black or dark colored background. Alternative terms: *reverse; dropout.*

lap	(1) The edge where one color overprints another. Alternative terms: *bleed; extended color; full bleed.* (2) The extra edge on one side of a signature gripped by binding equipment during the inserting process. Alternative term: *lip.*
lap lines	Unwanted lines that are visible when two images from adjacent pieces of film are assembled to appear as one image. Exposing these adjacent films onto a single piece of film or plate can yield a lap line where the films touch each other. Alternative term: *butt lines.*
lap register	Overlapping two colors at their junction to improve image fit and lessen image distortion on the press.
lateral reversal	The transposition of text and display type or illustrations so that they will appear as a "mirror image." The conversion of right-reading material to wrong-reading material.
lay	The arrangement and position of printed forms on a press sheet.
lay sheet	The first of several sheets run through the press to verify lineup, register, type, and nonimage areas.
layback	The nonprintable distance from the edge of the printing plate to beyond the gripper margin.
layout	A guide prepared to show the arrangement and location of all the type, illustrations, and line art that are combined together to compose the film flat.
layout sheet	The imposition form that indicates where to place negatives on a film flat in locations corresponding to the printed page on the press sheet or a folded dummy.
leaf	(1) A separate, usually blank, sheet of paper in a book. (2) A pigmented stamping material used to decorate book edges.
letter fold	A sheet folded several times in the same direction with two or more folds wrapping around the inner leaf.
letterpress	The method of printing in which the image, or ink-bearing areas, of the printing plate are in relief, i.e., raised above the nonimage areas.

light table   A glass-topped work area illuminated from underneath and used for pasting up layouts, stripping, opaquing, and otherwise viewing images with transmitted light.

line gauge   A ruler scaled in picas and points for a typographer's use. Line gauges come in different sizes, materials, and configurations and may include other scales such as inches, agate lines, etc.

line up   In lithographic stripping and platemaking, to square and position all of the printing detail on the negatives or positives so that the elements are properly aligned.

lip   The additional paper on the side edges of a signature that extend beyond the trim size of the pages. Lips are included so that binding equipment can grab and insert the signature into a magazine or book. Alternative term: *folio lap.*

lith film   A high-contrast orthochromatic material used for photomechanical work in the graphic arts. Alternative term: *camera film.*

lithography   A printing process in which the image carrier is chemically treated so that the nonimage areas are receptive to water (i.e., dampening or fountain solution) and repel ink while the image areas are receptive to ink and repel water. The image carrier is said to be *planographic,* or flat and smooth.

lithography, waterless   A planographic printing process that relies on special surface properties of the printing plate, instead of a water-based dampening solution, to prevent ink from adhering to nonimage areas of the plate. The nonimage areas of this "waterless" plate consist of an ink-repellent silicone rubber layer. The process also requires special inks and temperature-controlled inking systems.

loose register   Term used when each color image on a press sheet is relatively independent of all others and slight variations in press register are inconsequential.

loose-leaf binding   A process in which individual sheets can be inserted and removed at will from a section of a larger document often held in a three-ring binder.

loupe	An adjustable-focus magnifier incorporating a precise measuring scale, with or without a self-contained light source. It is used to inspect fine detail.
makeup	Assembling text, illustrations, graphs, charts, rules, tabular material, and running heads or feet into a completed page. Stripping, pasteup, and electronic pagination are all forms of makeup. Alternative term: *page layout.*
margin	The white space extending from the edge of the printed image to a page's trim edge.
marks	The lines on films, flats, printing plates, and press sheets that serve as guides for positioning, registering, printing, and binding a job.
masking material	A material opaque to light used to cover image areas in a flat not to be exposed to a plate for a given color.
master marks flat	A flat used in process-color film assembly on which the trim marks, center marks, and fold marks are assembled, rather than putting the marks on all of the individual color flats. It is used as a complementary flat to each color flat. Alternative terms: *master flat; marks flat.*
mechanical	The assembly of all page elements, including text and line art, properly proportioned and positioned, in camera-ready form. Alternative term: *pasteup.*
misregister	Printed images that are incorrectly positioned, either in reference to each other or to the sheet's edges.
moiré	An undesirable, unintended interference pattern caused by the out-of-register overlap of two or more regular patterns such as dots or lines. In process-color printing, screen angles are selected to minimize this pattern. If the angles are not correct, an objectionable effect may be produced.
mortising	In stripping, to cut out incorrect text and replace it with the correct text on film cut to fit the space without overlapping.
multiple exposure	Combining the detail of each color from different film flats by double printing during platemaking. The combined exposures will produce the complete printed image if each flat is exposed

successively in register onto the sensitized surface. Alternative term: *complementary image assembly.*

multiple layout   A layout with two or more duplicates of the same image on one plate. Alternative term: *step-and-repeat layout.*

Mylar   DuPont's registered tradename for its clear polyester film, which is used in stripping operations.

negative   A photographic film or plate that is exposed and processed to provide a reversed image of the tones found on the original— highlights and shadows or color values (i.e., white as black).

negative-working plate   A printing plate that is exposed through a film negative. The plate areas exposed to light become the image areas.

notch binding   Small serrations cut in the spine of a perfect-bound book and filled with glue. This method eliminates the need to mill material off the spine of the book.

octavo   A sheet folded to form 8 leaves or 16 pages, or a book prepared from sheets so folded. The page size varies with the sheet dimensions, but this binding term is sometimes used to designate a page that is approximately 8×5 in. Alternative terms: *8vo or 8°.*

offline converting   Coating, cutting, folding, embossing, stamping, or otherwise altering newly printed sheets or rolls of material to form the final printed piece or product on a machine separate from the printing press. Printing plants may have dedicated converting equipment or they may send the work to companies that specialize in converting.

offpress proofing   Producing a simulation of the final printed piece by photochemical methods (such as an overlay of dye or pigment images on transparent film base) instead of photomechanical methods (ink on paper).

offset printing   An indirect printing method in which the inked image on a press plate is first transferred to a rubber blanket, that in turn "offsets" the inked impression to a press sheet. In offset lithography, the printing plate has been photochemically treated to produce image areas and nonimage areas receptive to ink and water respectively.

OK sheet
A press sheet that closely matches the prepress proof and has been approved by the customer and/or production personnel. It is used as a guide to judge the quality of the rest of the production run.

one-up
Printing a single image once on a press sheet.

orientation
The direction in which a page is printed, i.e., the portrait (vertical) or landscape (horizontal) mode.

outline
(1) To opaque out the background around the margins of an object in a halftone negative. (2) To box in an illustration with a line border. (3) A silhouetted reproduction. (4) Open characters as opposed to those that are solid color.

overlay
A sheet of translucent or transparent tissue, acetate, or Mylar attached over the face of the primary artwork (pasteup) and used to indicate surprints, knockouts, overlapping or butting flat colors, placement of alternate or additional copy, or previously separated color art.

overlay proof
Thin, transparent pigmented or dyed sheets of plastic film that are registered to each other in a specific order and taped or pin-registered to a base sheet. Each film carries the printed image for a different process color, which, when combined, creates a composite simulating the final printed piece.

overprint
(1) A color made by printing any two of the process inks (yellow, magenta, and cyan) on top of one another to form red, green, and blue secondary colors. (2) Solid or tint quality control image elements that are printed over or on the top of previously printed colors. Overprint patches are used to measure trapping, saturation, and overprint color densities. Like other quality control elements, overprints may be measured from a color bar in the trim of a press sheet or from the printed image itself.

page
One side of a sheet or leaf of paper.

page description language
In an electronic publishing system, the format by which all of the elements to be placed on the page, their x-y coordinates (respective position on the page), and the page's position within the larger document are identified in a manner that the output device can understand.

page layout   (1) A computer program that allows the user to position type and other elements automatically so that fully paginated electronic output can be generated. (2) Manual placement of art, type, photos, etc. into page positions by adhering each element to a "board" ready for camera work. Alternative term: *page makeup.*

page proof   A sample of type elements assembled into page form.

pagination   (1) The process of page makeup. (2) Numbering pages with associated running heads and feet, sometimes including trim marks. (3) Breaking down an electronic file or printed galley into individual pages. (4) Imposition.

paperback   A book with a flexible paper binding. Alternative term: *softcover.*

parallax   The apparent shift in alignment or register between two photographic images or superimposed films or flats when the viewing angle changes.

parallel fold   A folding succession in which all folds are made parallel to each other.

pasteup   The camera-ready assembly of type and line art (drawings), e.g., line copy prepared manually or electronically for photographic reproduction. Alternative terms: *mechanical; photomechanical.*

perfect binding   The use of glue to hold the pages of a book or magazine together. Alternative term: *adhesive binding.*

perfecting   Printing both sides of a sheet sequentially in the same pass through a sheetfed printing press. In xerography, perfecting is called duplexing.

perforating   Punching a row of small holes or incisions into or through a sheet of paper to permit part of it to be detached; to guide in folding; to allow air to escape from signatures; or to prevent wrinkling when folding heavy papers. A perforation may be indicated by a series of printed lines, or it may be *blind;* in other words, without a printed indication on the cutline. Alternative term: *perf.*

pickup	Film, photos, or type from a previously printed job that is marked for reuse in an upcoming job.
pin register	The use of standardized register pins and holes to ensure accurate register of copy, film, and plates during prepress; especially for process-color printing. Alternative term: *pin registration.*
pinbar	A long metal strip that contains several carefully spaced register pins.
pinhole	A small, unwanted, transparent area in the developed emulsion of a negative or positive. It is usually caused by dust or other defects on the copy, copyboard glass, or the film.
plastic binding	A form of mechanical binding using plastic strips, combs, or coils in place of stitching. The binding edge is punched with slots or holes through which the formed plastic material is inserted.
plate	A thin metal, plastic, or paper sheet that serves as the image carrier in many printing processes.
platemaking	Preparing a printing plate or other image carrier from a film or flat, including sensitizing the surface if the plate was not presensitized by the manufacturer, exposing it through the flat, and developing or processing and finishing it so that it is ready for the press.
portable document format (PDF)	A computer file format that preserves a printed or electronic document's original layout, type fonts, and graphics as one unit for electronic transfer and viewing. The recipient uses compatible "reader" software to access and even print the PDF file.
position proof	A color proof in which text, graphics, and pictures are combined and checked for location and registration before printing.
positive	A photographic reproduction with tonal values similar to those in the original artwork. The image areas on the film or plates are represented by opaque dot values.

positive-working plate	An image carrier that is exposed through a film positive. Plate areas exposed to light become the nonimage areas because they are soluble in the presence of developing agents.
post binder	A loose-leaf binding method in which straight rods are used instead of rings to hold the pages together. The binder can be expanded as the bulk of the contents increases. The front and back covers are separate pieces.
PostScript™	Adobe Systems, Inc. tradename for a page description language that enables imagesetters and other output devices developed by different companies to interpret electronic files from any number of personal computers ("front ends") and off-the-shelf software programs.
preflighting	An orderly procedure using a checklist to verify that all components of an electronic file are present and correct prior to submitting the document for high-resolution output.
prepunched film	Photographic film in which holes have been cut in advance to fit a specific lugging or pin-register system.
printer's spread	A pair of pages in the order necessary for printing, folding, and binding to yield the desired results.
proof	A prototype of the printed job made photochemically from film and dyes, or digitally from electronic data (offpress proofs) or photomechanically from plates mounted on a printing press (a press proof). A proof serves as a sample for the customer and as a guide for the press operator.
proof, progressive	A set of press proofs from the separate plates used in process color work, showing the printing sequence and the result after each additional color has been applied. (Press proofs of each individual process color and black; each combination of two process colors; each combination of three process colors; and all four process inks combined.) Alternative term: *progs*.
proofreaders' marks	A series of symbols and abbreviations used by a proofreader to mark errors on copy and the corrections to be made.
proofreading	Checking galleys, proofs, and bluelines for errors and marking where corrections should be made.

quality control   The day-to-day operational techniques and activities that are used to fulfill requirements for quality, such as intermediate and final product inspections, testing incoming materials, and calibrating instruments used to verify product quality.

rapid-access film   A blue- or green-sensitive film with a high-density continuous-tone emulsion providing the fastest means of producing film intermediates.

raster image processor (RIP)   The device that interprets all of the page layout information for the marking engine of the imagesetter or platesetter. Post-Script™, or another page description language, serves as an interface between the page layout workstation and the RIP.

rasterization   The process of converting mathematical and digital information into a series of variable-density pixels.

reader's spread   A pair of pages positioned across the binding edge, or gutter, from each other after the book is assembled; e.g., pages six and seven of a book.

recto   The right-hand page of an open book, usually an odd-numbered page; sometimes the first or cover page.

reflection copy   A photographic print, painting, or other opaque copy used as original art for reproduction. Such copy is viewed by the light reflected from its surface and can only be photoreproduced with front illumination (as from a graphic arts camera).

register   The overall agreement in the position of printing detail on a press sheet, especially the alignment of two or more over-printed colors in multicolor presswork. Register may be observed by agreement of overprinted register marks on a press sheet. In stripping, film flats are usually punched and held together with pins to ensure register. The punched holes on the film flat match those on the plate and press specified for the job. Alternative term: *registration*.

register marks   Small reference patterns, guides, or crosses placed on originals before reproduction to aid in color separation and positioning negatives for stripping. Register marks are also placed along the margins of negative film flats to aid in color registration and correct alignment of overprinted colors on press sheets.

relief printing   A printing process using an image carrier on which the image areas are raised above the nonimage areas.

reverse-reading   Photographic negative or positive that reads from right to left when viewed from the emulsion side. Alternative term: *wrong-reading*.

right-reading   A photographic negative, positive, or printing plate that reads from left to right (top to bottom) when viewed from the emulsion side.

roomlight films   Silver-based photographic films that can be handled under yellow safelights or tungsten and fluorescent lights.

rosettes   The patterns formed when halftone color images are printed in register at the correct angles.

rounding and backing   Shaping a book to fit its cover. Rounding gives the book a convex spine and a concave fore-edge. Backing makes the spine wider than the thickness of the rest of the book to provide a shoulder against which the cardboard front and back covers rest. It also provides the hinge crease for the joints of the book.

Rubylith   The Ulano Company's trademark name for a thin red or amber plastic film used by graphic artists, designers, and strippers to indicate placement and size of illustrations. The Rubylith is adhered to a pasteup board or acetate base and cut to shape, forming a "window" for the illustration. This window appears as a black "mask" on orthochromatic photographic materials. Alternative term: *masking film, peelable*.

saddle-stitching   Binding multiple sheets by opening the signatures in the center and gathering and stitching them with a wire through the fold line. The folded sheets rest on supports called saddles as they are transported through the stitcher. Booklets, brochures, and pamphlets are most often bound this way. Alternative term: *wire-stitching*.

screen angle   The position of the rows of dots on halftone screens in relation to a reference grid with horizontal and vertical lines. The most dominant color screened is positioned at a 45° angle to the reference grid.

screen printing   A printing process in which a squeegee forces ink through a porous mesh, synthetic, or silk image carrier, or screen, covered by a stencil that blocks the nonimage areas. The ink pressed through the open image areas of the screen forms the image on the substrate.

screen tint   A halftone film with a uniform dot size throughout. It is rated by its approximate printing dot size value, such as 20%, 50%, etc.

self-cover   A book binding composed of the same paper used for the inside text pages.

semi-concealed cover   In mechanical binding, a single piece of material that is scored and slotted or punched and combined with the actual binding device to form a closed backbone on bound units.

setback   The distance from the front edge of a printing plate to the beginning of the image area with a space allotment for the gripper margin and for fastening the plate to the cylinder. This distance varies with different press makes and sizes.

shadow   The darker or denser areas of an original, film positive, or halftone reproduction.

sheetfed press   A printing press that feeds and prints on individual sheets of paper (or another substrate). Some sheetfed presses employ a rollfed system in which rolls of paper are cut into sheets before they enter the feeder; however, most sheetfed presses forward individual sheets directly to the feeder.

sheetwise imposition   A printing layout in which separate plates (and film flats) are used to print the front and the back of a single press sheet. Completely different pages appear on each side of the sheet.

side guide   A device that serves as part of the register system of a sheetfed printing press. Side guides move the sheet sideways to facilitate register.

side-guide mark   A vertical line approximately 0.875 in. (22 mm) long with a 0.1875-in. (5-mm) horizontal line used for monitoring sheet-to-sheet register during a pressrun.

side-sewing

A book binding method in which the entire book is sewn as a single unit, instead of as individual sections. Side-sewn books will not lie flat when open.

side-stitch

A method of binding in which the folded signature or cut sheets are stitched along and through the side close to the gutter margin. The pages cannot be fully opened to lie flat. Alternative term: *sidewire.*

signature

One or more printed sheets folded to form a multiple page section of a book or pamphlet. Signatures are most commonly grouped as four, eight, sixteen, or thirty-two pages. Various combinations of multiple page signatures create the full complement of pages needed in the printed piece.

spine

The back, or bound, edge of a book.

spiral binding

A mechanical binding method in which a continuous wire coil is run through a series of closely spaced holes near the gutter margin of loose sheets.

spread

(1) A line image with edges that have been moved slightly outward to allow a color or tint to intentionally overlap. Alternative term: *"fatty."* (2) An image that extends across two facing pages in a book or magazine, crossing over the binding. Alternative terms: *crossover; reader's spread.*

stamping

Using a die and often colored foil or gold leaf to press a design into a book cover, a sheet of paper, or another substrate. The die may be used alone (in blank stamping) if no color or other ornamentation is necessary. Special presses fitted with heating devices can stamp designs into book covers.

step-and-repeat

Making multiples of a single image by assembling the image into a flat and exposing it repeatedly in different places on the printing plate.

stochastic screening

A halftoning method that creates the illusion of tones by varying the number (frequency) of micro-sized dots (spots) in a small area. Unlike conventional halftoning, the spots are not positioned in a grid-like pattern. Instead, the placement of each spot is determined as a result of a complex algorithm that statistically evaluates and distributes spots under a fixed set of parameters. With first-order stochastic screening, only the number of dots in an area varies, but with second-order stochastic screening, both the number and size vary. Alternative terms: *FM dots; FM screening.*

stripping   The act of combining and positioning all of the copy elements from all of the film negatives or positives together as a negative for platemaking. Alternative term: *image assembly.*

superimpose   To position negatives or positives on a new film flat that is prepared directly over another flat to obtain exact registration between them. This is frequently done when stripping up complementary color flats.

surprint   The overprinting of images during double printing, as when line detail overprints on a halftone or tint.

tabloid   The newspaper page size, approximately 11.75 in. wide and from 15 to 17 in. long, or about half of the standard newspaper page size.

tagged image file format (TIFF)   A file format for exchanging bitmapped images (usually scans) between applications.

tail   The back end of a sheet or printed image opposite the gripper edge.

tail pin   On a pin-register system, the pin at the back edge of the flat or plate.

text   The body matter of a page composed in column or paragraph form. Display matter, headings, and illustrations do not fall into this category.

thumb edge   The outside edge of a book, directly opposite the binding edge.

thumbnail sketch   Crude, small layouts sketched in pencil to develop the initial concept for a design.

tint   An image element with an even shading produced by either a halftone dot screen of various shapes and sizes or fine parallel lines. Tints produced with halftone dot screens are often used to measure dot area, dot gain, and print contrast while tints produced with parallel lines are used to measure slur.

tissue overlay   A thin transparent sheet of paper placed over artwork or the pasteup to protect it. Instructions, corrections, and color breaks are usually indicated on the overlay.

trapping   (1) Printing a wet ink over a previously printed dry or wet ink film. (2) Creating thin overlaps between adjoining colors to compensate for misregister in prepress and press operations. If the colors are not trapped, the misregister may result in small areas of unprinted paper where colors would normally abut.

trim   The excess area of a printed form or page in which instructions, register marks, and quality control devices are printed. The trim is cut off before binding.

trim margin   The white space on the open side of a signature.

trim marks   Guide marks on the original copy and the printed sheet to indicate where the sheet will be cut.

trim size   The final dimensions of a page.

trimmer, three-knife   A cutting machine with three knives, two parallel and one at a right angle, used to trim books or booklets. It operates automatically, usually at the end of a saddle-stitcher, perfect binder, or casebound book binding system.

trim-out   The area between two books that is removed when a job bound two-up is cut apart by the fourth and fifth knife of a trimmer.

truck   Two pages of a book, tabloid, or newspaper set up and processed together. Alternative term: *double truck*.

two-on binding   Two books trimmed one on top of the other.

two-up   Printing two identical pages on the same press sheet.

two-up binding   Binding two units at a time, then cutting them apart and trimming them.

undercut   The spread of light beyond the transparent design areas of a negative or positive during exposure. This problem results frequently if the film and plate are not in proper contact.

vacuum frame

A device that uses vacuum to hold the imaged and the photo-sensitive materials, such as film and plates, together for exposure.

web

A roll of any substrate that passes continuously through a printing press or converting or finishing equipment.

web offset

A lithographic printing process in which a press prints on a continuous roll of paper instead of individual sheets.

window method

A procedure in which a sized adhesive-backed red masking material is placed on the pasteup board wherever a halftone or separate artwork will print. When photographed, the mask produces a clear area on the negative into which the halftone or artwork is stripped during image assembly.

work-and-roll

An imposition (layout) in which the front and back of a form is printed from a single plate. After the first run through the press, the stock pile is inverted so that the back edge becomes the gripper edge for the second printing. Work-and-roll differs from work-and-turn in that the gripper edge changes, often leading to misregister unless the stock has been squared accurately. Alternative term: *work-and-tumble*.

work-and-turn

A common printing imposition or layout in which all the images on both sides of a press sheet are placed in such a way that when the sheet is turned over and the same gripper edge is used, one half of the sheet automatically backs up the previously printed half. When the sheet is cut in half parallel to the guide edge, two identical sheets are produced. Work-and-turn impositions are preferred over work-and-tumble impositions for accuracy because the same gripper edge and the same side of the press sheet are used to guide the sheet twice through the press. Alternative term: *work-and-flop*.

wraparound

A folio or insert placed around a signature prior to stitching and binding.

wrong-reading image

In Western countries, printed type that reads from right to left, or an image printed backwards from its normal orientation. Wrong-reading film images are read from right to left when the film is viewed from the base side.

Index

About the Author

Hal Hinderliter is the director of the Center for Imaging Excellence (CIE), an electronic prepress training and production facility at the Graphic Arts Technical Foundation. As director of the CIE, Hinderliter is responsible for managing the CIE's equipment and facilities, as well as managing GATF's internal prepress production workflow. He creates and conducts GATF workshops, custom training programs, and seminars throughout the industry on a variety of graphic communications, information technology, and prepress issues. His seminars are frequently given at major trade shows, such as Seybold and Graph Expo.

Hinderliter, with seventeen years of experience in the printing industry, also performs Technical Plant Assessments (TPAs) for member companies, observing and evaluating prepress production operation methods, techniques, and equipment. Prior to joining the Foundation in 1995, he was a prepress supervisor and DTP computer operator with Hoechstetter Printing, one of Pittsburgh's premier commercial printers. He has held positions in stripping, camera work, press operation, design, and commercial photography.

About GATF

The Graphic Arts Technical Foundation is a nonprofit, scientific, technical, and educational organization dedicated to the advancement of the graphic communications industries worldwide. Its mission is to serve the field as the leading resource for technical information and services through research and education.

For 74 years the Foundation has developed leading edge technologies and practices for printing. GATF's staff of researchers, educators, and technical specialists partner with nearly 2,000 corporate members in over 65 countries to help them maintain their competitive edge by increasing productivity, print quality, process control, and environmental compliance, and by implementing new techniques and technologies. Through conferences, satellite symposia, workshops, consulting, technical support, laboratory services, and publications, GATF strives to advance a global graphic communications community.

The GATF*Press* publishes books on nearly every aspect of the field; learning modules (step-by-step instruction booklets); audiovisuals (CD-ROMs, videocassettes, slides, and audiocassettes); and research and technology reports. It also publishes *GATFWorld,* a bimonthly magazine of technical articles, industry news, and reviews of specific products.

For more detailed information on GATF products and services, please visit our website *http://www.gatf.org* or write to us at 200 Deer Run Road, Sewickley, PA 15143-2600 (phone: 412/741-6860).

Orders to:
GATF Orders
P.O. Box 1020
Sewickley, PA 15143-1020
Phone (U.S. and Canada only): 800/662-3916
Phone (all other countries): 412/741-5733
Fax: 412/741-0609
Email: gatforders@abdintl.com